W9-CCY-737

HARRY POTTER
&
IMAGINATION

THE WAY BETWEEN TWO WORLDS

TRAVIS PRINZI

This book has not been prepared, approved, or licensed by any person or entity that created, published, or produced the *Harry Potter* books or related properties. Harry Potter, characters, names, and related indicia are trademarks of Warner Bros. and *Harry Potter* Publishing Rights © J. K. Rowling

Harry Potter & Imagination
Copyright © 2009 Travis Prinzi
Allentown, PA

All rights reserved. Except in the case of quotations embodied in critical articles or reviews, no part of this book may be reproduced or transmitted in any form or by any means, electronic or mechanical, including photocopying, recording, or by any information storage or retrieval system, without written permission of the publisher. For information, contact Zossima Press www.Zossima.com

Zossima Press titles may be purchased for business or promotional use or special sales.

10-9-8-7-6-5-4-3-2-1

Zossima
Press

ISBN   0-9822385-1-7
ISBN-13 978-0-9822385-1-6

FOR TRICIA AND SOPHIA,
WHO HAVE TAUGHT ME TO
IMAGINE BETTER

Table of Contents

Introduction

Harry Potter for Real Life?

Fairy Tales matter. That's quite the assertion, but there it is. Far from being cute, fanciful stories meant to excite kids or perhaps distract adults who haven't succeeded in growing up into what is called "real life," fantastic literature often imagines a more accurate and edifying vision of reality than what the so-called "realists" give us. Despite protestations from academics, realists, and religious zealots, *Harry Potter* is for real life.

When J.K. Rowling wrote the *Harry Potter* series, she wrote a beautiful, sprawling mess of a story that will undoubtedly have profound historical reverberations. What do I mean by "a beautiful, sprawling mess?" It defies one-volume analysis, unless that volume is a tome, because Rowling has drawn from so many different genres of fiction and strictly followed the rules of none. It would be folly to criticize Rowling for not being faithful to one particular genre, because in order to do that, a critic would first have to pin her down on a genre (fairy tale? mystery novel? school story?) and then deal with the very simple fact that Rowling did not intend to play by the rules of that genre. But somehow, it all works and tells a beautiful story. Other works will no doubt abound on the detective novel, the school story, and other elements of Rowling's fiction. This present work will explore *Harry Potter* as fairy tale and fantastic literature, which is both shaped by and a shaping force in culture.

It's impossible to say the series shapes "our" culture or "Western" culture exclusively, because the series has been an international success, serving as a veritable icon of postmodern multicultural sentiment. To examine the Harry Potter series as a global phenomenon is a work of its own, and this volume does not attempt that, either. Quite simply because its author is part of Western, U.S. culture, and because Rowling writes as a Western person, *Harry Potter & Imagination* approaches the series from that point of view.

When approaching mythopoeic literature in the Western world, Tolkien is a great starting place. Since he wrote of the "Cauldron of Story" in his famous essay, "On Fairy-Stories," the concept has been oft-used in the analysis of various works of literature. Tolkien believed that the fairy-story answers "primordial human desires," and that each new fairy-story writer is not starting completely afresh, but is adding elements of each age and culture to an ever-brewing cauldron of a story which has been simmering since the beginning of human consciousness.

The cauldron is a particularly apt metaphor for Rowling's work, since cauldrons themselves play an important role in the *Harry Potter* series. Rowling once explained that she viewed C.S. Lewis's "world between worlds," wherein portals to various worlds can be found, as a metaphor for a library (Fry, "Living with Harry Potter"). Perhaps her use of many ingredients producing a wide variety of fantastic potions is just as poignant a metaphor for the brewing of many good stories, all of which answer the longings and help to heal the hurts of human beings.

Tolkien did not write of many cauldrons, but of one, into which many ingredients were cast. He wrote,

> So with regard to fairy stories, I feel that it is more interesting, and also in its way more difficult, to consider what they are, what they have become for us, and what values the long alchemic processes of time have produced in them. (9)

Tolkien explains, quoting Dasent, that "We must be satisfied with the soup that is set before us, and not desire to see the bones of the ox out of which it has been boiled" (9). A systematic sorting of all the ingredients, the "bones," that are both in the cauldron and that have been added by Rowling has already been done in the plenty of guidebooks to the *Harry Potter* series.[1] This work is about the *Harry Potter* soup itself. Why does it taste so good? Why do readers keep coming back for more?

The answer to that question is that the soup satisfies what Tolkien called "primordial human desires." The millions of excited fans who lined up for midnight releases of the *Harry Potter* books weren't just looking for a good story; they were starving people, and the bookstores were the soup kitchens. A true fairy story isn't just a fun distraction for children, and it isn't just a morality tale; it is rooted in the human condition, the very meaning of being a human.

Tolkien gets to the point of the Soup analogy:

> Speaking of the history of stories and especially of fairy-stories we
> may say that the Pot of Soup, the Cauldron of Story, has always
> been boiling, and to it have continually been added new bits, dainty
> and undainty (12-13).

This Cauldron has "always been boiling" because it contains the stories that satisfy the ancient desires; the fairy-tale element of story "is there...waiting for the great figures of Myth and History, and for the yet nameless He or She, waiting for the moment when they are cast into the simmering stew, one by one or all together, without consideration of rank or precedence" (14). As such, the Cauldron exists independently of the writer; it is comprised of stories that existed long before the writer put pen to paper, and it will bubble on long after.

Into the Cauldron of Story, J.K. Rowling threw Harry Potter, perhaps the most potent ingredient to be added since Tolkien himself tossed in hobbits, orcs, a white wizard, and a ranger from the north. Rowling was fully aware of many of the ingredients already boiling in the soup; she borrowed from a vast array of fairy tale and mythological works and translated them into her own world. For example, her particular recipe has turned Cerberus, guardian of the Underworld in Greek mythology, into Fluffy the three-headed dog, guardian of the Philosopher's Stone. Far from being simple "derivation," Rowling has joined the circle of cooks around this Cauldron and done in the postmodern 21st century what greats like George MacDonald, G.K. Chesterton, C.S. Lewis, J.R.R. Tolkien, and Madeleine L'Engle have done in the past.

Those five authors, whose views on the fairy tale are invoked for Chapter One, were all writers who were also Christians. As Rowling has professed Christian faith, albeit one with which she sometimes struggles, it is not out of place in the least to put her work into the context of Christian thinking about fairy tales. The perception sadly exists that when one adds a Christian element to academic analysis, serious scholarship is being subverted by religion. Against that objection I submit the simple fact that it's impossible to remove Rowling from her own tradition, being both a Christian personally and writing in a tradition of British literature which is manifestly Christian.

Part One of this book contains six chapters analyzing the way Rowling's world fulfills the call for the satisfaction of "primordial human desires." The nature of truth and truth-perception, the literary power of magic, and the resolution of fear and evil with courage and self-sacrificial love are examined in detail. As Rowling's books are primarily character-driven, Part Two examines, through the lens of mythological archetypes, the series' four primary characters: Harry Potter (hero), Voldemort (shadow), Albus Dumbledore (mentor), and Severus Snape (shapeshifter). Other characters and archetypes (trickster, mother, herald) are examined in the context of analyzing those primary four. We will look at the ways Rowling utilizes and transforms stock characters, or archetypes, to create a dynamic story. Part Three brings the *Harry Potter* series into conversation with postmodern social justice concerns by examining the social vision of J.K. Rowling's stories.

In Rowling's 2008 Harvard commencement speech, she quoted Plutarch: "What we achieve inwardly will change outer reality." That is the trajectory of *Harry Potter*, and that is the trajectory of this book: from the great themes of Part One through the character transformation of Part Two and into the social vision of Part Three, *Platform 9 ¾* sends the reader through the magical barrier between two worlds to be transformed inwardly, and so to become an agent of outward change.

Madeleine L'Engle, in her classic work on faith and art, *Walking on Water*, quoted Jean Rhys:

> All of writing is a huge lake. There are great rivers that feed that lake, like Tolstoy and Dostoyevksy. And there are mere trickles, like Jean Rhys. All that matters is feeding the lake. I don't matter. The lake matters. You must keep feeding the lake. (16)

Only history will tell the size of the river that Rowling has contributed to the lake with her *Harry Potter* series. Whatever the size, the purpose of the book you hold in your hands is to throw you into the River of Rowling, and to let it carry you to that lake.

Rowling made another important statement in that commencement speech, which captures the heart of *Harry Potter & Imagination*:

> We do not need magic to change the world, we carry all the power we need inside ourselves already: we have the power to imagine better. (http://harvardmagazine.com/go/jkrowling.html)

Imagine better. That is the great delight and duty to which fantastic literature calls us. Our imaginations are re-awakened by a journey into Faerie, and we return from there, with our vision transformed able to see our own world differently, and to imagine, and therefore to act for, a better world.

We begin with the journey into Faerie.

Introduction Notes

1   David Colbert, *The Magical Worlds of Harry Potter;* George Beahm, *Fact, Fiction, and Folklore in Harry Potter;* Colin Duriez, *A Field Guide to Harry Potter.*

PART 1

FAERIE

Chapter One

The Tales of Rowling the Bard
Harry Potter as Fairy Tale and Truth

"I have been hardly more than a wandering explorer (or trespasser) in the land, full of wonder but not of information" (Tolkien 2). So J.R.R. Tolkien wrote as he began his study of the fairy tale in his classic essay, "On Fairy-Stories." But why gather information, and is there really reason to explore the land and be "full of wonder" in the first place? Aren't fairy stories told for children, for good-hearted fun and simplistic moral lessons? Why do stories matter? These questions must be addressed as we begin to look at J.K. Rowling's *Harry Potter* series; for there are many people in our day who care only about information as brute fact, and are no more full of wonder at the fairy tale than the sea is filled with milk. And if you mentioned a sea of milk to such people, they would scoff at your childish foolishness.

Harry Potter contains elements of many genres of story – detective novels, school stories, 19th century British literature, adventure stories. But *Harry Potter* is primarily a fairy story – not according to the strict definition which distinguishes it from myth, legend, and heroic romance, but insofar as it brings readers into an encounter with Faerie, the magical "land" in which Tolkien called himself a "wandered (or a trespasser)." As such, in this chapter *Harry Potter* will be brought into conversation with great fairy tale authors and thinkers who wrote stories during a time when fairy tales were taken less and less seriously and relegated to a supposedly unimportant place in the nursery. *Harry Potter* is a fairy tale, and fairy tales matter. Fairy tales are true.

Reactions to the *Harry Potter* books have contained no shortage of derision, and while some mount academic complaints against the book, others attack the genre altogether, like this man did in a write-in section for the *Times-Mail News*:

> I recommend that people stop wasting their time reading fiction (lies) for entertainment, and that parents teach their children by good example to spend more time reading wholesome nonfiction with literary value (including the Bible) for education. ("Potter debate still brewing," 3 Aug 2007)

The example is not as extreme as one might think. That fiction is a "lie" is not very wide of the mark when it comes to truth-concepts in our modern age. Enlightenment rationalism – the belief that rational philosophy and scientific inquiry have replaced the need for "superstitions" like myth, religion and magic – has left in place the notion that anything that is really "true" must be objectively, verifiably so. If it cannot be repeated in a laboratory, doubt must be cast upon it. At best, modern-day lovers of fiction can distinguish between what is a harmful lie (one told to hurt somebody) and what is an unharmful one (a created story for entertainment value); and this will not do at all. This painfully limited definition of "truth" is a misuse of science and reason, and it is ultimately subversive to the quest for truth.

Enlightenment philosophy is rooted in the rationalists of the 18th century (Kant, Hume, among many others) and produced a subsequent period emphasizing natural philosophy and expansive scientific discovery and progress known as modernism. To oversimplify, the belief was that human progress fueled by scientific discovery and rational inquiry into human ethics would produce eventual universal freedom, peace, and prosperity; the old, outdated dependence upon religion was to be seen as an unnecessary superstition. Modernism's philosophical underpinnings have been criticized over the past half a century by "postmodern" philosophers. There are, of course, positive things that came out of Enlightenment philosophy, such as more widespread belief in freedom, democracy, individual rights. Not all Enlightenment thinkers fell into absolute anti-supernaturalism. On the other hand, the exaltation of the rational human mind and scientific observation began to push out the need for myth, fairy tales, religion, and anything else that could not be verified in a laboratory. Those were silly superstitions of the past – myths that people leaned on for comfort because they didn't know any better. Science and philosophy would lead to truth and a better world; if there was a god at all, he was the proverbial clockmaker, creating the world and letting it run on its own.

The two worlds, supernatural and natural, were two separate worlds; they did not cross paths. There was certainly no Platform 9 3/4, and no train to the magical parts of the universe.

Truth is something far more deep and dynamic than scientific fact alone; and one cannot exactly offer a scientific proof for that statement! Two points of view clash: One claims that what can be discovered through scientific and rationalistic inquiry is all that can be know, and perhaps all that there is. The other claims that there are other ways of knowing – spiritual, even magical ways – which come from outside the human being's five senses. The fairy tale, by nature, belongs to the second view. The fairy tale is a protest against the Enlightenment Project.[1]

To get a better handle on this, we turn to five great fairy-tale philosophers. Against rationalistic, Enlightenment thinking come the great fairy tale thinkers of previous generations: George MacDonald, G.K. Chesterton, C.S. Lewis, Madeleine L'Engle and J.R.R. Tolkien.[2] Why these five in particular? Because these five great storytellers all argued against the equating of bare scientific fact with ultimate truth, and in response, they wrote fairy tales and defenses of fairy tales. One might object here on the grounds that these five are somewhat arbitrary, and that there are many more "giants" of the study of fairy tales to be consulted. The second point is granted, but to the first I would argue that these five are particular predecessors of Rowling's in that (a) they posit the fairy tale elements of the world squarely against the misuse of overly-rationalist scientific fatalism, and (b) they are heavily influenced by the Christian story. If it can be demonstrated that Rowling stands in the tradition of these five giants, then she has written a true and worthy fairy tale indeed.

MacDonald: "New Embodiments of Old Truth"

Tolkien, Lewis, and L'Engle all claimed George MacDonald as a mentor. MacDonald's essay, "The Fantastic Imagination," takes up objections to the fairy tale, the first of which is, "You write as if a fairytale were a thing of importance: must it have meaning?" One would imagine a reply from the likes of the gentleman quoted earlier to sound something like this: "No, it does not have any meaning, except to deceive; it is not true at all, and is the vain imagination of futile human thinking." Or perhaps a more common, but just as unhelpful response would be: "No, it's just an opportunity to escape from the real world." MacDonald's answer is quite different:

It cannot help having some meaning; if it have proportion and harmony it has vitality, and vitality is truth. The beauty may be plainer in it than the truth, but without the truth the beauty could not be, and the fairytale would give no delight. Everyone, however, who feels the story, will read its meaning after his own nature and development.

The words MacDonald uses when discussing truth are much different than the ones we hear today. "Proportion," "harmony," "vitality," "beauty," and the story's being "felt" are much different descriptions than "fact," "observed," "objective," and "verifiable." That the harmony and vitality of truth are things that the reader "feels" is a much different notion of truth-perception than bare scientific observation. Indeed, to communicate truth by means of the fairy tale is not merely to pass along verified information to someone, but to "wake up the things that are in [them]...to make [them] think things for [themselves]" (MacDonald). Truth as scientific fact does little to rouse humans beings to seek their full potential; truth as a force to be felt, as a reality to be inwardly perceived, shapes them for good.

Rowling's fairy tales fall squarely in line with MacDonald's description of truth, best illustrated by the materialistic Dursleys, who are caricatures of Enlightenment rationalists. Albus Dumbledore, the series' powerful, wise wizard, shows up on their doorstep in *Half-Blood Prince* to take Harry away and to rebuke the Dursleys for mistreating both Harry and their son Dudley, albeit in different ways (neglect and spoiling, respectively). Their incredulity at being confronted with the truth of their mistreatment of Dudley ("Us — mistreat Dudders? What d'you — ?") serves as a sufficient illustration of their strictly rationalistic mentality (*Prince* 55). So blinded were they by their hatred of anything that did not act in a scientifically verifiable way that they would not see the deeper truths of life. Appalled at the weird wizard who stood before them, they could not ponder for a moment that what Dumbledore was saying to them might be true. In fact, their anti-supernaturalism is responsible for their strict materialism, and spoiling "Dudders" with stuff was one of their biggest parenting problems. One might criticize Rowling for writing very two-dimensional, flat characters in the Dursleys. But it would be more appropriate to criticize the Dursleys themselves for being so flat, for those who forsake beauty and harmony for cold, hard fact in the pursuit of truth become little more than what the Dursleys are.

Fairy tales, for MacDonald, are "new embodiments of old truth," told in a created world wherein the laws of that world are consistently obeyed ("Fantastic Imagination").[3]   Rowling's magical world is vastly complex, and it is evident that she put significant research into setting parameters to that world, particularly in her study of alchemy (Simpson). Rowling is on record as stating that she tries "to be meticulous and make sure that everything operates according to laws, however odd, so that everyone understands exactly how and why" (Renton). While one might find ways to poke holes in the use of this or that spell over the course of the seven novels, it is on the whole an amazingly consistent world. And furthermore, there is one magical force that drives the whole story, that satisfies MacDonald's desire for the new embodiment of old truth, and that is altogether consistent throughout the series: Dumbledore's insistence that the most powerful form of magic is Love (*Prince* 444). Love, Dumbledore says, is "a force that is at once more wonderful and more terrible than death, than human intelligence, than forces of nature" (*Order* 843).   Dumbledore's description of love bears out in the series' conclusion, and indeed gives us a new, fascinating embodiment of the old truth about love.

Chesterton: "The World is Wild"

One of G.K. Chesterton's maxims could sum up the entire point of this chapter in five simple words: "Not facts first, truth first" (quoted in Pearce, *Man and Myth* 45). In *Orthodoxy*, Chesterton takes up the subject of the fairy tale in Chapter IV, "The Ethics of Elfland." He certainly did not believe fairy tales were unimportant, trifling little stories for children.

There are, in Chesterton's view, necessary ethical lessons to be learned by children and adults from fairy tales. When Jack kills the giant, the reader learns to launch an assault against pride. From Cinderella, humility is learned. From Beauty and the Beast, that "a thing must be loved before it is lovable." But Chesterton believed the fairy tale had a more important value than just the ethical lessons. At a higher level than the moral lessons is the philosophy of life espoused by the fairy tale believer, and that is this – that life is much better explained by magic than it is by laws, scientific or otherwise.   He writes,

> My first and last philosophy, that which I believe in with unbroken
> certainty, I learnt in the nursery. I generally learnt it from a nurse;
> that is, from the solemn and star-appointed priestess at once of
> democracy and tradition. The things I believed most then, the things

I believe most now, are the things called fairy tales. They seem to me to be the entirely reasonable things. They are not fantasies: compared with them other things are fantastic. ("Elfland")

Chesterton believed the fairy tale oriented him toward two firm convictions: (1) "that the world is a wild and startling place, which might have been quite different, but which is quite delightful," and (2) "before this wildness and delight one may well be modest and submit to the queerest limitations of so queer a kindness" ("Elfland"). The alternative that Chesterton saw in his day was "scientific fatalism," which is not very different than the belief that anything not scientifically verifiable is not worthy to be called "true." Chesterton profoundly illustrates the difference: the scientific fatalist believes "the leaf on the tree is green because it could never have been anything else…. [T]he fairy-tale philosopher is glad that the leaf is green precisely because it might have been scarlet" ("Elfland").

Or we might say that motorbikes travel at a fast pace on the ground because they might have flown instead. "MOTORCYCLES DON'T FLY!" Vernon Dursley shouted at Harry when he told him of his dream (*Stone* 25). For Vernon, motorcycles don't fly because they just don't; they never could, and they never will. For Harry, the fascinating possibility exists of a flying motorbike, a possibility that fairy-tale philosopher and Elfland creator J.K. Rowling brings into existence in her story. Natov rightly notes that in instances like these, "Rowling emphasizes the preeminence of the imagination of childhood and the need for children to question and dream" (312). Chesterton believed this very thing – indeed, that what he learned from the fairy tales in the nursery were "the entirely reasonable things."

What Rowling has done with the character of Arthur Weasley is precisely what Chesterton imagines the fairy-tale is designed to do: cause us to remember "that life is not only a pleasure but a kind of eccentric privilege" ("Elfland"). This is what Tolkien refers to as Recovery (Sturgis, "Hobbit" 6). Arthur is a man whose job it is to help maintain the division between the Wizarding and Muggle worlds, to make sure that Muggle objects don't get used magically. Yet, quite apart from magic altogether, Arthur is absolutely fascinated with scientific discoveries and inventions like the "eckeltricity" that runs the Dursley's fireplace (*Chamber* 46), and his "dearest ambition" is "to find out how airplanes stay up" (*Prince* 86) – which reminds us to ask *ourselves*, how *do* those heavy objects stay up without magic? And if objects as heavy as airplanes can fly, why not motorcycles?

Tolkien: Escape to Faerie,
and to "More Permanent Things"

Tolkien's classic essay, "One Fairy-Stories," is an important and informative study of the fairy tale. Tolkien himself has clearly become a gold standard in fantasy fiction since his epic *The Lord of the Rings* was written. Does *Harry Potter* work as a fairy tale according Tolkien's definition? That is somewhat difficult to answer, because Tolkien never gives a strict, positive definition of the fairy story. There is plenty of time spent on what a fairy tale is *not,* but Faerie itself defies any strict definition. It is an experience, a "particular mood and power."

Amy H. Sturgis has argued that the *Harry Potter* series meets Tolkien's criteria for a Fairy-Story on the grounds that (1) the story is an encounter with "Faerie," (2) the magic is taken seriously, (3) "primordial human desires" are satisfied, and (4) all four of the "gifts of the fairy-story" – Fantasy, Recovery, Escape, Consolation – are provided (3-8). "Fantasy" refers to a believable alternative world, or "sub-creation" (see below for more on this); "Recovery" is the same as Chesterton's notion of restoring the idea that the world is an exciting place; "Escape" refers to the move from the transient things of our world to meditation on the more "permanent things"; "Consolation" is the way in which the "primordial human desires" are satisfied.[4]

The reader encounters Faerie in the *Harry Potter* world.[5] In *Philosopher's Stone,* we begin with Harry in the world of Privet Drive, where life is comprised of a muddled malaise of manicured lawns and mundane, mechanical, middle-class, monetary Muggle matters. When Dumbledore arrives on the scene, we get our first glimpse of Faerie; but when Harry is suddenly whisked away to the Wizarding World, we encounter that certain "mood" and "power" that characterizes the land of Faerie. Like Smith from Tolkien's *Smith of Wootton Major,* we leave our normal daily life to spend time in a land of magic; then we return, unable to theorize academically about Faerie, but having experienced "sophisticated, serious, and even life-changing events" (Sturgis 4).

And the escape to Faerie is not mere "escapism." The notion of storytelling, whether by book, television, or film, as a means of "escape" from the so-called "real world" is part of the cause of the modern trivialization of the fairy tale. Tolkien believed that Escape was one of the four primary gifts of the fairy-story. The question about Escape is, *from* what, *to* what? Tolkien notes that it is hardly a bad thing to escape from the "transient...street lamps" to more "permanent and fundamental things," like Lightning, which are found in the fairy tale (30). The subject matter of fairy tales, then, frequently contains more consequential matters of Truth than do the details of nonfiction or even "realistic" fiction. *Harry Potter* is no different; while readers escape, with Harry himself, into the Wizarding World, we find that as they travel with Harry, we encounter many of the "same social conundrums as us Muggles" (Franklin 170). Yet these social conundrums happen in this other magical world and can therefore be approached by Fantasy.[6]

The *Harry Potter* novels most definitely "have the flavour of fairy-story," satisfying "certain primordial human desires" (Tolkien, "On Fairy-Stories" 6). In order to satisfy those desires, Rowling taps into the "Cauldron of Story;" she has borrowed from and built upon the folklore and mythologies of the past in creating her story. She has been quite up front about this in the interviews she has given:

> I've taken horrible liberties with folklore and mythology, but I'm quite unashamed about that, because British folklore and British mythology is a totally bastard mythology. You know, we've been invaded by people, we've appropriated their gods, we've taken their mythical creatures, and we've soldered them all together to make, what I would say, is one of the richest folklores in the world, because it's so varied. (Fry, "Living")

This "bastard mythology" is appropriated by Rowling to answer the "ancient desires" that Tolkien – and humans in general – want from the fairy tale. Alice Mills pinpoints the human longing that is the central theme of the *Harry Potter* novels; noting many mythological elements in the series, she writes, "All of these mythic figures...are linked to the human longing to transcend time and death" (4). Indeed, of the many human longings explored by Rowling, the fear of death is the central element in each, and Rowling appropriates elements of folklore and myth in the satisfying of those "primordial human desires." How one responds to the fear of death is the central conflict of the story; the fundamental difference between Harry and Voldemort is how each one approaches the reality of their own mortality. This is why Rowling says she included the two Bible verses on the graves of the Dumbledores and the Potters; they are about "living beyond death," and they "sum up" the entire message of the series (Adler, "Christian Imagery, *MTV.com*, October 15, 2007).

The story's Consolation, communicated through its *eucatastrophe*, is powerfully felt in *Harry Potter and the Deathly Hallows*. J.K. Rowling did excellent work leading up to that book's release, as evidenced by the ongoing debates, in between books 6 and 7, concerning Harry's fate. Would Harry die? The prominence of the debate meant that Rowling successfully created enough dramatic tension that Harry's death was a real possibility in the minds of her readers.

That possibility became a reality in *Deathly Hallows*, as Harry accepted the inevitability of his own death in the book's climax. As the reader comes to terms with Harry's death, hears Dumbledore's pronouncement that Harry is "not dead," and then returns with Harry to defeat Voldemort once and for all, the *Harry Potter* series provides precisely the type of *eucatastrophe* that Tolkien believes is a fundamental part of the fairy tale:

> Endings of this sort suit fairy-stories, because such tales have a greater sense and grasp of the endlessness of the World of Story than most modern "realistic" stories…. In its fairy-tale-or otherworld-setting, it is a sudden and miraculous grace: never to be counted on to recur. It does not deny the existence of dyscatastrophe, of sorrow and failure: the possibility of these is necessary to the joy of deliverance; it denies (in the face of much evidence, if you will) universal final defeat and in so far is evangelium, giving a glimpse of Joy, Joy beyond the walls of the world, poignant as grief. ("On Fairy-Stories" 34-35)

It is Harry's miraculous and unique return to life that is J.K. Rowling's greatest ingredient in the Cauldron (34).[7]. This is *Harry Potter's* Consolation, its "good catastrophe," the "sudden joyous turn" that "all complete fairy-stories must have." *Harry Potter*, it stands to reason, is a "complete fairy tale."

Lewis: "Awe and Bewilderment"

C.S. Lewis paints a beautiful picture of the power and truth of fairy tales in *Prince Caspian*. King Miraz calls the tales of the "Old Days" of talking animals, Naiads, Dryads and Fauns "nonsense, for babies" (43). Prince Caspian, the story's protagonist and rightful heir to Narnia's throne, is forbidden from talking or even *thinking* about "all those silly stories" (44). Miraz's reason is fairly simple: he knows those stories and the reality that they reflect contain the power to topple his murderous, unjust regime. Doctor Cornelius, Caspian's mentor, knows this, too, and that is why he tells Caspian the stories, even after being forbidden.

Lewis, like Chesterton and Tolkien, saw a problem with the way certain people – mainly those who had secured power and influence – utilized science in the dehumanization of people for manipulation and the creation of a "post-humanity," an engineered reality in which principles of eugenics determine just what a human should and should not be (Lewis, *Abolition* 86). It's important to note that it was not science[8] itself that Lewis and the others opposed, but misusers of science "who feel that the object, stripped to its qualitative properties and reduced to mere quantity, is wholly real" (82). Lewis here uncovers the false dichotomy about truth perpetuated by the fact-finders who have no use for deeper truth, or "deeper magic," as Lewis might call it (*Lion* 178-79) – whose naturalistic minds refuse to see that there is magic even in the written laws of the universe.

Science and magic are not at all diametrically opposed; as Lewis argued, "the serious magical endeavor and the serious scientific endeavor are twins" (*Abolition* 87). C.S. Lewis, whose writing was influenced by the medieval view of the "Seven Heavens" (both Narnia and the Ransom Triology) and alchemy (Ransom Trilogy), took a similar tack. "As Lewis points out in English Literature in the Sixteenth Century, astrology and astronomy were not really distinguishable until the Copernican revolution" (Ward).[9] Furthermore, alchemy and chemistry have common roots; Rowling's use of alchemy underscores the principle.[10] Many have also noted distinct parallels between Rowling's magic and Muggle technology.

The point of it all is this: both true Muggle science and true Faerie magic should be aimed at the uncovering of truth both in quantity and quality, in fact and fantasy, in logic and love. If one goes digging around the Narnia series asking, "Is it true?" and searches the whole world for the wardrobe, the painting, or the schoolyard that served as entrances to that enchanted land, that would be silly. But it would not be silly to ask, "Is it true? Can the death of one on behalf of another really bring healing, forgiveness, and restoration?" That would be a worthy pursuit of truth.

Lewis wrote fairy tales and many important essays on fairy tales, and there is much to commend to the careful reader in them; but one paragraph in particular is so apropos as a description for *Harry Potter*, it might be said that one of the best comments on the Potter books was written 40 years ago:

> Another very large class of stories turns on fulfilled prophecies – the
> story of Oedipus, or *The Man who would be King*, or *The Hobbit*. In

most of them the very steps taken to prevent the fulfillment of the prophecy actually bring it about.... Such stories produce...a feeling of awe, coupled with a certain sort of bewilderment such as one often feels in looking at a complex pattern of lines that pass over and under one another. One sees, yet does not quite see, the regularity. And is there not good occasion both for awe and bewilderment? We have just had set before our imagination something that has always baffled the intellect: we have *seen* how destiny and free will can be combined, even how free will is the *modus operandi* of destiny. The story does what no theorem can quite do. It may not be 'like real life' in the superficial sense: but it sets before us an image of what reality may well be like at some more central region. ("On Stories" 17)

What Lewis is getting at here is fundamental to the fairy tale – it immerses us in wonder-invoking reality that theories cannot comprehend. What "has always baffled the intellect" is "set before our imagination." The imagination perceives, through story, paradoxes of reality that the intellect cannot reconcile. This is Lewis against modernism, against the Enlightenment Project. Narnia, Middle Earth, Hogwarts – these are all places which, if we let ourselves experience their accompanying "awe and bewilderment," will teach us more about being human than any scientific or even philosophical propositional-truth statement.

Harry Potter is exactly the kind of story Lewis mentions here: it all turns on a prophecy, and indeed, the very actions Voldemort took to prevent its fulfillment resulted in its fulfillment. Rowling herself was rather excited to be exploring that theme (Anelli and Spartz, 2005), and while taking the clear side of "free will," nevertheless, as the story stands, it gives us the same thrill and awe that Lewis accredits to the prophecy story (more on this in chapter 11). We are able to experience, along with Harry, some of the most fascinating and befuddling of life's paradoxes, and that is worth all the effort put into reading the books.

Madeleine L'Engle: "What is Real?"

Madeleine L'Engle's contribution to the world of fantasy, both in her stories and in her writings on faith and art, have been significant and deserve close attention when considering how truth can be found in story. She, like other fairy tale-tellers before her, was confronted with the mentality that one cannot find truth in a "story," but that the "real world" is only found in "instructive books" (*Walking* 56). Of fairy tales and truth, she writes, "The world of fairy tale, fantasy, myth...is interested not in limited laboratory proofs but in truth" (57). Her *Time* stories bear this out in their unique combination of speculative quantum physics, myth and magic, all blending seamlessly together. Her call for artists to believe in and search for an "archaic understanding, a willingness to know things in their deepest, most mythic sense" (98) hearkens back to Tolkien's "primordial human desires." The opposite of this is escapism, story as mere entertainment leading to storytelling as consumerism, and literary vapidity.

L'Engle did not see tellers of tales as fringe folk who need to be discarded by the mainstream in order to get on with real life; neither did she see them as having their simple niche in the world among many other cute and enjoyable hobbies. She saw storytellers as absolutely vital to life on earth, as the ones who preserve some kind of meaning in life: "When the powers of this world denigrate and deny the value of story, life loses much of its meaning" (56). In other words, were it not for Frodo, Gandalf, Aslan, the Pevensies, Meg Murray, Charles Wallace, Harry,[11] and a host of so many other fairy tale heroes acting as preservatives, life would have lost meaning for many people long ago.

L'Engle believed not only that story was vital to meaning-making, but that it was crucial to survival during a "century of war;" "story was in no way an evasion of life, but a way of living life creatively instead of fearfully" (55). The marks of war upon the fairy tales of the last century is evident. There has been voluminous discussion of the influence of the World Wars on Tolkien's work. The Pevensies' adventure begins by escaping London in World War II. The central conflict of L'Engle's *A Swiftly Tilting Planet* is looming nuclear war. The influence of the world's current multi-faceted conflicts with international terrorism are evident in the latter half of the *Harry Potter* series.[12] Story is survival, precisely because it calls on us to imagine a world where these conflicts can be ended by love, by acts of bravery, and that all the dark chaos that has resulted from war can be countered with the peaceful quiet of the Shire, the coronation of kings and queens in Cair Paravel, the magical flight of a unicorn, and resurrection from the dead.

In *A Wind in the Door*, the second in her *Time* Quintet, she introduces a heavenly Teacher who challenges Meg on the perception of reality. Every time Meg or Charles Wallace are tempted to say something like, "It was just a dream; it wasn't real," the Teacher responds with a question (to which L'Engle provides no immediate concrete answer): "What is real?"

(62, 74, 83). Proginoskes, the cherubim, speaks of himself and observes of humans, "I'm real, and most earthlings can bear very little reality" (92). The Teacher's frequent, unanswered, pointed question, "What is real?" causes Meg and Charles Wallace to rethink reality itself and how it is perceived, so that they can become earthlings who can bear reality.

In the series' final "Dumbledore Denouement," at King's Cross in *Deathly Hallows*, Dumbledore makes a statement that gets at the heart of L'Engle's question, "What is real?" This passage will be treated in greater detail in chapter two, but for now, observe the point Rowling is making which is similar to L'Engle's:

> "Tell me one thing," said Harry. "Is this real, or has this been happening inside my head?" …
>
> "Of course it is happening inside your head, Harry, but why on earth should that mean it is not real?" (*Hallows* 723)

Dumbledore is challenging the way reality is perceived; Harry is not objectively, scientifically observing something. And yet the scene is quite real, and the choice he has to "go on" or to return to fight Voldemort is very real.

It turns out this was not just a clever line Rowling had in a moment of inspiration while writing *Deathly Hallows*. It was a message she wanted to get across when she first conceived the story:

> That dialogue is the key; I've waited seventeen years to use those lines. Yes, that's right. All this time I've worked to be able to write those two phrases; writing Harry entering the forest and Harry having that dialog. (Cruz)

Rowling falls right in line with L'Engle, then, on the simple fact that reality is not limited to the information one gathers with the five senses.

L'Engle didn't think literature derived primarily from the writers themselves. Quite the opposite. She believed the story held sway over the writer. In the introduction, we saw her use of Jean Rhys' "lake" illustration for literature. All writers are contributing to something greater than themselves; they are all rivers contributing to the great lake of literature. L'Engle drew from this that, rather than the story being completely in the hands of the writer, the writer must be a servant of the story. Rowling has spoken in an interview in such a way that indicates that, to some extent she believes this as well:

Q: What did she [Rowling's daughter, Jessica] tell you after she read the books?

A: She asked me why I did this thing or another, and I my answer was that *that's the way it had to be.* Yes, sometimes you can give an automatic answer, like some things were made up as literary mechanisms, elements that helped the plot. In other cases, is harder to explain the process of writing. I wrote it because it came up that way. *Sometimes I wrote as if something or somebody was saying it to me.*

Q: Could you describe what that something was?

A: There are so many answers to that question. I could say: "It was me, it was my subconscious." Yes, it was my subconscious, so what I've written comes from everything that I've done and all the people I've known because everything and everyone are somewhere in my head. *Or I could say it was the muse, and I like to think it was the muse, because that means the writer is not aware of the origin of what they're writing,* or at least is not fully aware of it, and I know it's a cliché word about the Harry Potter books, but they're magical. (Cruz, emphasis added)

J.K. Rowling has a sense that what she was creating was greater than herself, and that it was, indeed, magical. L'Engle argued, "When the artist is truly the servant of the work, the work is better than the artist" (*Walking* 17). In much the same way that Tolkien believed the true fairy tale-teller put his or her ingredients into an already simmering Cauldron of Story, so L'Engle believed that all true artists are rivers heading to a lake which is far greater and far more important than the river itself.

As such, anyone coming to a theory of Story from a Christian perspective will discover that the Christ-story finds its way into stories, sometimes quite unexpectedly, when the artist is willing to "listen," as L'Engle said, and to let her work be a servant to the story itself. We should not be surprised, then, when crucial elements of the Christ-story are found in the plot and symbolism – even in places where they were not necessarily intended by the author. One need not adopt a Christian worldview to believe this. Philip Pullman, atheist and author of the *His Dark Materials* trilogy, said the following in an interview with Peter Chattaway, who asked him about this very phenomenon of the Christian "mythology" working its way into the writing of "gifted storytellers:"

I was brought up in the Church of England, and whereas I'm an atheist, I'm certainly a Church of England atheist, and for the matter of that a 1662 Book of Common Prayer atheist. The Church of England is so deeply embedded in my personality and my way of thinking that to remove it would take a surgical operation so radical that I would probably not survive it. (Chattaway, 28 November 2007)

If it can happen to Pullman, it can happen to anyone. It might be objected that this "looking for the Christ story in every story" will result in interpretive chaos – that we can then go reading any and every influence into the artist's work that we like. MacDonald gives wisdom on this point that should be heeded:

It may be better that you should read your meaning into it. That may be a higher operation of your intellect than the mere reading of mine out of it: your meaning may be superior to mine....

"But a man may then imagine in your work what he pleases, what you never meant!"

Not what he pleases, but what he can. If he be not a true man, he will draw evil out of the best; we need not mind how he treats any work of art! If he be a true man, he will imagine true things; what matter whether I meant them or not? They are there none the less that I cannot claim putting them there! One difference between God's work and man's is, that, while God's work cannot mean more than he meant, man's must mean more than he meant. For in everything that God has made, there is a layer upon layer of ascending significance; also he expresses the same thought in higher and higher kinds of that thought: it is God's things, his embodied thoughts, which alone a man has to use, modified and adapted to his own purposes, for the expression of his thoughts; therefore he cannot help his words and figures falling into such combinations in the mind of another as he had himself not foreseen, so many are the thoughts allied to every other thought, so many are the relations involved in every figure, so many the facts hinted in every symbol. A man may well himself discover truth in what he wrote; for he was dealing all the time things that came from thoughts beyond his own. ("Fantastic Imagination")

Tolkien saw this happen with his own work. Over four years after he finished *The Lord of the Rings*, but prior to its publication, Tolkien had asked Father Robert Murray to read parts of the epic, and Father Murray had responded by saying that the story had "a positive compatibility with the order of Grace," and he compared Galadriel to the Virgin Mary (Pearce, *Man and Myth* 101). Tolkien's response is telling: "I have been cheered specially by what you have said ... because you are more perceptive, especially in some directions, than anyone else, and *have revealed to me more clearly some things about my own work*" (101, emphasis added).

Shippey argues, "*The Lord of the Rings*, then, contains within it hints of the Christian message, but refuses just to repeat it" (175). Tolkien himself says that the story is "a fundamentally religious and Catholic work," but it is not so in the specific details; he either did "not put in," or he "cut out practically all references to anything like 'religion,' to cults or practices.... For the religious element is absorbed into the story and the symbolism" (quoted in Shippey 175).

As with *The Lord of the Rings*, so with *Harry Potter*. The greatest mistake in some of the "fundamentalist Christian" analysis of the *Harry Potter* series has been the expectation that if it's truly "Christian," it must be as blatant as the *Left Behind* series, or at least as obvious as *The Lion, the Witch, and the Wardrobe*. But if this is the case, *The Lord of the Rings* needs to be removed from the approved list of Christian reading.

All three authors – Tolkien, Rowling, and Lewis – have spoken or written of their stories in a way that hints at L'Engle's theme of serving the work, specifically when discussing the origin of their ideas. Tolkien explained that while grading papers for his students, he suddenly found himself writing down a simple line: "In a hole in the ground there lived a hobbit." Lewis wrote of images that had intrigued him: "a fawn carrying an umbrella, a queen on a sledge, a magnificent lion" ("Sometimes Fairy Stories" 36). Rowling said that Harry popped into her mind "fully formed." All three expressed a certain compulsion to write, based on their initial inklings. Tolkien decided that he better find out what a hobbit was after writing that line. Lewis wrote of story ideas suddenly "bubbling up," and though he believed it necessary to critique the ideas that bubble up, he nevertheless allowed the whole story to be "pulled together" by Aslan.[13] Rowling, when suddenly faced with the realization that she was not writing about "Harriet" Potter (i.e., writing a feminist novel) chose to obey the initial image, saying "It was uncontrived. It wasn't conscious. That's how he happened. So I kept him that way" (King). All three, with L'Engle, believed their work to be more important than themselves, and the Christ story finds its way into all of their works. Lewis wrote of smuggling the gospel through his stories to "steal past those watchful dragons" ("Sometimes Fairy Stories"). It might just be said, as a corollary, that sometimes the gospel smuggles itself right past the author's conscious intentions and onto the page.

The Tales of Rowling the Bard

Rowling has written no academic defense of fairy tale and myth, but she has embedded her beliefs in the story itself. The most potent defense of the fairy tale comes in *Deathly Hallows*, with Dumbledore's bequest to Hermione: a copy of "The Tales of Beetle the Bard." The gift, like all the others, is met with confusion by Hermione. What help could a collection of children's stories provide in the hunt for Horcruxes? After examining the book for months for hidden, secret messages, the time finally comes to visit Xenophilius Lovegood, who wore the very same symbol that Hermione had found in the book and on the gravestone of Ignotus Peverell. Upon hearing the children's story about Death's gifts of the Hallows to the three brothers, Hermione expresses incredulity.

Before examining their argument about the children's story, observe the trick Rowling has played on her readers. There has already been quite the argument between Hermione and Mr. Lovegood about the horn mounted on the wall, Xenophilius insisting it belonged to a (non-existent) Crumple-Horned Snorkack, Hermione insisting (correctly) that it is an Erumpent horn (401). The reader has been led to believe that Hermione's logical, fact-finding, book-quoting precision is to be believed over the imaginative foolishness of Xenophilius, who once published an article arguing that Sirius Black was really rock singer Stubby Boardman (*Order* 191-93). Rowling has put us squarely on the side of Hermione, the logician, so that when she asks, "Mr. Lovegood, how can you *possibly* believe – ?" the reader is inclined to be as skeptical as she. Mr. Lovegood, though clearly discredited on a number of counts throughout the series, is not too far off the mark when he calls Hermione "painfully limited" (*Hallows* 410). As the argument ensues, and Hermione challenges the existence of the Resurrection Stone, Xenophilius challenges Hermione, in return, to prove that the Stone does *not* exist.

Hermione looked outraged.

"But that's – I'm sorry, but that's completely ridiculous! How can I possibly prove it doesn't exist? Do you expect me to get hold of – of all the pebbles in the world and test them? I mean, you could claim anything's real if the only basis for believing in it is that nobody's proved it doesn't exist!"

"Yes, you could," said Xenophilius. "I am glad to see that you are opening your mind a little." (411-412).

Strictly speaking, Hermione's point is correct. Correct, but "painfully limited," because it sets scientific verification as the standard of evidence for any claim to truth or existence. Rowling here is channeling the beliefs of one of her favorite authors, Edith Nesbit, who wrote as narrator in *Five Children and It,* "Grown-up people find it very difficult to believe really wonderful things, unless they have what they call proof'" (13) – only in this situation, Rowling has made the teenager the unbeliever, and the grown-up the believer. While Xenophilius's "open mind" has resulted in a lot of absurdities, he does hold Chesterton's view that "the world is a wild and startling place." This is his starting point, for he believes Hermione begins to open her mind once she is open to the possibility that the world could be another way than it currently is, or is perceived to be, or have been "proven" to be.

Before the Trio leaves Mr. Lovegood's, the Erumpent horn has exploded, just as Hermione had said that it would, and the reader is left once again on the side of skeptical Hermione, who has disproved Xenophilius's claims about the Crumple-Horned Snorkack. Harry, having believed in the Hallows, then drifts off into an obsession with them, which seemingly distracts him from the task at hand; Hermione tries in vain to call him back to the Horcrux hunt. She makes blatantly modernistic appeals to common sense and reason. When Ron protests, "The Chamber of Secrets was supposed to be a myth, wasn't it?" Hermione's response is emphatically, "But the Deathly Hallows *can't* exist" (426). In this, Hermione has taken a huge step backward, and Rowling has played another trick on her readers. Hermione, whose brilliant opinions we have come to trust, is set up here by Rowling as someone who has grown too old for fairy tales; for it was Hermione who was arguing with Professor Binns about the Chamber of Secrets just five years earlier:

"I deal with *facts*, Miss Granger, not myths and legends." [...]

"Please, sir, don't legends always have a basis in fact?"

And after many exchanges between the two, Professor Binns makes an argument that sounds just like Hermione's response to "The Tale of the Three Brothers:"

"That will do," he said sharply. "It is a myth! It does not exist! There is not a shred of evidence that Slytherin ever built so much as a secret broom cupboard! I regret telling you such a foolish story! We will return, if you please, to *history*, to solid, believable, verifiable *fact!*" (Chamber 152)

Professor Binns is a rationalist, despite the amusing irony that he is a *ghost*; legends and myths are "foolish." There is subtle commentary on Rowling's part here: as soon as Professor Binns departs from myth and returns to history and fact, "within five minutes, the class had sunk back into its usual torpor" (152). But the real story here is Hermione, who at one point argued that truth can be found even in fantastical stories. She's grown up a little too much, and by Book 7, she believes that something so mythical as the Deathly Hallows "just *can't* exist."

Why *can't* they, Hermione?

To what standard is Hermione appealing in her bald assertion that they *can't* exist? Strangely, though she has lived in a world of magic for seven years, she appeals to reason and scientific fact in trumping the fairy tale: "The Tale of the Three Brothers is a story," said Hermione firmly (426).

A story. End of discussion. She's been wearing the Invisibility Cloak – one of the three Hallows she believes don't exist – for six years; but her own experience doesn't seem to matter. "Fictional" stories don't matter in the pursuit of truth, for Hermione – only facts found in nonfiction books. Hermione, of course, is wrong; she's on a slow progression toward becoming like Susan Pevensie, who quit believing Narnia, because she was all "grown up," and grown-ups don't believe silly kid's stories (Lewis, *The Last Battle* 169). The Deathly Hallows do indeed turn out to be real, though in all fairness to Hermione, Dumbledore notes that the more fantastic events of the story – Death himself giving the gifts to the Peverell brothers – are probably not factually accurate (*Hallows* 714).

Dumbledore is the one who gets the point of the fairy tale right; he gave the copy of *The Tales* to Hermione "in the hope that she will find it *entertaining* and *instructive*" (126, emphasis added). Potter scholar John Granger has consistently argued that Rowling falls in line with Lewis and Tolkien, who believed "that the best books 'instruct while delighting'" (*Looking* xix-xx). This is precisely Rowling's use of "The Tale of the Three Brothers," and precisely what the *Harry Potter* series accomplishes.

It might be here objected that Rowling said she did not intended to write morality stories; but this is to radically misread her statements on the matter. In an interview in 1999, she was asked about the books' morality by James Naughtie (there's irony there):

> No, I've never at any point sat down and thought, what will be this book's moral? Having said that, a *moral normally emerges* fairly rapidly as I write, so it's not a conscious thing, it tends to evolve as I do the books. (emphasis added)

In 2003, Rowling said: "I've always believed that Harry Potter books *are highly moral*" ("Fighting in a Battle," emphasis added). Again, in 2005: "I never think in terms of What am I going to teach them? ... Although, undeniably, *morals are drawn*" (Grossman, emphasis added). Not only this, but she calls her books "*more moral* than Dahl's" (Nicol, "Boy wizard," emphasis added). When Rowling says she does not sit down to write morality tales, she does not mean she's writing *amoral* tales (which would be quite impossible), nor that her tales do not "instruct while delighting." Instruction is not her primary goal in the writing; it happens along the way.

In both "The Tale of the Three Brothers" and the *Harry Potter* series, "morals are drawn" about the way death should be approached, and therefore deep and vital truth can be gained from Rowling's "fairy tale."

Dumbledore powerfully underscores Rowling's belief about fairy tales in the final Dumbledore denouement:

> "And his knowledge remained woefully incomplete, Harry! That which Voldemort does not value, he takes no trouble to comprehend. Of house-elves and children's tales, of love, loyalty, and innocence, Voldemort knows and understands nothing. *Nothing.* That they all have a power beyond his own, a power beyond the reach of any magic, is a truth he has never grasped." (*Hallows* 709-710; emphasis in original)

The greatest and most blatant expression of evil in the series had a glaring weakness: he failed to understand the power of ridiculed persons and ideas like house-elves, love, loyalty, innocence – and, yes, children's tales. The power of a children's tale can bring the greatest evil to its knees. J.K. Rowling thinks every bit as highly of the fairy tale as MacDonald, Chesterton, Tolkien, Lewis, and L'Engle. The fact that she's allowing her five "Beedle the Bard" fairy tales to be published underscores Rowling's love of fairy tales.[14]

Rowling, Subcreator

A final challenge to the fairy tale should be addressed. The man quoted at the beginning of this chapter considered fiction to be "lies" and nonfiction to be "wholesome" and of "literary value." One could imagine his reasoning looking something like this: Why does one have to craft an untrue story in order to communicate a truth or a moral? Why does one need Aslan or Harry to explain the power of self-sacrificial love? Why not simply state the principle, "You should live a life of self-sacrificial love," and make sure, by repetition, that humans get the message? And are there not plenty of factual, historical stories that can illustrate the moral?

Tolkien would have answered that humans are "Subcreators," that "fantasy is a natural human activity," because, being created in the very image of a Creator, we were made to create (11, 27-28). And if we are Subcreators, made in a Maker's image with the desire and ability to create worlds, it is altogether likely that when we create, the Truth of our own world will be reflected in the ones we craft. This is why Tolkien writes, "History often resembles 'Myth,' because they are both ultimately of the same stuff" (14).

Rowling eschews the terminology like "merely myth," as seen by the Peverell story as well as by the legend of the Chamber of Secrets. Though factual historian Professor Binns is put out by having to teach about anything that cannot be objectively proved, he turns out to be quite wrong, and the Chamber quite real. By writing these fairy tales within a fairy tale, Rowling has constructed a creative defense of fairy tales, complete with lessons on how to read them by observing the important lessons Harry learns as the result of each, as well as how *not* to read them, illustrated by the reactions of Hermione, Professor Binns, and above all, the Dursleys.

Not only this, but as the entire *Harry Potter* saga is itself a fairy tale, it contains powerful elements of truth and transformation, opening the hearts of millions to the beautiful magic of courageous, self-sacrificial love. For Chesterton, the moral of the fairy tale was important, but more important still was the broader philosophy assumed by the fairy tale. Hermione understood that "The Tale of the Three Brothers" told a moral, but she had lost the grander vision; quite ironically, she had lost the magical meaning, that the world is wild, and doesn't fit into the categories of the strict logician or the scientific fatalist. Before moral lessons of courage and love can be expounded, it's important to recognize that in reading a fairy tale, we let ourselves encounter the Perilous Realm. As the protagonist of George MacDonald's *Phantastes* experiences while traveling through Fairy Land, we are to enter the story to the point where we feel that we truly are in the story – we experience the story as thought it were our own. Our next stop on the journey explores how the reader encounters this magical realm while traveling with Harry.

Chapter 1 Notes

1   The obvious counter to this statement will be that fairy tales were around long before the Enlightenment. Granted. But on the ideological level, Fairy Tales are protests against Enlightenment-type thinking, *and* the perpetuity of the genre throughout modernity and into postmodernism is in view. Certainly, the fairy stories of MacDonald, Chesterton, Lewis, Tolkien, L'Engle, and Rowling are protest against the Enlightenment Project.

2   These five authors will be consistently invoked throughout the remainder of this book.

3   Lewis makes this point well in "On Stories," in which he tells the story of a man who believed that everything in a fairy-tale is "arbitrary." Lewis writes, "His error was profound. The logic of a fairy-tale is as strict as that of a realistic novel, though different" (13). The man's error was so profound for the simple reason that it was informed by the belief that anything magical like a fairy-tale must not be logical, but random.

4   For a more detailed examination, see Amy H. Sturgis's excellent article, "Harry Potter is a Hobbit" in *CSL:The Bulletin of the New York C.S. Lewis Society*. Ed. by Robert Trexler. May/June 2004, Vol. 35, No. 3. pp. 1-10.

5   Chapter Two will give added attention to how the reader encounters Faerie in the *Harry Potter* books.

6   Part III of this book rests on the assumption that, having escaped into the magical world, we can return to our own Muggle world and have much-needed conversations we were unwilling or ill-prepared to have before.

7   King's Cross in *Deathly Hallows* will be treated at length in Chapter Two. The meaning and significance of Harry's "death" will be explored in Chapter Six.

8   Tolkien has the same complaint against the misuse of science. He writes in "On Fairy-Stories" about the "sense of separation" caused by the Fall: "As far as our western, European, world is concerned, this 'sense of separation; has in fact been attacked and weakened in modern times not by fantasy but by scientific theory. Not by stories of centaurs or werewolves or enchanted bears, but by the hypotheses (or dogmatic guesses) of scientific writers who classed Man not only as "an animal"-that correct classification is ancient-but as "only an animal." (33)

9   Galileo, ironically, made the same point as Lewis about science and magic in his "Letter to the Grand Duchess Christina."

10   For discussion of the alchemical framework of the Harry Potter series, see John Granger, *Unlocking Harry Potter* (Zossima, 2007).

11   We must consider L'Engle's response to *Harry Potter*, for some readers will be familiar with it and think that her response to the series renders this entire section moot. In *Newsweek* in May 2003, L'Engle was asked whether or not she had read *Harry Potter*. Her response: I read one of them. It's a nice story but there's nothing underneath it. I don't want to be bothered with stuff where there's nothing underneath. Some people say, 'Why do you read the Bible?" I say, 'Because there's a lot of stuff underneath.'" The key element here is that she had only read one book, assumedly the first book. As such, it's impossible to accept her criticism as valid, simply because it was not fully-informed. Many, many readers missed the deeper, underneath meaning until later books fleshed it out a bit more. Further, Potter fans need not be harsh on her either, for she had, after all, only read one. It would have been interesting to have heard L'Engle's opinion on the series as a whole, but sadly, that can never be.

12   J.K. Rowling's commentary on Terrorism is explored in Chapter 15.

13   Dr. Michael Ward has proven that Lewis was more than a little cagey when expressing these seemingly innocent "I don't know where the story came from" sentiments in his book *Planet Narnia*. But having a specific framework (in Lewis's case, the medieval "seven heavens") doesn't negate the author's "serving the work."

14   *The Tales of Beedle the Bard*, at the time of the publication of *Harry Potter & Imagination*, are not yet available; publication date December 4, 2008.

Chapter Two

Between Two Worlds
Encountering Faerie with Harry

What a tale we have been in, Mr. Frodo, haven't we? I wish I could hear it told! Do you think they'll say: *Now comes the story of the Nine-Fingered Frodo and the Ring of Doom?* And then everyone will hush, like we did, when in Rivendell they told us the tale of Beren One-Hand and the Great Jewel. I wish I could hear it! And I wonder how it will go on after our part. ~ Samwise Gamgee, *The Return of the King*

Samwise Gamgee understands point of the fairy tale. For Sam, the story itself is important, and the telling of tales is filled with wonder and inspiration. But to actually be a part of one! That is a tremendous dream in the heart of everyone who loves myths and fairy tales. For most people, day to day life is not filled with the wonder of Faerie, and being able to enter one is the kind of healthy "escape" that Tolkien requires of the fairy tale. But most of the time, the subcreated world seems too far distant from our own; it's a tale we hear while staying in Rivendell, not one that we experience back home in the Shire. The trick is to find ways to Rivendell on a daily basis; indeed, to live each day between two worlds – the mundane one that we're told is true, and the magical one that we *know* is true, that needs to invade the mundane. We are the places where those worlds intersect.

In the art of subcreation, there is a lot of room to play, particularly with the nature of the magical world which is being created. Tolkien's Middle-Earth is essentially our own world, but the time frame is ages ago, so to serve as England's mythological foundation. Lewis places Narnia in a different dimension altogether, and Narnia's magic is not to occur in the primary world. Lewis rewrote his first draft of *The Magician's Nephew* because he had initially written Diggory with the ability to do things in the primary world one could only do in Narnia (Duriez 107). In L'Engle's *A Wrinkle in Time*, other worlds are found through the tesseracts, which have a scientific, if still fantastical, explanation; but in subsequent books in the *Time* Quintet, elements of Faerie enter into the primary world itself in the forms of cherubim, Echthroi, and unicorns. Philip Pullman writes an alternative history to our own world in *His Dark Materials*. Many other fantasy writers start with the subcreation as the primary world (i.e., Ursula K. Le Guin's *Earthsea* books), usually referred to as high fantasy. J.K. Rowling puts the two worlds very close – in fact, her subcreation is hiding right underneath the primary world. *Harry Potter*, then, is a wainscot fantasy, because the Wizarding World is a "wainscot society" (Clute 991). Wainscot societies are "invisible and undetected societies living in the interstices of of the dominant world" (991). That's a good description of Rowling's subcreation.

For someone who's written such effective fantasy, J.K. Rowling has a rocky relationship with fantasy fiction:

> In fact, I don't really like fantasy. It's not so much that I don't like it, I really haven't read a lot of it…. It didn't occur to me for quite a while that I was writing fantasy when I'd started "Harry Potter," because I'm a bit slow on the uptake about those things. I was so caught up in it. And I was about two thirds of the way through, and I suddenly thought, This has got unicorns in it. I'm writing fantasy! (Jones)

She has cited Edith Nesbit, Elizabeth Goudge, Paul Gallico, Clement Freud, and C.S. Lewis as influences; while she admires Tolkien, she's stated rather clearly he's not one of her favorites (Nel, "Is There a Text" 250, 252). Upon realizing that she was writing fantasy, she made the statement that she was trying to "subvert the genre" (Grossman). If Rowling did not set out to write fantasy, discovered she was writing it along the way, and then attempted to "subvert the genre," what do we make of Rowling's magical world?

Tolkien had strict criteria for the fairy-story when it came to the distance between the primary world and the subcreation, or secondary world. Given the proximity of the Wizarding and Muggle worlds, it could be questioned whether Rowling's books would meet Tolkien's "distance" criterion which he applied to "travelers' tales," namely, that if the wonders of the magical world can be found by traveling somewhere in our own world, it is not strictly a fairy-story (6). Rather than being a world in which "our fates are sundered, and our paths seldom meet," the Wizarding World exists right under the nose of the Muggle world and is in constant interaction with it, even if Muggles don't realize it (5).

While there are many barriers and clear boundaries which keep Muggles out of Wizarding World, they are in place primarily because of the Statute of Secrecy, which is based on the premise that Muggles can, and in fact do, regularly cross paths with the Wizarding World. Memory modification is frequently used to erase the Muggle memories of these events. In *Fantastic Beasts and Where to Find Them*, the story is told of a seven week meeting held in 1692 by the International Confederation of Wizards with the sole purpose of deciding which beasts would be hidden from Muggles, and how that would be done (Scamander xv). In *Deathly Hallows* we learned that there were certain places in the past where Muggles and Wizards lived side-by-side without conflict (*Hallows* 319). As such, the boundary between our own world and the Wizarding one may not be considered the natural or ontological boundary between our world and Faerie, but one imposed by the possessors of magic in our own world. In classic Rowling style, she's take a traditional fantasy-fiction concept – in this case, the ontological boundary between Faerie and the Muggle world – and turned it into a social justice issue.[1]

Still, there is something concrete about the separation between the two worlds. Rowling comments in an interview:

> Narnia is literally a different world, whereas in the Harry books you go into a world within a world that you can see *if you happen to belong*. A lot of the humour comes from collisions between the magic and the everyday worlds. (Renton, emphasis added)

Contained in this quote is the unique paradox of the world Rowling has created: you cannot "see" it if you don't "belong," yet there are frequent "collisions" between the two worlds nonetheless. It could be argued that Rowling's work is properly a fairy story, because while a Muggle can get *to* the Wizarding World, he or she cannot do what they do there, or be a part of that world. You have to already belong, similar to Tolkien's story, *Smith of Wootton Major*, in which Smith could not enter Faerie without the Star, his key to belonging. The separation is more concrete in *Smith* than in *Harry Potter*, but it remains impossible for any Muggle to truly participate in and belong to the Wizarding World. Just ask poor Aunt Petunia.

So there is, after all, something of an ontological break between the Wizarding and Muggle worlds which contributes to the fairy-tale nature of the series. In fact, there is both an ontological and a contrived break between the two worlds. One pertains to the very nature of being magical (witches and wizards will never be Muggles, and Muggles will never be witches or wizards), and the other pertains to a social justice issue – the divide imposed by the Wizarding World because the Muggle world hated and persecuted the it.

This places *Harry Potter* firmly into the category of "wainscot fantasy," meaning that the fantasy element of the story is found in a sub-world within the primary world.   Even as wainscot fantasy, however, Rowling is doing something a bit different. Kerrie Anne Le Lievre, in an article called "Wizards and wainscots," has argued that *Harry Potter* contains a high fantasy scenario within a wainscot fantasy setting (1). Rowling's Wizarding World has "a complexity not often seen in wainscot fantasy," with a long, historical conflict that is being played out within that secondary world at the time when Harry Potter arrives on the scene (1). So while Rowling is not writing strictly high fantasy, she has brought all its complexity into her wainscot fantasy, making it a powerfully effective story. Its complexity allows readers to explore the various social issues raised not only by the Wizard-Muggle divide but also by the issues within the Wizarding World itself.

Ultimately, whether or not the break between the Muggle World and "Faerie" is as clear-cut as Tolkien required misses the point. As readers travel with Harry, they encounter Faerie. As Amy Sturgis has argued, the reader encounters that certain "mood and power" of the Perilous Realm, a world where the magic is taken seriously, feels humanity's "primal desires," and experiences Fantasy, Recovery, Escape, and Consolation" ("Hobbit" 5-6). This is nowhere more evident than in the way that the magic of "love" is treated in the stories. "Love" is the magic that most marks *Harry Potter* as a fairy-story, because there is something about the Wizarding World that has potential to communicate it, to incarnate love in a way that the Muggle world cannot. It's true that this most powerful form of magic is something that is accessible not only to the Wizarding World, but to Muggles also. Love is available to all, and powerful for all. Nevertheless, love, in the *Harry Potter* stories, is manifested in the Wizarding World in a way that it cannot possibly be manifested at Privet Drive, apart from the work of Albus Dumbledore. Harry's being saved by his mother's love has no Muggle parallel; this is something that can only be manifested by magic.

It's unlikely Rowling would be too troubled even if Tolkien *did* deny *Harry Potter* the official status of fairy tale. She's been quite up front about the fact that as far as fantasy goes, she's attempting to "subvert the genre" (Grossman, "Hogwarts"). This is precisely what is happening when the postmodern social justice issue trumps, or at least stands alongside the traditional, ontological break between the Wizarding and Muggle worlds, between Faerie and our own world. Rowling is arguing through *Harry*

Potter that most magic doesn't make the world any better whatsoever; the magic itself isn't saying anything in particular about the goodness or badness of the world. This is why after the series' turning point at Voldemort's return, Harry's whole world gets turned upside down; he learns by the end of his fifth year at Hogwarts that because of Dumbledore's invocation of the ancient magic, it's actually the mundane, Muggle world of 4 Privet Drive where he's safe, and what he thought was his "home," the magical world, where he is in danger, and even at times the outcast.

The Realm of Magic

The interweaving of these two worlds is fundamental to the effectiveness of the *Harry Potter* series, particularly for postmodern readers. Rowling has written into her story many places in which two realms – whether Magic and Muggle realms, or Life and Death – are surprisingly close. The King's Cross scene in *Deathly Hallows* is the most profound example, bringing together both the Life/Death and Magic/Muggle divides, and it will be treated in depth later in this chapter. The usual King's Cross at Platform 9 and 3/4, the Leaky Cauldron, the phone booth at the Ministry, the store front at St. Mungo's, and just about any fireplace – if a witch or wizard is carrying flue powder – all serve as transition points between the Muggle and Magic worlds. The veil in the Department of Mysteries is a profound picture of the proximity of Life and Death.

Even when the main characters are fully embedded in the Wizarding World as opposed to the Muggle world, they are at Hogwarts, "the transitional world situated between childhood and adulthood" (Natov 318). Rowling has consistently emphasized the fact that her characters were going to "grow up," and the Hogwarts setting is a transitional world in which this seven-year maturing process happens.

The atmosphere at Hogwarts stands in stark contrast with the Muggle world. Michael Ward quotes C.S. Lewis's belief about the medieval world in relation to its cosmology: "the medieval universe was 'tingling with anthropomorphic life, dancing, ceremonial, a festival not a machine'" ("Star"). Recalling the theme of the first chapter, "a festival not a machine" is central to the idea that truth about life is more than an industrial project or a scientific fact. Hogwarts School plunges the reader into the "tingling" world Lewis was fascinated by, and it is the exact opposite of the monotony of Privet Drive. Hogwarts itself is filled with life, not least in the Room of Requirement, which changes itself based entirely on a student's choice.

Rowling is not the first author to have created a Wizarding boarding school as the place for the training of young wizards. Ursula K. Le Guin's *A Wizard of Earthsea* tells the story of young Ged, a powerful wizard whose life is shaped by the egregious error of pride he makes while learning his craft at a wizarding school. The mentors of Roke instruct him in wizardry and teach him humility and wisdom, turning him into the legendary wizard he becomes.

Le Guin has noted with a bit of irritation the reaction to the *Harry Potter* stories as opposed to her own:

> I'm glad kids are reading. But when grownups sit around saying that there's never been anything like Harry Potter, well, gee, I had a wizard school in 1968. These people simply haven't been reading this stuff. They've been sneering at fantasy until the huge success of a fantasy made them read it. And then they say there's nothing like this, and it breaks my heart. When I think of all the great fantasies around. And Rowling has certainly read me; it's obvious she's read me. (quoted in Pennington 92)

It is lamentable that Le Guin's masterful *Earthsea* books have not received more attention, and without a doubt she's correct that critics have been "sneering at fantasy" for a long time, and unjustifiably so. But there are profound differences in Rowling's work, even with the superficial similarities, which give the *Harry Potter* series greater popularity than *Earthsea,* and the fundamental point of divergence is Rowling's use of two closely intertwined worlds as opposed to Le Guin's self-contained world of Earthsea. With Ged, the reader starts off in an entirely different world, has to get used to that world and the way that it works, and find points of emotional relationship with Ged. With Harry, the readers start off in a world not unlike their own, with its seemingly boring repetition and technology-driven pace, empathizes the "unfair" treatment he receives, and is suddenly whisked away from that world to a place where, with Harry, they are valued, loved, and full of excitement about new possibilities. This interplay between the Muggle and Wizarding Worlds make, literally and metaphorically, a world difference.

"Something New:" The Spirit of Faerie

So far, we've seen that Rowling, while bearing some similarities to other well-known fantasy writers, she is doing something a bit different than all of them. She's got two different worlds, like *Narnia* and unlike *The Lord of the Rings* and *Earthsea*; but magic invades the primary world, unlike Lewis, because her worlds are not different dimensions. There is a clear, ontological break between her two worlds, but they could probably co-exist peacefully if not for the oppressive anti-magic metanarrative of the Muggle world.

It is precisely this difference, this "something new" (Cockrell 15), this "doing something slightly different" (Lydon), that makes Rowling's series unique and loved by readers of all ages. Because Rowling has in some ways subverted the genre, she has freed herself from the artistic fault of so many other fantasy writers: copying Tolkien. Rowling never cites him as an influence and though she admires him and read *The Lord of the Rings* when she was "about twenty" she says, "I've never re-read it, which is revealing (usually with my favourite books I re-read them endlessly)" ("Red Nose Day Chat," 2001). It would be difficult indeed to argue that she's borrowing much from Tolkien at all.[2] She said in 2000:

> In fact, I don't really like fantasy. It's not so much that I don't like it, I really haven't read a lot of it. I have read *Lord of the Rings*, though. I read that when I was about 14. I didn't read *The Hobbit* until I was in my 20s - much later. I'd started *Harry Potter* by then, and someone gave it to me, and I thought, Yeah, I really should read this, because people kept saying, "You've read *The Hobbit*, obviously?" And I was saying, "Um, no." So I thought, Well, I will, and I did, and it was wonderful. (Sheepish smile)
>
> It didn't occur to me for quite a while that I was writing fantasy when I'd started *Harry Potter*, because I'm a bit slow on the uptake about those things. I was so caught up in it. And I was about two thirds of the way through, and I suddenly thought, This has got unicorns in it. I'm writing fantasy! (Jones)

Not everyone sees Rowling's peculiar relationship with fantasy fiction as a good thing. John Pennington, in "From Elfland to Hogwarts" in *The Lion and the Unicorn* 2002, claims that Rowling "violates the integral rules of the fantasy game, never capturing the integrity of the very fantasy tradition that she is mining for riches;" and in doing so, she fails in the fantasy genre (78).

Philip Nel has answered the complaint well in his 2005 article, "Is There a Text in this Advertising Campaign?" (*The Lion and the Unicorn*), by noting that comparing Rowling to Tolkien and concluding that Tolkien did fantasy better is hardly a sufficient method of analyzing Rowling in the first place (250). While Tolkien's philosophy of the fairy-story is helpful for understanding why readers love *Harry Potter*, which was demonstrated in Chapter One, Rowling's own primary fantasy influences, Nel argues, are authors like Edith Nesbit and Elizabeth Gouge (250-52). Pennington claims that unlike Tolkien, Rowling fails to create "wonder" because her secondary world keeps bumping into the primary one, and Nel counters effectively that this is precisely what we find in Nesbit's fantasy (251). Not only this, but "Rowling's frequent juxtaposition of ordinary and extraordinary creates a fantasy that has a deliberately everyday quality" (251). In other words, what Pennington complains about is, in reality, the most effective part of *Harry Potter*; the interplay of the two worlds is what lets readers encounter Faerie.

Rowling's rule-breaking is very much like that of her own creation: the rules aren't as important as the spirit of the thing. So when Harry is faced with the choice to either follow a school rule or to travel once again to the corridor where Fluffy is guarding the entrance to the path that leads to the Philosopher's Stone, the morally correct paradoxical choice is: break the rule and do what is right. Like Harry, Rowling breaks a few fantasy rules but accomplishes what has become the first epic and most influential "fairy tale" since the advent of postmodernism, creating a story which brings the virtues and beauties of older, traditional, rule-following fantasy into the hearts and minds of postmodern readers. The subversion of the genre might have been necessary in order to accomplish the spirit of the fairy story with this kind of success in our time. *Harry Potter* has become the gold standard for how to transport postmodern readers to Faerie; in true postmodern fashion, you just might need to break a few rules to get there.

One thing is evident: Rowling really means it when she says she's writing exactly what she wants to write, and nothing else. Her stories are influenced by fantasy, but she breaks its rules; they are influenced by the detective novels, but she freely admits to breaking those rules as well (just like Dorothy Sayers, she says) (Anelli and Spartz). One wonders whether critiquing Rowling for breaking fantasy rules is even a logical thing to do, as she has been quite up front about it. She doesn't play by the rules, because the experience of the story is the point. John Granger is on the mark here in noting that "genre blurring" is part and parcel of Rowling's style and comprises one of the key postmodern elements of the series (*Unlocking*, 153-54).

The Battleground for Grace and Evil

Having said all that, there is a sense, thematically, Rowling isn't succeeding in her subversive attempt, because Tolkien and Lewis saw magic in much the same way as Rowling. In both Middle-Earth and Narnia, magic is just as easily used for evil as for good. Magic underscores the principle that there is more to this world than naturalism suggests, but magic, in and of itself, is not the solution to problems in the world. What Paul F. Ford wrote of Lewis's *Narnia* series could be applied directly to Rowling's *Harry Potter* series:

> In short, the *Chronicles* do not present a battle between the ordinary, natural world and dark, unnatural magical powers. The ordinary, natural world is rather the battlefield on which the good magic confronts the bad, just as ultimately the human heart is the stage on which the mystery of grace wrestles with the mystery of evil. (304)

There is a strong parallel here between *Narnia* and *Harry Potter.* Lewis's "deeper magic" is what gives Aslan the victory over the White Witch; it's the divine trump card that overrules her claim. Likewise, the self-sacrificial love, first of Lily, then of Harry is the power that defeats Voldemort. Love is called the greatest magic by Dumbledore, and even "old magic" by Voldemort himself, so ultimately Rowling's world is, like Narnia, a stage on which the deeper magic of love meets the dehumanized magic of selfishness.

Not only this, but Harry's heart becomes the battleground for these two mysteries, grace and evil. The piece of Voldemort's soul residing in Harry makes his very existence a literal battle between what is best and what is worst in the world. This is nowhere more evident than in *Order of the Phoenix*, as Harry battles with his anger. In the end, grace triumphs in the battle: "It was your heart that saved you," Dumbledore told Harry after his love for Sirius expelled the possessing Voldemort from himself (*Order* 844). By the time Harry begins to feel hope again in *Deathly Hallows*, he has so won the battle in his own heart that he can invade Voldemort's mind without the Dark Lord's knowledge, giving him the edge he needs to complete his mission.

For Lewis, magic is the realm in which gnostic dualism is done away with, and heaven and earth draw closest together. In attempting to explain the Christian celebration of the Eucharist in *Letters to Malcolm: Chiefly on Prayer,* he writes:

I find no difficulty in believing that the veil between the worlds...
is nowhere else so thin and permeable to divine operation. Here
a hand from the hidden country touches not only my soul but my
body.... Here is big medicine and strong magic. Now the value, for
me, of the magical element in Christianity is this. It is a permanent
witness that the heavenly realm, no less than the natural universe
and perhaps very much more, is a realm of objective facts – hard,
determinate facts, not to be constructed *a priori*, and not to be
dissolved into maxims, ideals, values, and the like.... Enlightened
people want to get rid of this magical element in favour of what they
would call the "spiritual" element. But the spiritual, conceived as
something thus antithetical to "magical," seems to become merely
psychological or ethical. (103-04)

Lewis is arguing that in the Christian Eucharist, the two worlds
– heaven and earth- are closest. This is "magic," he says, and magic is not
simply spiritual or simply physical; magic is the place where the spiritual
and physical meet most profoundly. It's no wonder that Lewis saw such
value in fantasy and fairy tale for telling the Christian story! The interplay
of two worlds is both the worldview of Christian theology and what fairy
story is all about.

There are at least five distinct responses to magic in the series. Firstly,
on the one extreme, there are the Dursleys who are adamantly opposed to
magic, because it is not "normal." Magical people are "freaks." The Dursleys
are utterly opposed to all wonder and imagination. Secondly, there are
Muggles who are completely oblivious to magic, who are so wrapped up in
the mundane and in the fast pace of modern living that they do not have
time to notice. Thirdly, there are Muggles who are fascinated with magic,
or at least accepting of it, like Hermione's parents. Wizards can be split
up into the other two camps: those who see magic as a responsibility to
be used wisely (Dumbledore and the Hogwarts staff) and those who see
magic as power, something that makes the Wizarding World more special
than the Muggle world (Voldemort, Fudge, Grindelwald). Magic is no
innocuous plot device.

What is most powerful about Rowling's magic is its combination with
her belief in children. Rowling was asked about the witchcraft controversy
in one interview:

Q: What are your feelings towards the people who say your books
are to do with cults and telling people to become witches ? (reader's
question, didn't give name)

Rowling: Alfie [a young boy]. Over to you. Do you feel a burning desire to become a witch?

Alfie: No.

Rowling: I thought not. *I think this is a case of people grossly underestimating children. Again.* ("World Exclusive," emphasis added)

The addition of "again" demonstrates that the underestimation of children is something that irks Rowling. In *Harry Potter*, magic opens up new worlds of possibility for children, as exemplified by the reader's association with Harry himself through the third person limited omniscient viewpoint, meaning, we're seeing things as though it were an objective, third person narrative, but in reality, most of the story is "limited" to Harry's perception. We experience the world as Harry does. Far from being about pagan manipulation of the world, as many Christian fundamentalists have falsely asserted, "Harry's supernatural powers invite children to imagine beyond the boundaries of their limitations" (Natov 315). In other words, in classic fairy tale form, Harry Potter is able to rise from the status of oppressed orphan to hero through the discovery that he has more potential than he ever realized, and Rowling is inviting her readers to do the same. She's tapping into her readers' imaginations, creating a space between Hogwarts and readers' hearts where magical wonder can inspire and transform.

The Choice at King's Cross

There is a moment in *Smith of Wootton Major* in which the protagonist stands at a moment of decision in a place between the two worlds, his primary world and Faerie. After many years of having the privilege of visiting Faerie, he is asked by the King of Faerie to pass the Fay-Star to a new person, so that someone else can travel there. This key moment of decision is central to the effectiveness of the entire story. It is the story's critical moment, its climax.

Likewise, Rowling places Harry between two worlds at various times during the series, the most potent of which is his conversation with Dumbledore in the divine waiting room before returning to duel Voldemort one last time. It is entirely appropriate that Rowling chose King's Cross as Harry's perception of this mysterious realm, because King's Cross functions in the series as the most powerful symbol of the barrier/gateway between the two worlds. There, Harry experiences his final Dumbledore denouement, the final deconstruction of his headmaster and mentor, and the forgiveness and healing of their relationship. And there Harry is faced with a very real choice: to "go on," to rest forever with Dumbledore, his parents, his loved ones; or to return and face Voldemort again.

We must assume that the choice is a very real one. The ambiguity comes in the final exchange between Harry and Dumbledore:

> "Tell me one thing," said Harry. "Is this real, Or has this been happening inside my head?" …
>
> "Of course it is happening inside your head, Harry, but why on earth should that mean it is not real?" (*Hallows* 723)

There are two ways to take this.[3] We could assume that Rowling is saying that something does not have to be factually real for it to have real meaning and truth, which is a correct statement in and of itself. On the other hand, we could assume that she is playing with the notion of *how reality is perceived*, or as we noted in Chapter One, with the notion of *what is real*.

In favor of the former reading, it has been argued by Edmund Kern that Harry really learns nothing in that moment at King's Cross other than what he already knew. Consider, for example, the fourteen times that Harry asks Dumbledore a question, and Dumbledore replies with some form of "you know," and then waits for Harry to work it out. This reading – that Harry experienced a near-death dream – argues that it was a moment of catharsis for him, coming to terms with his beloved headmaster, and putting all the pieces together. But it is, after all, a conversation that Harry is having with *himself*, and not with Albus Dumbledore at all.

There are several reasons to accept the latter view as the better reading – that the King's Cross scene actually *happened*, even if how it happened is left ambiguous. In the first place, for Harry's choice to return to face Voldemort to *mean* anything at all, the choice has to be viable; and if there's any clear moral lesson from the Harry Potter series, it's that our *choices* matter. Rowling has reinforced this theme over and over again in the books and in interviews. In a post-*Deathly Hallows* F.A.Q. section of her website, she writes about this scene in particular,

> It is important to state that I always saw these kinds of magic (the very deepest life and death issues) as essentially un-scientific; in other words, there is no "Elder Wand + Lily's Blood = Assured Survival" formula. What count, ultimately, are Harry and Voldemort's own choices. (jkrowling.com)

So Harry, like Smith of Wootton Major, reached a primary moment of decision while between the two worlds to which they belonged, Harry's arguably far more consequential. His choice to return to face Voldemort again has tremendous force. After all the pain he's suffered, the temptation to be done and at peace – especially after having just walked with his parents, Sirius, and Lupin in the forest – was undoubtedly strong. But in true hero form, Harry sacrifices himself once again to do what is right. Sitting with his mentor who taught him to choose what is right over what is easy, he follows Dumbledore's plan to the end and deals the final blow to the Dark Lord. It is in this moment, between two worlds, that Harry most clearly fulfills Dumbledore's lesson from Cedric's at the end of *Goblet of Fire* to choose what is right over what is easy.

And this theme of choice is leads us to what is perhaps the most important argument in favor of the view that Harry and Dumbledore really did have a conversation. Throughout *Deathly Hallows*, Harry is being driven to a point where he needs to make a choice to believe in things which, for him, are severely in doubt: Dumbledore's love, and Dumbledore's plan. Twice he is presented with the challenge to make a choice to believe in Dumbledore's love and guidance, and twice he balked at the idea. Elphias Doge exhorted Harry not to believe what Rita Skeeter had written about Dumbledore:

> Harry looked into Doge's earnest, pained face and felt, not reassured, but frustrated. Did Doge really think it was that easy, that Harry could simply *choose* not to believe? Didn't Doge understand Harry's need to be sure, to know *everything*? (*Hallows* 153)

Later, at 12 Grimmauld Place, Hermione encouraged Harry to take Doge's advice, reminding him of Rita Skeeter's abysmal reporting record. Harry couldn't take that advice, either:

> He looked away, trying not to betray the resentment he felt. There it was again: Choose what to believe. He wanted the truth. Why was everybody so determined that he should not get it? (*Hallows* 185)

Harry is the Enlightenment rationalist here; he wants facts about Dumbledore's life, not exhortations to believe without ironclad evidence. He needs objective, verifiable proof. But when the time comes that Harry finally does make the decision to follow Dumbledore's plan – when he was standing in Dobby's grave – he still did not have the facts he needed. He chose what to believe, because he had just witnessed the true power of self-sacrificial love; Dobby had just given his life for Harry. In that moment in the free elf's grave, without the answers he had demanded in response to Doge and Hermione, he thought of Dumbledore four separate times, and he made his decision to follow Dumbledore's plan. He chose what to believe, apart from the factual evidence.

Not only this, but when the facts were finally laid before him by Aberforth Dumbledore, Harry's plan did not alter. Despite Dumbledore's reputation being tarnished in his mind, he believed Dumbledore loved him and set a plan before him that would bring down Lord Voldemort. By the time Harry is walking toward the forest – despite understanding Dumbledore's actions as "betrayal" (*Hallows* 692) – he has come full circle, and is "Dumbledore's man through and through" once again. Talking to Neville, overcome with emotion about the possibility of his dear friends' deaths,

> ...he pulled himself together again: This was crucial, *he must be like Dumbledore*, keep a cool head, make sure there were backups, others to carry on. Dumbledore had died knowing there three people still knew about the Horcruxes; now Neville would take Harry's place. There would still be three in the secret. (696, emphasis added)

An important tangent must be followed here: this set-up for Harry's choice to believe is one of Rowling's best postmodern elements in the entire series. Three people gave an account of Dumbledore's life: Elphias Doge (faithful friend), Rita Skeeter (conniving journalist), and Aberforth Dumbledore (bitter brother). Not one of them, despite their access or lack thereof to Dumbledore, gave Harry an objective view of Albus Dumbledore. In the end, nobody could. The views of all were skewed by their own personal perspectives and motivations. Doge wrote a hagiography for Albus, because he thought so highly of him. Skeeter wrote a biography which, despite giving more accurate facts than Doge, was twisted and interpreted to look as scandalous as possible and cast Albus in a terrible light. Aberforth was so bitter about what happened to Ariana that he was jaded and cynical, unable to find hope or forgiveness. No one had the objective facts, because there are none; all interpret the facts through their own personal experience. In the end, Harry chose what to believe, and even went so far as to argue with Aberforth about his own brother.

This is where we come to theme of choice being the most important argument for the view that King's Cross really happened. It happened, because Rowling wants us to choose to believe it happened. Edmund Kern is correct that Rowling left the text ambiguous; it could be interpreted as a dream or a literal occurrence. The facts are not before us. We are left to choose. John Granger, in *The Deathly Hallows Lectures,* has demonstrated that King's Cross is the moment when Harry finally sees everything as he should; his vision has been transformed. No longer the Enlightenment rationalist, he can see reality as he should – and that is the true meaning of Dumbledore's statement, "Of course it is happening inside your head, Harry, but why on earth should that mean that it is not real?" Having traveled and been transformed with Harry, the reader is also in the place to see things rightly to choose what to believe.

After the release of *Deathly Hallows,* Rowling commented on the Scripture verses on the grave stones of the Dumbledores and Potters, which were about as Hermione said, life after death: "I think those two particular quotations he finds on the tombstones at Godric's Hollow, they sum up — they almost epitomize the whole series." She commented further about her own beliefs:

> On any given moment if you asked me [if] I believe in life after death, I think if you polled me regularly through the week, I think I would come down on the side of yes — that I do believe in life after death. [But] it's something that I wrestle with a lot. It preoccupies me a lot, and I think that's very obvious within the books. (Adler, October 17, 2007)

The facts are not all there when it comes to a subject like life after death. One has to choose what to believe. It's difficult to imagine that Rowling would struggle with faith in life after death, put that struggle into her story, and come down on the opposite side of what she usually believes in the weekly J.K. Rowling Life-After-Death Poll. But it's just as hard to imagine that she'd make the issue easy in the text; she's not going to cheat the difficulty of the issue. She leaves it ambiguous for the simple reason that she wants the reader to choose what to believe. And this brings us to the real heart of encountering Faerie with Harry: the transformation of the reader.

The Reader is the Place Between Two Worlds

What does the interplay between two worlds accomplish? Meeting at King's Cross in this divine waiting room, where the deceased Dumbledore and not-dead Harry converse, and the option is presented to return or to "go on," several worlds meet at once. As already noted, King's Cross is the primary "between two worlds" symbol in the series. Furthermore, *this* particular manifestation of King Cross is a meeting point for life and death, for this present world and "the next great adventure." Harry and Dumbledore are literally between the two worlds of life and of life-after-death – or the realms of heaven and of earth.

Returning one more time to Tolkien's short story, *Smith of Wootton Major*, we can unpack the way Rowling brings us to Faerie with Harry – and why her method is so effective. Harry is not precisely like Smith. Smith moves from Wootton Major to Faerie, and in doing so, he learns about the supernatural reality, the permanent things upon which the world is really founded, but that are hidden by the world's fallenness into sin. Harry is, on the other hand, part of Faerie itself, being ontologically magical. He goes through the experience of discovering that there is more to him than he ever realized, but no Muggle can experience any such thing. At the same time our experience with Harry is precisely the point of the fairy-story – it reminds us that this world is a more fantastical place than we realized, and that we belong to something greater and more magical than our mundane daily experiences. Readers identify with Harry, the wizard, and as such, our imaginations explore the wilder aspects of the world through participation in Faerie. After all, Faerie exists to reminds us we belong to a world that is greater than the physical world around us; we belong both to heaven and to earth.

It was argued in Chapter One that through characters like Arthur Weasley, Rowling fulfills Chesterton's purpose of the fairy tale, namely, to restore in our minds a wonder for the world's wildness. The way this happens in *Harry Potter* is found in the interweaving of the two worlds. Natov suggests that this "interdependence" of the two worlds reminds us that that we live "on more than one plain, with the life of the imagination and daily life moving in and out of our consciousness" (313). It is precisely the fact that Rowling created two worlds so uncomfortably close together that makes them so accessible to postmodern readers. They are simultaneously entering a new world, a subcreation, *and* experiencing the possibility, even probability, that our own world is far more exciting and full of wonder than we imagined.

Hogwarts itself is a challenging place for the reader to be. Somehow, we are drawn to a world that is far, far removed from ours – where quills and parchment replace pens, paper, and computers; torches and candles replace the electric light; and long staircases with trick steps replace escalators. Throughout the course of seven books we are removed from our technology-driven world and placed into a pre-modern realm of activity. This underscores an important principle of reading literature, particular of the fairy tale variety: the individual reader is the bridge between two worlds – the one we live in, and the one we're visiting. The individual reader *is* every place and moment in which a wizard and a muggle cross paths. The reader's heart and mind is King's Cross; the reader stands at Platform 9 and 3/4, and the space between the text and the reader is the Hogwarts Express. When readers choose to board that train, to crack open and enjoy a *Harry Potter* story, we enter a magical experience that will inform our own lives.

What is accomplished in the space between two worlds? Rowling sums it up nicely:

> It's important to have light and darkness, it's a very conventional mechanism, but to be able to create a transition between a mundane universe and the cruel and oppressive existence adds shadows. As the story moves forward what I was hoping to reach was that what used to be going to the Dursleys became something comical. As Harry gets older and keeps gaining power and confidence he find himself better with the Dursleys, and the place of darkness and evil is exactly what used to be the world of light and magic. This family goes from being cruel to be funny and in book seven it even becomes pathetic when we found out that his Aunt was a jealous woman and even, from Harry's point of view, a broken one. (Cruz)

In alternating between two worlds, Rowling is able to introduce us to the "shadows," to the paradoxes of good and evil that exist both in the world around us and in ourselves. Shadows confuse things and provide little in the way of hard-and-fast rules and descriptions of life; but then again, this is far more realistic. We turn now to consider those shadows.

Chapter 2 Notes

1　In the coming chapters, we'll see how she does this with classic "scary" and "evil" creatures, making werewolves, giants, and goblins not malevolent monsters but victims of oppressive structures in the Wizarding World.

2　The similarities that do exist between Rowling and Tolkien will be explored in chapters three and six.

3　For a lengthy and eye-opening discussion of this scene, see chapter 5 of John Granger's book, *The Deathly Hallows Lectures,* Zossima Press 2008.

Chapter Three

Hogwarts, a (Haunted) History
Fear and Supernatural Horror in Harry Potter

"The oldest and strongest emotion of mankind is fear, and the oldest and strongest kind of fear is fear of the unknown," wrote H.P. Lovecraft, godfather of the modern horror story, in his essay, "Supernatural Horror in Literature." While there is room for disagreement with his statement as it pertains to fear being the "oldest and strongest,"[1] it certainly fits under Tolkien's term "primordial human" emotion (even if it is not particularly a "desire"), and therefore naturally finds an important place in the world of literature. Rowling delivers some fascinating material related to ghosts and "supernatural horror."

Fear and supernatural terror have been part of literature as long as tales have been told, making it a potent ingredient in the Cauldron of Story. Lovecraft wrote, "Cosmic terror appears as an ingredient of the earliest folklore of all races, and is crystallised in the most archaic ballads, chronicles, and sacred writings" ("Supernatural Horror"). What ingredients did Rowling throw into the cauldron, and what already existing ingredients did she work with?

Ghosts Need A History

How many times does Hermione reference *Hogwarts, A History* in the span of seven books? That textbook is so important to her that she feels she needs to bring it on their Horcrux-hunt, despite her persistent belief that returning to Hogwarts would be a bad idea. "Even if we're not going back there, I don't think I'd feel right if I didn't have it…" (*Hallows* 96).

Indeed. None of us should feel right if we are detached from our histories. Rowling has been careful to construct a world that has a rich history and a certain rootedness, and this even works its way into the two companion books to the series. *Quidditch Through the Ages* is obviously a book of history, and *Fantastic Beasts and Where to Find Them* contains a brief ("liar") history behind the classification of beasts. In other words, Rowling sees historical context as important to her world, so much so that all 9 Potter-related books have a distinct historical character and purpose within her story. There are many things that are important about the construction of a meaningful historical context, but for the present purposes, we should simply note this about fear and horror in stories: history and haunting go together. Lovecraft understood that, and he researched and constructed careful and detailed histories for his horror stories. Even sensational ghost-finding television programs realize the importance of haunting and history; the paranormal experts always turn to the haunted house's history in order to explain which apparition is still walking the halls of the spooked place. It's the same with movies where hauntings are present; if the house is haunted, it just might be that the house was built on a graveyard.

Washington Irving embedded a poignant piece of wisdom into his classic ghost story, *The Legend of Sleepy Hollow:*

> There is no encouragement for ghosts in most of our villages, for, they have scarcely had time to finish their first nap, and turn themselves in their graves, before their surviving friends have travelled away from the neighborhood; so that when they turn out at night to walk their rounds, they have no acquaintance left to call upon.

While this is profoundly true of much of the Western world, Rowling has written a school with a history that is remembered and that bears heavily on the storyline, and that is the perfect atmosphere for ghosts, one of the primary ingredients of gothic literature. Of course, there is nothing frightening about the ghosts of Hogwarts. They provide comic relief more than anything else. Even Peeves, who is a poltergeist (which traditionally haunts children in folklore) flies about the castle wreaking humorous havoc, often as much for the adult teachers as for the children. Rowling has a penchant for not using traditionally scary creatures as her conduits for fear. Yet the supernatural element of ghosts plays a significant role in the story, not least in the climax of the entire series. Without the historical account of Rowena Ravenclaw's diadem, involving two ghosts who had been right under the reader's nose for the entire series, Harry might never have realized the location of the final Horcrux.

Why Lovecraft?

J.K. Rowling has never cited Lovecraft as an influence. We don't even know if she's ever read his work. Why spend so much time on Lovecraft? It's obvious, isn't it? The Giant Squid in the lake next to Hogwarts is Cthulhu! Cthulhu is the monstrous, squid-like creature from outer space who, in what has become known as Lovecraft's Cthulhu mythos, lurks under the water until the time he'll return to the surface to destroy humankind.

It's a humorous thought for fans of both Rowling and Lovecraft – but, of course, a stretch.[2] So, returning to the question: Why Lovecraft?

H.P. Lovecraft, though in many ways different from the authors invoked in chapter one, is something of an ally to their point of view. MacDonald, Chesterton, Tolkien, Lewis, and L'Engle all saw the fairy tale playing a special role in literature and in life; these stories are not merely kids' tales out of which we must grow. They are superior, in many ways, to more "realistic" fiction, because of the creative gifts they provide to the reader. Though Lovecraft was nowhere near as optimistic about the world as these five, yet he also saw what he called "imaginative fiction" as being superior to "romantic" or "realistic" fiction, because the writer of the imaginative tale writes outside of the "everyday world experienced by us all" and moves on toward "full creativity, license to pursue 'art in its most essential sense'" (Sturgis, "Art")[3]. Lovecraft believed that he belonged to a small and special group of people who understood the importance of the imaginative tale (Sturgis). Recall from chapter one that MacDonald believed fairy tales give us "new embodiments of old truth;" that Chesterton believed that all he learned about the world he learned from the "nursery;" that Tolkien believed that Faerie contains "more permanent things" than what is found our own world; that Lewis believed children's fairy stories lead us to truth; and L'Engle believed that magical stories were essential for survival. All five were devoted to works of the fantastic imagination in much the same way Lovecraft was, and to that extent, Lovecraft was a kindred spirit. And, as we've already demonstrated, Rowling belongs in this tradition. Lovecraft wrote in his essay, "In Defense of Dagon:"

> Pleasure to me is wonder – the unexplored, the unexpected, the thing that is hidden and the changeless thing that lurks behind superficial mutability. To trace the remote in the immediate; the eternal in the ephemeral; the past in the present; the infinite in the finite; these are to me the springs of delight and beauty.

This is a great summary of the heart of imaginative literature as explained by our five great fairy-tale philosophers of chapter one. Imaginative literature is a doorway to other worlds, to more permanent things, to greater visions reality, and ultimately, to the changed mind that can see the present world as more than bare scientific fact. Lovecraft's disdain for unimaginative science can be seen in his literature. In "The Colour Out of Space," for example, a strange object from outer space lands in the field of Nahum Gardner. At first, the scientists from the nearby college were interested in the stone, which never cooled off but shrunk in size. When the stone disappeared entirely, they moved on to other studies, having discovered nothing about it. But the effects of the stone continued on Nahum's farm, causing large, bitter fruit, strange weather behavior (such as snow melting quicker only around the area where the meteorite had fallen, and strange-colored, monstrously-shaped skunk cabbages. The scientists from the college were called to examine the situation, and Lovecraft writes this narrative:

> One day they paid Nahum a visit; but having no love of wild tales and folklore were very conservative in what they inferred. The plants were certainly odd, but all skunk-cabbages are more or less odd in shape and hue. Perhaps some mineral element from the stone had entered the soil, but it would soon be washed away. And as for the footprints and frightened horses – of course this was mere country talk which such a phenomenon as the aerolite would be certain to start. There was really nothing for serious men to do in cases of wild gossip, for superstitious rustics will say and believe anything. And so all through the strange days the professors stayed away in contempt.

Later in the same story, as the police are examining the supernatural devastation wrought by the evil power at work on Nahum's farm, Lovecraft writes of the investigators, "They had heard the common country talk, it is true; but could not believe that anything contrary to natural law could have occurred." Lovecraft is expressing in narrative form the sentiment of Chesterton, that the scientific fatalist is unable to see the wonder of the world, because supposed fixed laws of science are unable to see possibilities other than the world as they've observed it and categorized it.

Tolkien and Lovecraft bear some particularly interesting similarities; both wrote around the same time and both hated the implications of modernity.[4] Both Tolkien and Lovecraft were "against the urbanisation and mechanisation of modern life" (Blackmore 12). Though anti-modernists, they responded to modernism in radically different ways.   Lovecraft embraced rationalism whole-heartedly, though this drove him to despair and meaninglessness; he wrote, then, of cosmic, unavoidable chaos and fear lurking just under the surface of the waters and deep beneath mountains. Tolkien, on the other hand, looked backward to premodernity and wrote of hopeful victories, glimpses of the final victory, in the midst of history's long defeat.   In Lovecraft's stories, lurking under the faux tranquility of modernity was unimaginable chaos; for Tolkien, seemingly hidden from the chaotic modern world, there was a hope that would some day be fully realized.   Rowling is far more in line with Tolkien than Lovecraft, for hope reigns supreme in her novels (while being realistic about the ongoing presence of chaotic, seemingly meaningless evil).[5]   But Rowling's anti-modernism is willing to embrace a little of both Lovecraft and Tolkien, and it's Lovecraft with whom we are presently concerned, for there are definite hints of dark, unexplained supernatural terror throughout *Harry Potter*.

Lovecraft is also important in analyzing Rowling because both authors give detailed historical foundations to their respective stories and mythologies. It has already been noted that Rowling developed a very detailed historical background to her Wizarding World. The primary conflict of the series has a thousand year old history. Magical history explores a wide range of issues and gives the sense that, despite Rowling's claim that she could never write an entire mythology, she's written a very intricately detailed and cohesive world. Lovecraft, while his stories are not as cohesive a vision as Rowling's 7-part series, also gives very close attention to historical detail.   Lovecraft understood the importance of rootedness in a place; his epitaph read, "I am Providence," by which he was referring to his hometown in Rhode Island. In his stories, family histories are explored ("A Shadow Over Innsmouth," "Rats in the Walls," "Some Facts Concerning the Late Arthur Jermyn"), local histories and mythologies are detailed ("The Call of Cthulhu," "The Case of Charles Dexter Ward" "The Haunter of the Dark"), even historical burial practices explained ("The Shunned House"). The historical foundations in both Rowling's and Lovecraft's works give the sense that the frightening aspects of the world are lurking just after the surface – and that they've been there a very long time.

The True Weird Tale – Appropriate for Children?

While history is of fundamental importance to supernatural horror, a simple ghost story will not create the desired effect of producing fear. In order to get a handle on how the horror tale works its way into *Harry Potter*, we do well to consider Lovecraft's explanation of the "true weird tale," as he called it:

> The true weird tale has something more than secret murder, bloody bones, or a sheeted form clanking chains according to rule. A certain atmosphere of breathless and unexplainable dread of outer, unknown forces must be present; and there must be a hint, expressed with a seriousness and portentousness becoming its subject, of that most terrible conception of the human brain -- a malign and particular suspension or defeat of those fixed laws of Nature which are our only safeguard against the assaults of chaos and the demons of unplumbed space.

The Wizarding World, by default, is a context in which the supernatural is expected, and therefore the mere presence of something outside the "natural" world is not fear-producing for wizards themselves (though the Dursleys, of course, experience terror at the mere mention of magic). Nevertheless, from the "Restricted Section" of the library in *Philosopher's Stone* to the attack of Nagini in Bathilda Bagshot's house in *Deathly Hallows*, Rowling creates multiple instances of "breathless and unexplainable dread of outer, unknown forces."

Rowling has been challenged frequently on the matter of the frightening nature of certain elements of the novels. Her response has been consistent:

> I feel very strongly that there is a move to sanitize literature because we're trying to protect children not from, necessarily, from the grisly facts of life, but from their own imaginations.

> I remember being in America a few years ago and Halloween was approaching, and three television programmes in a row were talking about how to explain to children it wasn't real. Now there's a reason why we create these stories, and we have always created these stories, and the reason why we have had these pagan festivals, and the reason why even the church allows a certain amount of fear... we need to feel fear, and we need to confront that in an controlled environment.

And also, what are we saying to children who do have scary and disturbing thoughts? We're saying that's wrong, that's not natural, and it's not something that's intrinsic to the human condition. That they're in some way odd or ill. (Fry, "Living")

Rowling perfectly blends Lovecraft and Tolkien here – or maybe better said, she answers Lovecraft with Tolkien. Lovecraft sees fear as an original human emotion, and Tolkien believes the fairy-story should address "primordial human desires." Rowling agrees that fear is part of "the human condition," *a la* Lovecraft. She also believes that the imagination is the place wherein fear is felt and resolved, and that *stories* are a perfect place for that to happen, *a la* Tolkien. In another interview, speaking of classic fairy tales, she says, "Folktales are generally told for a reason. They're ways for children to explore their darkest fears" ("Diane Rehm Show" 1999).

Rowling does not shy away from Lovecraftian fear in her stories, because she believes fairy tales allow children to enter into them via their "own imaginations" and deal with their fears there. Indeed, as Lovecraft presumedly calls fear the "oldest human emotion," because without it we would not have learned to survive those things that *should* be feared (Lovecraft was an atheist and therefore believed in naturalistic evolution), Rowling also calls fear a "healthy thing" and a "survival thing" ("J.K. Rowling Interview," CBC News World, 2000). These are similar statements about fear, for Lovecraft is clearly appealing to an evolutionary mindset when claiming fear as the "old human emotion;" it would be the emotion most necessary for survival!

Natov, discussing the fear element in the *Harry Potter* novels, invokes Maurice Sendak, the author who had to defend the monsters he included in *Where the Wild Things Are*:

> Most frightening to children is to dream their own figures of fear and find no analogue in anything they hear about or read. Children need to see their feelings, particularly the darkest ones, reflected in their stories. Mitigating the darkness of the fairy tale takes away their power to reassure children that they are not alone in their fearful imaginings, that they are shared and can be addressed. (320)

This is Rowling's argument precisely. L'Engle also noted that "children are taught fear early;" while some of this is absolutely necessary for safety, she wrote, "there's a fine line between essential prudence for the child's sake and the destruction of creativity" (*Walking* 114). Rowling believes, as L'Engle did, that in creativity – in stories – children learn about and deal with fear in a healthy way.

Fear in *Harry Potter*

Harry Potter is not primarily a horror story. No one reads the series for the same reasons one would read *Dracula* or watch a scary movie. Rather, *Harry Potter* fits the kind of story that Lovecraft describes in which supernatural horror can be found "appearing in memorable fragments scattered through material whose massed effect may be of a very different cast" ("Supernatural"). According to Lovecraft, even in an otherwise abysmal work, if the "least mundane" portion produces an "atmosphere" of supernatural horror, then it "must be admitted on its own merits as weird literature."[6]

The *Harry Potter* stories, for good reason, provide fear-facing and fear-resolving opportunities in their multiple moments of mysterious malevolence. There are many varieties of fear present in the series, not all equal to the others. Some play significant roles in the plot, while others are merely part of the ongoing movement of the story. C.S. Lewis is helpful to get a handle on the place of fear in the fairy tale, having outlined various types of fear created in literature in his essay, "On Stories." They are: a fear which is twin sister to awe; a fear which is twin sister to disgust; taut, quivering fears; dead, squashed, flattened, numbing fears; fears not of danger at all (8). All five are found in Rowling's work. Let's examine them one by one.

"A fear which is twin sister to awe"

The greatest failure of the 2005 film adaptation of *The Lion, the Witch, and the Wardrobe* was the portrayal of Aslan, quite simply because the awe of Aslan which dominates the book is largely absent from the movie. "Aslan is on the move" was replaced by Father Christmas's remark that the coming of the *children* had set into effect a series of events that would bring down the White Witch. Absent from the film is this awe-inspiring fear of Aslan, the "not safe but good" king, in whose presence one both trembles and is inexplicably drawn closer.

There is one character who commands the reverent sort of fear to which Lewis is referring and which he successfully created with Aslan:

Albus Dumbledore. For the most part, the first three books portray a sort of quirky, funny old man who is respected because of his achievements (faithfully chronicled on his chocolate frog card). Only in one brief moment in *Philosopher's Stone* – when Hermione proclaims that Dumbledore is the only one the Dark Lord ever feared – do we get a glimpse of the awe-inspiring power of Dumbledore. This changes from *Goblet of Fire* onward, and though he is deconstructed in the final book, there are several moments throughout the series in which this sense of awe is powerfully present.

At the climax of *Goblet of Fire*, we begin to see why Dumbledore is feared by Voldemort, Fudge, and many others in the Wizarding World. As Faux Moody is about to kill Harry, Dumbledore arrives on the scene and emanates an aura which is awe-inspiring:

> At that moment, Harry fully understood for the first time why people said Dumbledore was the only wizard Voldemort had ever feared. The look upon Dumbledore's face as he stared down at the unconscious form of Mad–Eye Moody was more terrible than Harry could have ever imagined. There was no benign smile upon Dumbledore's face, no twinkle in the eyes behind the spectacles. There was cold fury in every line of the ancient face; a sense of power radiated from Dumbledore as though he were giving off burning heat. (*Goblet* 679)

He commands the same kind of awe in *Order of the Phoenix*, both in his escape from Fudge and Umbridge in his office, and in the battle with the Death Eaters and Voldemort in the book's climax.

"A fear which is twin sister to disgust"

Rowling taps into this fear at multiple moments throughout the series, not least when Harry is repulsed by the creature that has become known in Harry Potter fandom as "Babymort," the rudimentary body to which Wormtail restores Voldemort in *Goblet of Fire* (see below for more). Ron's fear of spiders fits into this category.

"Taut, quivering fears."

These are fears like Harry's first experience on Buckbeak, riding the thestrals, or the escape from Gringotts on the back of the flying dragon. It's a thrill-like fear, and it carries with it a sense of adventure, something exceedingly important to the Harry Potter series. The latter of the three cited examples illustrates the fear well:

Behind [Harry], whether from delight or fear he could not tell. Ron kept swearing at the top of his voice, and Hermione seemed to be sobbing. After five minutes or so, Harry lost some of his immediate dread that the dragon was going to throw them off, for it seemed intent on nothing but getting as far away from its underground prison as possible; but the question of how and when they were to dismount remained rather frightening. He had no idea how long dragons could fly without landing, nor how this particular dragon, which could barely see, would locate a good place to put down. He glanced around constantly, imagining that he could feel his seat prickling. (*Hallows* 544)

"Dead, squashed, flattened, numbing fears."

This is the fear that grips a witch or wizard who is unequipped to handle a boggart – much like Mrs. Weasley when faced with the boggart who continually transformed into her greatest fears: dead family members. Molly, a witch powerful enough to defeat Bellatrix LeStrange, is completely paralyzed at a mere boggart. It's the kind of fear the dementors represent, leading to depression, numbness, inability to act. Harry experienced this kind of numbness at the end of Book 5, when he stood before the killing curse without making a move – "Harry had not even opened his mouth to resist. His mind was blank, his wand pointing uselessly at the floor" (*Order* 813). It's the kind of fear produced at the mere mention of Voldemort's name, and any thought about the Dark Arts.

"Fears not of danger at all."

This is evident in the early moments of *Philosopher's Stone*, when the "ickle firsties" have their first experiences with ghosts, who clearly present no danger, but cause quite a chill whenever they suddenly and unexpectedly pass through a student. Their first encounter with ghosts is a perfect illustration:

Then something happened that made him jump about a foot in the air -- several people behind him screamed.

"What the --?"

He gasped. So did the people around him. About twenty ghosts had just streamed through the back wall. Pearly-white and slightly transparent, they glided across the room talking to one another and hardly glancing at the first years. (*Stone* 115)

There's nothing to fear from Hogwarts ghosts, but they produce a sort of fear nonetheless. When the Fat Friar asks the new students if they're about to be sorted, Rowling writes that "a few people nodded mutely," and the whole experience makes Harry feel "oddly as though his legs had turned to lead" (116).

So Rowling does a fine job of introducing a broad spectrum of fears to be encountered throughout her series. It should also be noted that the type of fear experienced depends very much on the person. For some, the boggart produces a "fear not of danger at all," because they are clever enough to realize that the boggart is not the *real* fear, while for others, like Molly at 12 Grimmauld Place, they can produce a "numbing fear." While ghosts are primarily a "fear not of danger at all," the Bloody Baron is no such thing for Peeves, who is unable to continue his mischief at a threat from the Baron (*Stone* 129).

Lovecraftian Elements: Introducing Fearful Things

Keeping an evil "unknown" is the key to maintaining fear in the story. As quoted earlier, Lovecraft believed the strongest kind of fear was fear of the "unknown." A fundamental part of creating the "unknown" is how one introduces the fearful element. If an author simply writes, "And then a big, ugly giant showed up out of nowhere," there is no mystery; we know a big, ugly giant has arrived on the scene. The element which is supposed to frighten us is explained in its entirety right from the start, and this removes any reason to be terribly afraid, and it certainly kills the atmosphere of the unknown. Lovecraft was a master at this; his patient storytelling, his slow introduction of lurking evil in such stories as "The Call of Cthulhu" (rumors of fearful cult activity, the distorted, unearthly geometrical shapes), "A Shadow Over Innsmouth" (the lore surrounding the town, the strange religion, and the eyes of its citizens), and "At the Mountains of Madness" (the strange new discovery and the response of the dogs) all create tension and fear precisely because he introduces evil slowly, steadily, and incompletely. Lovecraft wrote about the importance of this for developing the fearful "mood." Sturgis writes:

> Lovecraft...discusses how the central mood of the weird tale – whether built upon the unnatural, barren immensity, time, or any other ingredient – can best be achieved. In "Notes on Writing Weird Fiction," he advocates devoting steadily increasing attention on the fantastic element of the story: "This marvel must be treated

very impressively and deliberately – with careful emotional 'build-up' – else it will seem flat and unconvincing." The "impossible, improbable, or inconceivable phenomena" must not be treated as "commonplace narrative of objective acts and conventional emotions," he argues. ("Art")

If a fairy tale writer is going to create effective fear, later to be resolved, she must not abandon Lovecraft's wisdom on this, even if her ultimate storytelling goals are different. The fear must be really felt, or its resolution is phony. Comparing passages from L'Engle, Le Guin, and Rowling, three fantasy fiction writers who handle well the issue of fear, will illustrate the effectiveness of this subtle introduction of evil; all three effectively do this in a way that produces immediate fearful reactions.

Madeleine L'Engle did this masterfully when she introduced her Echthroi – demonic beings – in *A Wind in the Door*. Walking out to find Charles Wallace late at night, she suddenly and unexpectedly runs into "Mr. Jenkins," her former principal and Charles Wallace's present principal. He had never visited the house before, and his presence took Meg by surprise. Furthermore, he was acting much differently than usual. After explaining his reason for looking for her, he reaches out his hand to Meg:

> In utter confusion she reached out to take his hand, and as she did so, Louise [the snake] rose up on the wall behind her, hissing and making a strange, warning clacking. Meg turned to the snake, looking as large and hooded as a cobra, hissing angrily at Mr. Jenkins, raising her large, dark coils to strike.
>
> Mr. Jenkins screamed, in a way she never knew a man could scream, a high, piercing screech.
>
> Then he rose up into the night like a great, flapping bird, flew, screaming across the sky, became a rent, an emptiness, a slash of nothingness.
>
> Meg found that she, too, was screaming. (50)

"Mr. Jenkins" turned out to be an Echthros, a demonlike creature that seems to embody evil and oppose all goodness. L'Engle introduces the Echthroi in this scene with a transformation so sudden and unexpected, the reader has to glance back; we are as shocked and taken by surprise as Meg is. The fact that the evil came out of a character we already knew makes it all the more frightening. Echthroi remain a supernatural power outside the normal realm of human experience, and a persistent threat throughout her Time Quintet. So successful is she in creating this element of fear that every time Charles Wallace and Gaudior take flight in *A Swiftly Tilting Planet*, the reader experiences with the two of them the fear that the Echthroi might be waiting. What enhances the experience of fear is how much Gaudior simply does not know.

This can be seen also in Ursula K. Le Guin's introduction of the Shadow in *A Wizard of Earthsea*. The first time we get a glimpse of evil things in Earthsea, it is when Ged, whose pride has been injured, attempts to read a spell to summon a spirit of the dead from his mentor Ogion's spellbook:

> As he read, puzzling out the runes and symbols one by one, a horror came over him. His eyes were fixed, and he could not lift them till he had finished reading all the spell.
>
> Then raising his head he saw that it was dark in the house. He had been reading without any light, in the darkness. He could not now make out the runes when he looked down at the book. Yet the horror grew in him, seeming to hold him bound to his chair. He was cold. Looking over his shoulder he saw that something was crouching beside the closed door, a shapeless clot of Shadow darker than the darkness. It seemed to reach out towards him and to whisper, and to call to him in a whisper: but he could not understand the words. (24)

Le Guin ably introduces fear into her book with Lovecraftian methodology: only say enough to create the initial experience of intrigue and fear. Later in the book when the shadow is "loosed," she employs the same method, and the shadow remains without a full explanation of its existence or nature until its defeat.

Rowling strikes this note of fear into her readers at multiple times throughout the series – the introduction of Voldemort in the forest, the first encounter with a Dementor, and the almost behind-the-scenes discussions of Inferi throughout *Half-Blood Prince*. Observe Harry's first encounter with Voldemort – though he doesn't realize who he's seeing at the time. He is walking with Malfoy and Fang, looking for the dead unicorn:

> Then, out of the shadows, a hooded figure came crawling across the ground like some stalking beast. Harry, Malfoy, and Fang stood transfixed. The cloaked figure reached the unicorn, lowered its head over the wound in the animal's side, and began to drink its blood....

Malfoy let out a terrible scream and bolted – so did Fang. The hooded figure raised its head and looked right at Harry – unicorn blood was dribbling down its front. It got to its feet and came swiftly toward Harry – he couldn't move for fear.

Then a pain like he'd never felt before pierced his head; it was though his scar were on fire. Half-blinded, he staggered backward. (*Stone* 256).

Before being able to get a handle on what he's seeing, Firenze comes onto the scene and rescues Harry. Harry and the reader now know there's something to be very afraid of, but even after learning its identity, we still know too little about it to have that fear resolved. In fact, Rowing introduces several fearful elements in this short encounter that will linger throughout most of the series – the supernatural acts of horror committed by those seeking immortality, the mystery of his scar (particularly relevant to Harry's fear and depression in *Order of the Phoenix*), and Voldemort himself.

The way Rowling handles Voldemort is particularly effective for creating this atmosphere of fear. For being the series' arch-villain, we don't see a lot of him. In fact, she's doing something very similar to what Tolkien did with Sauron. Pearce explains Sauron's "evil presence" as "always felt though always in the background (Peace, *Man and Myth* 108-09). Voldemort and Sauron are both evil, brooding presences in the story's background, creating an aura of impending danger and a sense of supernatural threat that might not be able to be defeated in the end. From a place entirely hidden, Voldemort sends armies of Death Eaters, Giants, walking dead, Dementors, and werewolves into the world to wreak havoc. Dumbledore's lessons with Harry in *Half-Blood Prince* in which he uncovers Voldemort's past are precisely for the purpose of removing the mystery, of humanizing the horror. The mystique of Voldemort reaches its climax when his snake tears itself free of Bathilda Bagshot's body in *Deathly Hallows* (but is torn down rather quickly thereafter by his arrogance concerning the hiding place of the tiara Horcrux; indeed, he looks something of a bungler by the series' end, and he is certainly not on par with Sauron as a baddie).

Lovecraftian Elements: An Atmosphere of Fear

Le Guin, L'Engle, Rowling, and other fairy tale writers are doing something different than Lovecraft, of course, which means that much that one fears is resolved later in the story. To be a writer of fairy stories, according to Tolkien, is to write a story with a happy ending. Indeed, part of Rowling's purpose in introducing fear elements to her story is to demonstrate the ability of courage to conquer those things. This is precisely why neither Rowling's nor Le Guin's nor L'Engle's works classify strictly as "weird tales," though they do most certainly fit Lovecraft's category of "imaginative tale" as opposed to romantic or realistic. But for Lovecraft, not being a strictly weird tale did not negate one from having success as a writer of such:

> We may say, as a general thing, that a weird story whose intent is to teach or produce a social effect, or one in which the horrors are finally explained away by natural means, is not a genuine tale of cosmic fear; but it remains a fact that such narratives often possess, in isolated sections, atmospheric touches which fulfill every condition of true supernatural horror literature. Therefore we must judge a weird tale not by the author's intent, or by the mere mechanics of the plot; but by the emotional level which it attains at its least mundane point. If the proper sensations are excited, such a "high spot" must be admitted on its own merits as weird literature, no matter how prosaically it is later dragged down. The one test of the really weird is simply this -- whether or not there be excited in the reader a profound sense of dread, and of contact with unknown spheres and powers; a subtle attitude of awed listening, as if for the beating of black wings or the scratching of outside shapes and entities on the known universe's utmost rim.[7]

There are several places in *Harry Potter* in which Rowling taps into the atmosphere of fear, exciting in the reader "a profound sense of dread, and of contact with unknown spheres and powers." Some very traditional fearful elements are subverted in Rowling's world. The Shrieking Shack, for example, is a classic haunted house, except that it's not really haunted, and there's nothing to be afraid of. Indeed, the "shrieks" came from the werewolf Remus Lupin when he was a student at Hogwarts, and in another subversive move, werewolves are also not something that one needs to inherently fear. It turns out werewolves are defined by their choices, just like every other sentient character in the story.

This leaves many of Rowling's own creations, some of which borrow from older ideas but are given new, frightening twists in *Harry Potter*. Several fearful elements should be be explored: boggarts, dementors, twisted family trees, Horcruxes, Inferi, and dark arts and ritual.

Boggarts and Dementors

Rowling introduces two fascinating magical creatures in *Prisoner of Azkaban* – dementors and boggarts. She introduces dementors first, but boggarts are far more innocuous on the whole. Boggarts are not an original creation of Rowling's, having appeared previously under the name "Clutterbumph" in Paul Gallico's *Maxnmouse* (1968) and in Susan Cooper's *The Boggart* (1993). But she uses them effectively within her own story. Boggarts are shapeshifters, converting into whatever their opponents fear most. Defense against the boggart is a charm, *ridikulus,* and laughter produced by the effects of the charm, which changes the boggart into something comical. The students learn to deal with boggarts earlier than dementors (Harry learns the Patronus charm in the same book, but no other student learns it until taught by Harry in the 5th year), and they are manifestly easier to tackle than the haunting dementors.

Dementors represent a psychological progression from fear to depression. Depression is fundamentally more difficult to counter than fear, because of the way in which it assaults judgment and destroys hope. Dementors represent a more insidious realm of fear than the boggart. If one is overly-susceptible to boggarts, it's quite possible one will fall all too easily to a dementor, because dementors represent the progression from fear to downright depression. What makes dementors so effective as scary creatures is Rowling's entire lack of explanation as to origins and nature. dementors are far and away Rowling's best Lovecraftian creation. Rather than being another species of oppressed magical brethren, they are naturally evil creatures.

The dementors are shrouded in mystery. Whence these dark, rotting, decayed creatures? Whence their power to destroy happiness by their mere presence, and more, to create a soulless existence, worse than death? We are never told. We know very little about them – only that Voldemort calls them his "natural allies" (*Goblet* 651) and that they are feared by all. If Voldemort's description is correct, and we have no evidence to the contrary, they are naturally evil, and no good can come from them. They do not fit into any categories in the Wizarding World, and their existence seems to be entirely dependent upon and rooted in human emotion.

Some of Lovecraft's most haunting bits of prose are moments when the knowledge and images of evil drive one to madness, such as in "A Shadow Over Innsmouth" and "The Rats in the Walls." The effect of the dementors is clearly a picture of madness. Their evil power results in depression, and those in Azkaban eventually go mad. Stan Shunpike and Knight Bus driver Ernie discuss this when talking about Sirius Black's laughter after allegedly killing Pettigrew:

> "Jus' stood there an' laughed. An' when reinforcements from the Ministry of Magic got there, 'e went wiv em quiet as anyfink, still laughing 'is 'ead off. 'Cos 'e's mad, inee, Ern? Inee mad?"

> "If he weren't when he went to Azkaban, he will be now," said Ern in his slow voice. "I'd blow meself up before I set foot in that place. Serves him right, mind you ... after what he did...." (*Prisoner* 39).

The fear leading to depression and mental illness motif is most strongly evident in Voldemort, who becomes a mentally ill person as a result of his fear of death (see Chapter Eight).

Twisted Family Tree

One of Lovecraft's best scary elements is the fear that one might not be able to escape one's own family genes.[8] Consider the protagonist of "A Shadow over Innsmouth." As unsettling as his experience is in observing and learning about the Shoggoths and the Esoteric Order of Dagon in Innsmouth, far more terrifying is the fact that after he escapes the town itself, he becomes just like its inhabitants, because he is descended from them. No matter how much he fears and loathes everything about that town's citizens, he becomes one of them and returns to the sea with the other Shoggoths. The same sort of shocking ending can be found in "The Rats in the Walls;" in one horrifying moment, the protagonist's family history commands in him an irresistible frightening insanity. The fear in "Some Facts Concerning the Late Arthur Jermyn" is of the same type.

Rowling plays with this fear as well. It is introduced in *Chamber of Secrets* as Harry, the Parselmouth, wrestles with the possibility of being Slytherin's heir, in which case, he's been wreaking havoc in the castle without consciously realizing it, for the sole reason that he belongs to a certain bloodline. This is a strong similarity with "Rats in the Walls," because the protagonist seems to be unaware of his moment of insanity, and has it explained to him after the fact. While Harry's fear is later dispelled by the realization that Voldemort himself was causing the attacks by possessing Ginny, the soul-fragment in Harry's head reignites the fear in *Order of the Phoenix* that an internal connection with Voldemort might have caused him to attack Arthur Weasley (Harry does not yet know it's a soul fragment, but the fear is there nonetheless). In wrestling with the inner Voldemort, Harry loses touch of what is real and what is a dream, and in the end, that confusion leads to Sirius Black's death. Lovecraft considered the confusion of "dream and waking worlds" to be "a basic and underlying horror" that effectively creates an atmosphere of fear in weird fiction (quoted in Blackmore 12). All of this comes from the fear that there might be something internal that might cause one to become evil against one's own will.

This element of fear continues in *Half-Blood Prince,* as we observe Tom Riddle's Slytherin line in action. They are clearly deranged, in part because of the Slytherin mentality, and in part because of intermarriages in order to keep the pureblood line intact. The question remains – and is never answered sufficiently – whether Voldemort ever had a choice to be anything other than what he was.[9] In *Deathly Hallows,* we learn that Harry and Voldemort were both descended from the Peverells, meaning that even Harry had some Slytherin in him. The line that broke from the Peverells and went to the Gaunts and Voldemort, of course, was far more evil than the one leading to the Potters.

Horcruxes

We also know very little about Horcruxes; while we will look at them in more detail in the next chapter, a few comments about them are in order here. They are called the "wickedest of magical inventions," and they are clearly feared by the majority of the Wizarding World. Slughorn seems to tremble even talking to young Tom Riddle, Jr. about them. Horcruxes are the result of an evil spell – one that is never described – in which a murderer places a bit of his or her soul, rent because of the murder committed – into an external physical object. Horcrux-creation dehumanizes a person, and in Voldemort's case, distorted his very appearance. It is terrifying magic, and it is the secret of Voldemort's power. But what makes it most frightening is that the dark magic is never explained. Most Potter fans, having become interested in the Horcrux plot in *Half-Blood Prince,* probably expected an explanation of Horcrux-creation in *Deathly Hallows.* No such explanation was given; and this probably should have been expected, given Slughorn's terror and the mere thought of the magic involved: "There is a spell, do not ask me, I don't know" (*Prince* 499).

In *Deathly Hallows*, there are only two living characters that we know for certain possess the knowledge of Horcrux-creation: Lord Voldemort and Hermione Granger.   Hermione had summoned Dumbledore's Horcrux books out of his office after his death, and *Secrets of the Darkest Art* had given the explicit instructions for Horcrux-making. It was such a disgusting and frightening prospect that when Hermione pulled the book out of her bag, "She looked a little nauseated and held it as gingerly as if it were something recently dead" (*Hallows* 102). She never explains the process of making a Horcrux, and this was a wise choice on Rowling's part. To keep the mystery and horror of the Horcrux intact, leaving the frightening process unknown was essential.

Inferi

Walking dead, or zombies, have held a firm place in classic horror, not least in the movies in films like *Night of the Living Dead*. In Rowling's world, Inferi are reanimated corpses, and while we have a basic idea of how these dead are walking – by use of a dark spell – much is left a mystery about these creatures and the magic which animates them. They are more than puppets on a string. The legion of Inferi waiting underwater in the cave – one of Rowling's best and most chilling scenes – were ready and prepared to attack anyone who attempted to take the locket horcrux. There seems to be indication in the text that had Harry been drowned by the Inferi, he would become one of them.

In *Half-Blood Prince*, Rowling paces herself well in building up to the horrific encounter with the Inferi at the lake, dropping hints about their existence early in the book with the Ministry's pamphlet and later in Snape's DADA class. By the time we are face to face with them, we have already been prepped to know they are frightening creatures. Indeed, they almost drag Harry to his death.

Not only this, but their symbolism is fearsome and evil. They represent a mockery of the dead; Voldemort thinks dead people are weak, and he uses weak people to his advantage. When Voldemort reanimates a corpse, he is mocking that person for dying. It's vile and disgusting. Perhaps one of the most fearful things about the concept of Inferi is that their number is massive; there are more dead people than living. Even the earliest mythology recognized this; Ishtar threatened the use of the dead in the *Epic of Gilgamesh*:

Father give me the Bull of Heaven,

So he can kill Gilgamesh in his dwelling.

If you do not give me the Bull of Heaven,

I will knock down the Gates of the Netherworld,

I will smash the doorposts, and leave the doors flat down,

and will let the dead go up to eat the living!

And the dead will outnumber the living!

It is said that in Voldemort's first rise to power, he had legions of Inferi at his command. Though Rowling did not tap into this potential in *Deathly Hallows*, the potential remains; it's a lingering fear in the Wizarding World than any dark wizard could utilize.

Dark Arts and Ritual

One of Rowling's most frightening images – and one which she never explains, adding to the fear – is what has become known in fandom as "Babymort," the small, vile, rudimentary body which Wormtail had given Voldemort prior to he rebirth. In the first place, we see this creature in the context of a dark, mysterious ritual, something employed by Lovecraft in his Cthulhu stories. In "The Call of Cthulhu," the protagonist's hearing of the rituals of a mysterious cult is fear-invoking. In "A Shadow Over Innsmouth," the mysterious Esoteric Order of Dagon is one of the most potent elements of fear. Cult rituals are powerful conduits for horror in a story, because they set the atmosphere of the dark unknown and of tampering with the unknown, cosmic, supernatural forces in the universe.

The particularly horrifying aspect of Babymort is the simple fact that it is described as an ugly baby. It is a visual corruption of innocence, a dehumanization at the earliest stage of life. When one looks at a baby, one knows for certain that he will not find there an image or symbol of the vilest of evil on earth. Babies represent new life and hope, new potential in the fight against evil. But this corrupted image is radically unsettling for Harry and for the reader, because the epitome of evil, the symbol of everything that is wrong in the Wizarding World, has taken the likeness of a deformed infant. Just as Granger has argued that "Death Eaters" might be a reference to the opposite of the Eucharist (*How Harry Cast* 176),[10] so this image is a perversion of the Incarnation.[11]

The Dark Arts themselves create an atmosphere of unknown dread. Knockturn Alley is not to be visited by any witch or wizard who hates the Dark Arts; the Restricted Section of the library is restricted precisely because of the knowledge of the Dark Arts contained therein. Snape, describing the Dark Arts, uses the language of supernatural, incomprehensible horror: "The Dark Arts are many, varied, ever-changing and eternal. Fighting them is like fighting a many-headed monster, which, each time a neck is severed, sprouts a head even fiercer and cleverer than before. You are fighting that which is unfixed, mutating, indestructible" (*Prince* 177).

One of the most frightening moments of the series is Christmas Eve in *Deathly Hallows* in the house of Bathilda Bagshot. The whole scene feels dark and trouble is looming as the old woman silently leads Harry up the staircase, a horrid stench throughout the place; Harry is suddenly faced with a giant serpent tearing itself out of the old woman's dead body, attacking Harry, and calling her master. It's a horrifying scene, and when Harry reflects upon it later, he remembers, "Lupin said there would be magic we'd never imagined" (*Hallows* 347). Indeed he had, and this simple fact, illustrated by the Christmas Eve terror, creates an atmosphere throughout *Deathly Hallows* of dread that comes from "unknown spheres and powers" (Lovecraft).

If anyone wonders whether J.K. Rowling has written effective moments of dread in her series, one can simply ask the most popular horror writer of our day. Stephen King himself said,

> Sometimes you get surprised into fright. When I picked up the *Harry Potter* books, I was not prepared for the depth of some of the frightening passages in there. Frankly, I was surprised by how scary the Death Eaters were. (Cheeser, "Transcripts")

To which Rowling responded, "I scared Stephen King!"

Conquering Fear

Rowling's stories are different than Lovecraft's. Sturgis writes, "Lovecraft ... did not want his reader to grow complacent in the worlds he devised. He did not wish for his readers to feel welcomed into his stories, but to run from them screaming" ("Art"). This is not Rowling's goal, even if, in moments, we want to escape as soon as possible – as in the Inferi-infested cave! But Rowling, far from seeing humanity as small and inconsequential, the victims of unfathomable cosmic forces and bound for despair as Lovecraft did, instead celebrates the world-changing potential of humanity and urges readers, through her characters, to realize how consequential acts of love and courage can be, especially in the face of acts of evil born of fear and cowardice. But one cannot demonstrate a courageous victory over evil without first creating an atmosphere of fear and evil to be conquered.

How, then, does Rowling accomplish the defeat of fear?

Naming

The first experience of genuine fear that confronts Harry, albeit a minor one, is in a conversation with Ron on the train to Hogwarts. Harry has learned the main points of his history from Hagrid – that his parents were killed by Voldemort, whose name no one in the Wizarding World dared to speak. Only Harry didn't learn not to speak it. But he quickly encountered a world that had, and in his first train ride to Hogwarts, he began realizing just how uncomfortable everyone was with the name. Harry apologized to Ron for using it, explained that he never really learned he "shouldn't," and then a curious thing happened: for the first time, Harry began to experience a "prickle of fear" when "You Know Who" was mentioned. Harry thinks that he was much more comfortable when he could just say the name. A parallel to the fear of Voldemort's name is found in the world of acrumantulas, who are as afraid to speak of the basilisk as wizards are afraid to name the Dark Lord.

Naming evil is the first step towards conquering fear of it; even Voldemort knows this, since he sought to create a name that all would fear. Likewise in L'Engle, the act of naming beings that previously caused fear results in the conquering of that fear. In one of the rare moments in which Echthroi are present but not feared, in *A Wind in the Door*, Meg is confronted with three Mr. Jenkinses, two of whom are Echthroi imposters. When she finally names the real Mr. Jenkins, the Echthroi are likewise revealed to be what they are rather than whom they are impersonating, and they are defeated. Le Guin's entire magical structure is built upon knowing the true names of things, and Ged is only able to defeat his shadow when he discovers its name.

Likewise, Harry is able to gain an edge over the Dark Lord by naming him, for he does not allow the mystique of that name to cause fear in him. By the end of the first book, Harry has still not quite learned not to say the name, and he corrects himself in front of Dumbledore, switching to "You Know Who." Dumbledore rebukes him: "Call him by his proper name, Harry. Lord Voldemort. Fear of a name only increases fear of the thing itself" (*Stone* 298).

Laughing

Boggarts are defeated not with the *ridikulus* incantation itself, but with the effect it produces: laughter. "The Boggart in the Wardrobe" does nothing less than equip readers with a method for dealing with fear: imagine the cause of that fear as something to be laughed at. In doing so, we strip the object of its power – or better said, we refuse to *give* it power, because in many cases, the object has no power other than the power we give it in allowing it to scare us.

We saw earlier how Rowling responded to the American "fear" over Halloween. Much of this has been fueled by the Christian fundamentalism that Rowling eschews. But Christians who do celebrate Halloween, costumes and all, do so in the very same way or for the very same reasons that Lupin's students defeated their boggarts. James Jordan, apologist for a Christian celebration of Halloween, writes,

> The concept, as dramatized in Christian custom, is quite simple: On October 31, the demonic realm tries one last time to achieve victory, but is banished by the joy of the Kingdom.
>
> What is the means by which the demonic realm is vanquished? In a word: mockery. Satan's great sin (and our great sin) is pride. Thus, to drive Satan from us we ridicule him. This is why the custom arose of portraying Satan in a ridiculous red suit with horns and a tail. Nobody thinks the devil really looks like this; the Bible teaches that he is the fallen Arch-Cherub. Rather, the idea is to ridicule him because he has lost the battle with Jesus and he no longer has power over us. ("Concerning Halloween")

Jordan's concept here also ties back into the naming concept; Voldemort is a Satan-like figure, in that the fear-inspiring, threatening mystique that he creates around himself is fundamental to his power. When Harry (and Rowling also) begins to mock Voldemort in his absurd arrogance, his mystique begins to crumble, and he's shown to be the fool that he is.

Remembering

Dementors are defeated by a Patronus charm, but once again, it is not the charm itself, but the power to conjure the charm that defeats fear and depression. This power comes from calling to mind one's happiest memory. Unlike boggarts, dementors have real, intrinsic power to cause fear and depression; it is part of their dark magical makeup, their very essence. Likewise, while the majority of things we fear in life are caused by our own inner paranoia, there are darker elements of the world that are fearsome, and there are moments in life that plunge us into despair. Christian theologians have written of the "dark night of the soul," in which depression seems to take over. Dementors represent this dark night, and in the midst of those moments, there is no present comfort. It must be found in memories of the past. "It was not always like this," Harry must say in the presence of a dementor. "I was happy once, and I can be happy again."

"What you fear most of all is – fear. Very wise, Harry."

For Harry, it is the wrong response to fear that he most fears. This is what Lupin is referring to when he calls Harry "wise" for fearing "fear" itself the most (*Prisoner* 155). The boggart turning into a dementor for Harry is a symbol of fear turning to depression, and it is this response to fear that Harry must overcome. Why? Because the wrong response to fear leads either to depression, or to evil.

It could be argued that the entire plot hangs on the difference between Harry's and Voldemort's response to "fear of the unknown." Voldemort is in unimaginative, uncreative, and in many ways a strict scientific rationalist. The tearing apart of his own soul is an "experiment." He believes that if he has the greater knowledge, he is the most powerful; that which is "unknown" is despised by Voldemort, because he fears it. Voldemort has no use for the Department of Mysteries except to gain what he believes will be the correct "knowledge" from the prophecy, which knowledge he'll use to defeat Harry. It was the information of the half-prophecy that caused him to attack Harry the first time. It never occurred to Voldemort to question the necessity or the mystery of the prophecy itself. His hatred, indeed, fear of the unknown became his downfall.

Harry, on the other hand, embraces the unknown by faith. Voldemort avoids death; Harry walks to his death. Voldemort avoids love; Harry loves deeply and self-sacrificially. Throughout *Order of the Phoenix*, Harry is translated back and forth between two kinds of knowledge: the cold, hard, Ministry approved theory and facts of Umbridge's pedagogy, and visions of the Department of Mysteries, where the most important, and simultaneously most mysterious elements of life are studied. Harry learns, in the moment of Dobby's death in Book 7, that the most important things are the mysteries – love and death, in particular – even if he can't completely understand them. Rather than responding to the unknown by despising and trivializing it, like Voldemort, he meets the unknown with steadfast faith and courage.

Harry knows what Voldemort does not: how one responds to fear makes all the difference in the world. Voldemort's fear leads to evil; Harry responds to fear with courage and love. And to those three issues – evil, courage, and love – we turn in the next three chapters.

Chapter 3 Notes

1 Edward T. Babinski disagreed strongly with Lovecraft's "philosophy of cosmic fear" on this point in particular, noting an inherent contradiction in the fact that Lovecraft's protagonists seem to be more curious than they are afraid. Were they not more curious – desirous to know the truth – than they were afraid, there would be no occasions in the story to experience fear. The protagonist would not be seeking out the truth behind the fear in the first place! Babinksi's article, "Lovecraft's Theology of Fear and Williams's Theology of Romance," can be found in *The Crypt of Cthulhu, Volume 2*, Number 5, 1983. pp. 16-22.

2 Amy Sturgis, upon reading this line, suggested that it's much less of a stretch to assume that Umbridge is from Innsmouth!

3 At the time of the writing of this chapter, Amy Sturgis's essay, "'Art in its Most Essential Sense:' H.P. Lovecraft on the Imaginative Tale" was in production, but not yet paginated. The essay can be found in *Cthulhu's Grandfather*, edited by Geoffrey Girard, Apex Books, 2008.

4 There is a surprising amount of similarity between Lovecraft and Tolkien, and Amy H. Sturgis has done excellent work on this in her article "The New Shoggoth Chic: Why H.P. Lovecraft Now?"*Apex Science Fiction and Horror Digest*, Vol. 1 Issue 4 (Winter 2005).

5 Again, Edward T. Babinki's article, "Lovecraft's Theology of Fear and William's Theology of Romance" is helpful here. Comparing Lovecraft and Williams, Babinski notes that while Lovecraft's more fantastic literature ("The Case of Charles Dexter Ward," "The Dreams in the Witch-House" pit "power versus counterpower, incantation versus counterincantation," in William's theology of romance, love itself is the power to banish evil and restore hope (20). As we saw in the last chapter, though *Harry Potter* certain has its share of incantation vs. counterincantation, Rowling's plan all along was to demonstrate that the clashing of spells – the magic itself – was not effective against evil. Like in Charles Williams – and in Tolkien, Lewis, and others in this tradition – Rowling sees love as the most powerful form of magic.

6 An interesting parallel to Tolkien's definition of the "Fairy Story" should be noted here. Tolkien made a similar point concerning certain tales which he would refrain from classifying strictly as "Fairy Stories," but which nevertheless satisfies primordial human desires and therefore "will approach the quality and have the flavour of fairy-story" (Tolkien, 6).

7 As a point of interest, here is another place where Tolkien and Lovecraft are similar. Both, while defending their genre – fairy stories and weird fiction, respectively – create a few ironclad rules about what "counts," but are more than willing to admit that other stories contain certain elements which accomplish the same purpose. Lovecraft's paragraph above should be read alongside Tolkien's

paragraph in "On Fairy Stories" in which he writes of those stories that, though not strictly fairy stories, still have the "flavour of fairy story."

8   Special thanks to Dr. Amy H. Sturgis for pointing me in this direction.

9   This question is explored in greater detail in Chapter 8.

10   In the Christian theology of the Eucharist, the communicant is a "Life Eater," one who finds spiritual life and strength in the body and blood of Christ.

11   The Incarnation refers to Christ's taking on flesh and becoming a man, which obviously has its beginning in the babyhood of Jesus.

Chapter Four

Dehumanization
Defining Evil in Harry Potter

You have a choice when you're going to introduce a very evil character. You can dress a guy up with loads of ammunition, put a black Stetson on him, and say, "Bad guy. Shoot him." I'm writing about shades of evil. You have Voldemort, a raging psychopath, devoid of the normal human responses to other people's suffering, and there are people like that in the world. But then you have Wormtail, who out of cowardice will stand in the shadow of the strongest person. (Rowling, in interview with *Entertainment Weekly*, 2000).

What does evil look like in the *Harry Potter* series? Whatever the various characteristics of evil, the different "shades" which we will explore below, there is an overarching theme under which they all fall: dehumanization. To be evil, on the path to evil, or to contribute to evil in the world, one has to be moving away from what it means to be truly human. The epitome of evil in the *Harry Potter* series, the guy with the "black Stetson," is Voldemort, perhaps one of the most gruesome and potent pictures of dehumanization in literature. Contained within Voldemort's character are the seeds of the various types that we find in other aspects of the story. Much more will be said about Voldemort, particularly in Chapter Eight, but here we give special attention to his dehumanization.

Harry and Hnau

The concern C.S. Lewis had in his little book, *The Abolition of Man*, was his perception that modern education was taking as foundational the assumption that humans are merely physical beings – a naturalistic view of humanity. It is the underlying belief, reflected in the English textbook "*The Green Book*" by "Gaius" and "Titius," that "nothing but the physically quantifiable can be real or objective," and it therefore "rules out precisely the central essence of human nature" (Williams 25). In other words, to deny the spiritual component of a human being is to deny the most important part of our existence, and to give a less-than-human, even inhuman definition to humanity. Lewis did not mince words in evaluating the consequences of accepting such a view: "The practical result of education in the spirit of *The Green Book* must be the destruction of the society which accepts it" (*Abolition* 39).

Donald T. Williams concludes in his essay "Sons of Adam and Daughters of Eve" (*Past Watchful Dragons*, 2007) that Lewis's argument is basically this: humans are animals with spirits, therefore "capable of reason and living under objective spiritual values;" if the spirit part is removed, dehumanization begins to take place – not that a person becomes ontologically less human, for merely *thinking* a soul is not there does not remove it; rather, he or she starts acting, believing, feeling, and thinking less humanly.

While the use of magic in literature symbolically serves to underscore a spiritual view of humanity, Rowling's world and plot (as Lewis's and Tolkien's) gives no special status to magic itself, while not neglecting to take it seriously. In other words, the magic is not a joke, but it is not the solution to the world's problems either. Voldemort can do magic, perhaps better than anyone else in the entire wizarding world, save Dumbledore; but Voldemort still denies the importance of the spiritual component of the human being. By dividing up his soul to maintain his physical life, he reveals himself to be exactly the kind of person who could have written a Wizarding version of *The Green Book* by Gaius and Titius, against whom Lewis was writing in *The Abolition of Man*. Rowling's most straightforward, "black Stetson" definition of a "bad guy" is Voldemort, and his acts of evil are fundamentally *dehumanizing*. We could argue, then, that Rowling's fundamental definition of evil is that which dehumanizes.

What makes dehumanization a definition of evil rather than simply a result of it? This can be answered much more easily in the works of writers like Lewis and Tolkien, because their mythologies have specific god-figures who created humans – indeed, both *Narnia* and *The Silmarillion* have specific creation stories. As such, evil can be defined as the subversion of created intent. The Genesis narrative – which surely informed the myth-making of both Lewis and Tolkien, describes creation as "good" and gives to humanity certain characteristics and purposes; the rejection of those characteristics and purposes is an act of evil against the Creator, because the fullness of humanity is an *image* of God, expressed by fulfilling created intent. To act in any way less than human is to tarnish the representation of God on earth.

When Aslan created Narnia, there were certain animals into which he imparted the ability to talk. These talking animals are the equivalent to humans in our own world, their King and Christ figure being the incarnate in the form of a lion, king of the beasts. Donald T. Williams notes that the relationship between Talking Beasts and humans is that of equals, even while Lewis shapes the story around the right of humans to rule in Narnia (29). In *Ransom Trilogy* language, they are all *hnau*. And *hnau* are not supposed to act in any other way than their created purposes. Aslan says to the Talking Beasts of Narnia:

> The Dumb Beasts whom I have not chosen are yours also. Treat them gently and cherish them but do not go back to their ways lest you cease to be Talking Beasts. For out of them you were taken and into them you can return. Do not so. (*Nephew* 140)

Aslan's command encapsulates the idea being argued for here: it is evil to *act* less than fully human, and in doing so, one *becomes* less than human. Dehumanization is first a rebellious act, and *then* a result of choices. Evil is dehumanization. This theme is found not only in Lewis, but in several other works of imaginative literature as well. In George MacDonald's *The Princess and Curdie*, people who are becoming evil are becoming more and more like animals, and Curdie is given special power to discern who is turning animalistic, by a touch of the hand. In some of H.P. Lovecraft's horror, humans affected by evil influence become physically and mentally transformed and often take on animalistic characteristics. In Le Guin's *A Wizard of Earthsea*, it is possible to lose one's humanity when transforming into an animal, because the animal can take over the soul.

Understanding evil as dehumanization harks back to Christian origin mythology, particularly the Fall. That we are living in a fallen world informed everything Tolkien wrote. Shortly after *The Lord of the Rings* was written, he wrote that being a Roman Catholic and a Christian, he did "not expect history" to be anything other than a "long defeat" in which we can catch glimpses of final victory. He saw evil as being rooted in the corruption of created intent – humans' deliberately choosing to be less than or other than they were so beautifully meant to be. Tolkien's orcs are a stark image of this, because they are distorted and corrupted elves, meant to be a mockery of elves; of course, orcs had their dehumanization forced upon them, yet another great dehumanizing evil to be explored below. Gollum, on the other hand, is the "dehumanization" of a hobbit by his own obsession with the Ring.

Defining evil as dehumanization works very nicely for Tolkien and Lewis. It's not quite as simple for Rowling. Despite the fact that by Rowling's own admission, there are Christian elements to her series, her mythological world contains no god or creation story. Can dehumanization still be a good definition of evil in *Harry Potter?* Yes, it can, primarily because the "black Stetson" baddie of the series commits deliberate acts of dehumanization.

Evil and the Soul

Horcruxes are the key to Rowling's definition of evil. Voldemort's dehumanization takes places in his soul, which is significant both in light of the Lewisian analysis above and Christian theology. Theologian Eugene Peterson writes the following:

> When we say "soul" we are calling attention to the God-origins, God-intentions, God-operations that make us what we are. It is the most personal and most comprehensive term for what we are – man, woman, and child.... "Soul" is a word reverberating with relationships: God-relationships, human-relationships, earth-relationships.... "Soul" gets beneath the fragmented surface appearances and experiences and affirms an at-homeness, an affinity with whoever and whatever is at hand. (37)

Though Rowling has likely not read Peterson, the applicability of this definition of "soul" to the situation with Voldemort is striking. The "soul" points to an origin and identity beyond ourselves, beyond this present life. And soul is fundamentally a relational word. Voldemort believes precisely the opposite: that his goal in life is to remain alive eternally and never to face death and "the next great adventure," and he isolates himself and avoids all relationship in the process. If "soul" refers to our relational capabilities, then it makes sense that Voldemort, who maintained no close relationships with anyone, would be less hesitant to chop his soul up into pieces. Evil is the evidence of a loveless life.

In his classic essay, "On Fairy Stories," Tolkien writes of the

> use of an ancient and very widespread folk-lore notion, which does occur in fairy-stories; the notion that the life or strength of a man or creature may reside in some other place or thing; or in some part of the body (especially the heart) that can be detached and hidden in a bag, or under a stone, or in an egg. At one end of recorded

folk-lore history this idea was used by George MacDonald in his fairy-story *The Giant's Heart*, which derives this central motif (as well as many other details) from well-known traditional tales. At the other end, indeed in what is probably one of the oldest stories in writing, it occurs in "The Tale of the Two Brothers" on the Egyptian D'Orsigny papyrus. There the younger brother says to the elder:

> I shall enchant my heart, and I shall place it upon the top of the flower of the cedar. Now the cedar will be cut down and my heart will fall to the ground, and thou shalt come to seek it, even though thou pass seven years in seeking it; but when thou hast found it, put it into a vase of cold water, and in very truth I shall live. (8)

Voldemort's Horcruxes follow in this tradition. Tolkien employed the same sort of idea in *The Lord of the Rings,* and there are striking parallels between the effects of Sauron's ring on its wearers and the effects of both the diary and the locket horcruxes on their possessors – particularly Ginny in *Chamber of Secrets* and Ron in *Deathly Hallows.* These perversions of the human soul not only corrupt their makers, but they begin a corrupting work on all who get too close to them.

The Horcrux itself, "wickedest of magical inventions," is a banned subject at Hogwarts, and the making of Horcuxes is such a horrifying, evil thing that Hermione, reading one of Dumbledore's books on Horcruxes, can't believe Voldemort had made six: "It warns in this book how unstable you make the rest of your soul by ripping it, and that's just by making one Horcrux" (*Hallows* 103). Horcruxes are Rowling's most potent and effective symbols of evil, and they perfectly fit the definition of evil being argued for at present: "A Horcrux is the complete opposite of a human being" (*Hallows* 104). In other words, "the wickedest of magical inventions" (i.e., the most evil form of magic) is "the complete opposite of a human being." Hence, in Rowling's world, even without a specific creation myth, evil is defined as dehumanization.

Interestingly, Rowling is no Gnostic dualist when it comes to the human being. While there is no unambiguous discussion about a future bodily resurrection in the Christian sense of the idea, Rowling shows tremendous respect for the body. When Mad-Eye is killed, there is no question in the minds of Bill and Lupin about what must be done:

> "Mad-Eye's body," said Lupin. "We need to recover it."
>
> "Can't it -- ?" began Mrs. Weasley with an appealing look at Bill.
>
> "Wait?" said Bill. "Not unless you'd rather the Death Eaters took it?"

Nobody spoke. Lupin and Bill said good-bye and left. (*Hallows* 81)

It's significant that the whole company accepted the argument that the recovery of Mad-Eye's body was so important that Lupin and Bill needed to head out immediately, so that the Death Eaters would not get to it first. There is nothing of the kind of dismissal of the body that we often hear at funerals: "Mad-Eye's not here. He's gone, his soul has left, and his body no longer matters." None of them seem to believe that the "real person" is the soul and that the body is just a shell. There is, of course, a fundamental belief that the soul *does* depart from the body. As Hermione says only a chapter later,

> "Look, if I picked up a sword right now, Ron, and ran you through with it, I wouldn't damage your soul at all....whatever happens to your body, your soul will survive, untouched." (*Hallows* 104).

But it does not follow from this that the body doesn't *matter*.[1] In fact, it appears that the body is fundamentally important for the constitution of the human being, because the Horcrux works quite oppositely: if the soul is placed inside another physical object other than a human body, "The fragment of soul inside it depends on its container, its enchanted body, for survival. It can't exist without it." (*Hallows* 104). In other words, a human soul in a human body works as it's supposed to. A human soul in anything other than a human body dehumanizes that soul fragment. Your soul remains human if it remains in your body and only leaves when the body dies; if it is encased in anything other than a human body, it is "evil," and it begins to act in a non-human way.

Images of Evil

Rowling does not depend heavily on traditional images of evil nor on traditional fantasy beastiaries for her evil creatures. Even when she does use traditional images like the snake, she subverts the symbol in places, such as with Snape and Slughorn, Harry's ability to speak parseltongue, and Harry's words to his son Ablus Severus at the end of *Deathly Hallows*. As far as the traditional evil creatures Rowling employs in her story, such as goblins, giants, dragons, and werewolves, none of them are inherently evil. The goblins of the Wizarding World are not primarily evil characters. In fact, the goblins turn out to be part of Rowling's postmodern message; they are a misunderstood group, a different culture. Likewise, giants are only considered "violent" and "evil," Dumbledore argues, because they have been mistreated by wizards; they work for Voldemort because, ironically, he is the only one willing to promise them any sort of freedom. Lewis argued that a good giant was "legitimate," even if "twenty tons of living, earth-shaking oxymoron" ("On Stories" 9), and Rumblebuffin proves the point. Nor are dragons necessarily evil creatures in and of themselves in the Wizarding World; they do not seem to have the humanlike intelligence they are given in many other works of fantasy fiction (Smaug in *The Hobbit*; the dragons in *A Wizard of Earthsea*). Werewolves fit the same category: not necessarily evil, but only so by choice. Remus Lupin and Fenrir Greyback are both werewolves, and as is usual with Rowling, the difference between them is the choices they make. Werewolves serve as a scapegoat for the Wizarding World's problems, rather than as an actual root cause of evil.

Like Tolkien, Rowling's most effective images of evil come from her own creations rather than traditional symbols of evil, and this is nowhere more evident than in the parallels between Ringwraiths and dementors. Shippey argues, "The Ringwraiths work for the most part not physically but psychologically, paralyzing the will, disarming all resistance" (125). Tolkien describes them in 'The Siege of Gondor' as "piercing the heart with a poisonous despair." Gunton writes, "Their touch brings a dreadful coldness, like the coldness of Dante's hell" (quoted in Peace, *Man and Myth* 117). The dementors, which we examined in detail in the last chapter, create much the same effect. The wraiths illustrate the dehumanization point more potently, however, for they were once humans, now corrupted by their lust for power. In Rowling, Voldemort represents this, while the dementors are his "natural ally," with Bellatrix LeStrange and the Death Eaters following in his path. And yet, the dementors' most potent act of evil is in the dementor's kiss, which renders a person entirely dehumanized – soulless, a fate worse than death.

Cowardice, the Root of Evil

Every character who does evil in the *Harry Potter* series is moved toward evil out of a cowardly response to fear. Cowardice is the root of the worst evils in the seven-book saga. That cowardice is the foundation for evil makes sense for Rowling's worldview; she has consistently voiced her opinion that courage is the most important virtue. If courage is at the heart of all that is virtuous, then its opposite is certainly at the heart of evil. Natov argues, invoking the boggart and dementor symbolism explored in the previous chapter, that by linking Harry's desire to see his parents in the mirror, and the effect that the boggart-dementor has on Harry, reproducing his mother's last moments of life, Rowling "connects despair with madness and suggests that it is the loss of hope that makes us demented, that promotes criminality and destroys the heart" (320).

Voldemort is the most obvious example, as his fear of death is at the core of his murders, his Horcrux-making, and his outright narcissism. Voldemort, of course, would never have said that he was *afraid* of death – only that he was more powerful than death. But the subconscious motivating factor behind Voldemort's maniacal pursuit of eternal earthly life is most definitely fear. Rooted firmly in his being abandoned by his mother, Voldemort sees death as something for the weak, the pathetic.

Pettigrew's fear is not much different than Voldemort's, though he does not have the same broken mentality leading him to Horcrux-making. Wormtail is afraid of Voldemort himself, which means he's afraid for his life. He always aligned himself with those who were most powerful, most able to protect him – following the Marauders at Hogwarts, and when Voldemort rose to power, betraying the Marauders and working for the Death Eaters.

The Death Eaters share Wormtail's fear also, it seems, for they have aligned themselves with the Dark Lord and taken on the name "Death Eater," which is a reference to Voldemort's quest to eliminate death itself.

There needs to be some nuance here. It is not the emotion, the feeling of fear that is evil. It is a cowardly response to fear. It's already been noted in the last chapter that Rowling sees some aspects of fear as a "survival thing." In other words, there are common sense things to do when one feels fear, some of which help us to know there is danger and to stay alive. But it is precisely the courageous response to fear that results in survival, not the irrational, cowardly responses that leads one to becoming a narcissistic, oppressive Dark Lord.

Abuse of Power

Speaking of which, another evil that comes from fear and leads to dehumanization is the Ministry's abuse of power. It leads to dehumanization precisely because it is an inhuman thing to deny the human rights of another person. It is a different version of Voldemort: Voldemort kills in order to stay alive; the Ministry takes away the power of others in order to maintain its own power. As Williams writes, "To make slaves of human beings...*is* to mistreat them, because it is to deny their God-given nature and force them to live a lie" (31). Even worse than dehumanizing oneself is dehumanizing others in the process.

Cowardice breeds abuse of power because cowardice is powerlessness without courage. If one lacks power, or feels vulnerable in a given situation, the coward's way is to deny vulnerability and grasp at power in order to maintain some sort of psychological homeostasis. Orwell links abuse of power and dehumanization in the conclusion of his book, *Animal Farm*, in which all who have selfishly grasped at power have become pigs, and no one can tell the pig farmers from the farmer pigs.

Rowling creates a paradox in *Deathly Hallows* with the simple phrase, "for the greater good," because the phrase is used simultaneously for Grindelwald's justification for his own racist actions, and for Harry's most courageous actions. It is true that there are sacrifices to be made "for the greater good." But when that phrase becomes a justification for taking power and sacrificing *others* "for the greater good," evil in the form of abuse of power is the result. This was the great sin of Grindelwald and young Albus Dumbledore, who believed, as they mused over the sacrifices they would have to force upon others, that it was all justified, because it was for the greater good of the Wizarding World. In fact, it might be argued that Grindelwald represents a more sinister evil than Voldemort, for Grindelwald thought he was working for the good of wizardkind, whereas Voldemort was working out of pure self-interest.

Abuse of power is also found in the multiplicity of bullies Rowling creates throughout her stories. Opening with Dudley, a steady stream of bullies are a regular part of Harry's struggles throughout each story. But it's at this point that Rowling introduces some of her best nuance when it comes to evil, for most of the bullies are not strictly evil characters like Voldemort. Draco, perhaps, comes the closest, but even he, when asked to commit a great act of evil in murdering Dumbledore, falters in the face of mercy (see Chapter Nine).

Severus Snape is a particularly nasty bully, and he might be the worst of them all, because he was loved, knew how to love, and because he was in charge of children. Rowling calls bullying students "the worst and shabbiest thing you can do" with specific reference to Snape (quoted in Fraser 21). Yet it's not as simple as Snape simply being a mean guy for the sake of it; he was bullied himself as a student, by no less than James Potter,

Harry's own father. Harry learns, much to his chagrin, that what he hated in Snape was found in his own father.

The same goes for Argus Filch, the caretaker at Hogwarts. We learn very quickly to hate Filch right along with Harry; he's the kind of guy who seems to like to push kids around, just because he's cranky. It turns out this is not the case. Filch is a squib – someone born to a wizarding family who cannot do magic – and there are clear hints of a history of ridicule. As soon as Filch's cat is found petrified, he is certain, despite no hard evidence at all, that Harry did it. Why? Filch's reasoning is simple: "He found out I'm a squib" (*Chamber* 142). What does that have to do with petrifying cats? Everything, in Filch's mind. The natural response to discovering Filch's non-magical status, in Filch's mind, was bullying. He most likely had a nasty history of getting bullied for being different.

None of this is to excuse bullying, of course, but Rowling is good at writing her "shades of evil." The bullies are abusing their power (strength, status, or authority) in order to feel in control, after having had control taken away from them, having been bullied themselves. It is a cowardly response to loss of control; but it is a conditioned response. The lesson seems to be that an atmosphere of love and acceptance is the remedy to bullies, to the abuse of power.

Bigotry

Bigotry is yet another evil that leads to dehumanization, and it is tied directly to the abuse of power. Bigotry denies someone their *status* as a human for superficial reasons. Again it must be emphasized that to take away the humanness of another person is to dehumanize oneself, for it is impossible to exercise the loving care of created intent or to have a soul-relationship with people while treating them as less than human. The Ministry's explanation of centaurs as having "near-human intelligence" is a poignant example in the Wizarding World. Rowling demonstrates through Dumbledore and through the centaur Firenze that centaurs are simply different, not inferior. In some realms and at some skills, they are far superior to wizards.

The Pureblood/Muggleborn metanarrative follows from the same twisted logic, that somehow Muggles – as well as witches and wizards born to Muggles – are inferior. This is how anti-Muggleborn legislation so easily goes into effect in *Deathly Hallows*, during a time of fear. Muggleborns are scapegoats as the Wizarding World is being taken over by Voldemort, and the similarity of the Ministry's and the Dark Lord's points of view on the matter are frightening. Umbridge and other Ministry officials willingly do the Dark Lord's bidding by getting rid of Muggleborns, all the while supposing that they are opposing him. Much more will be said both of bigotry and of institutionalized oppression in Part III.

The End of Evil

Rowling does not write a story in which all evil is neatly wrapped up and dealt with in the end. Injustice is still rampant. House-elves are still enslaved, the Ministry has a lot of cleaning up to do, and even then, it will still be a bastion of inequity. But Rowling does give us a striking image of what ultimately happens to evil, and that image is found at the heavenly King's Cross.

The first thing Harry notices after he wakes up from Voldemort's killing curse is described as follows:

> "[Harry] recoiled. He had spotted the thing that was making the noises. It had the form of a small, naked child, curled on the ground, its skin raw and rough, flayed-looking, and it lay shuddering under a seat where it had been left, unwanted, stuffed out of sight, struggling for breath…. 'You cannot help' [said Dumbledore]." (*Hallows* 706-07)

It's a very unsettling picture, especially because of Dumbledore's repeated insistence that nothing can be done for the creature. What is the creature that is not to be pitied or helped?

Clearly, the creature is Voldemort himself. Two interpretations seem possible here: either it's the piece of Voldemort's soul that has finally been severed from Harry, or it is Voldemort himself (since, as Harry comes back to consciousness, it becomes evident that Voldemort has been unconscious for just as long). Rowling herself seems to have intended the latter, though the text itself leaves both options open. How do we know from the text that it's Voldemort? In the final confrontation with Voldemort, Harry says this:

> "It's your one last chance," said Harry, "it's all you've got left…. I've seen what you'll be otherwise…. Be a man … try … Try for some remorse." (741)

This means that for Voldemort, once he dies, there is no longer any hope. Is Rowling giving us a picture of Hell? It would appear so. What does that picture look like? N.T. Wright and C.S. Lewis, both Anglicans (which is important, because this is the theological context in which Rowling deliberately placed herself as a teenager) offer insight that might get us close to Rowling's point. Wright, quoting Lewis, reminds us that there will be a time when God says to the unrepentant, "*Thy* will be done" (Wright, *Surprised* 180). In other words, Voldemort isn't getting anything other than what he chose – final, eternal dehumanization.

This is the very idea that N.T. Wright presents as Hell in his book, *Surprised by Hope*. Rather than describing Hell as though the figurative descriptions of the New Testament were meant to be literal depictions of Hell, Wright proposes this idea:

> When human beings give their heartfelt allegiance to and worship that which is not God, they progressively cease to reflect the image of God. One of the primary laws of human life is that you become like what you worship; what's more, you *reflect* what you worship not only back to the object itself but also outward to the world around.... My suggestion is it is possible for human beings so to continue down this road, so to refuse all whisperings of good news, all glimmers of true light, all promptings to turn and go the other way, all signposts of the love of God, that after death they become at last, by their own effective choice, *beings that were once human but are now not*, creatures that have ceased to bear the divine image at all. (182)

C.S. Lewis wrote about the same sort of idea:

> To enter heaven is to become more human than you ever succeed in being in earth; to enter hell, is to be banished from humanity. What is cast (or casts itself) into hell is not a man: it is "remains". To be a complete man means to have the passions obedient to the will and the will offered to God: to *have been* a man – to be an ex-man or "damned ghost" – would presumably mean to consist of a will utterly centred in its self and passions utterly uncontrolled by the will. It is, of course, impossible to imagine what the conciousness of such a creature – already a loose congeries of mutually antagonistic sins rather than a sinner – would be like. There may be a truth in the saying "hell is hell, not from its own point of view, but from the heavenly point of view." (*Pain* 112, emphasis in original)

This is not the place for a theological evaluation or debate about the merits of such a view. Wright's and Lewis's idea, rather, is not presented here as a matter of theological certainty, but as a commentary on what Rowling has done with Voldemort's downfall. But final judgment isn't something one falls accidentally into for Rowling. The redemption of Severus Snape is enough to demonstrate that. Voldemort chose eternal dehumanization.

But images of eternal damnation are hardly central to Rowling's world, and her story emphasizes quite the opposite: redemption by self-sacrificial love at work throughout the entire Wizarding World. It is a "more excellent way" (1 Cor. 13:3) and to that we turn in the next two chapters.

Chapter 4 Notes

1   Christian theology, which is not Gnostic, accepts the same premise. In making a point about faith and works in his epistle, James takes it as a given than "the body without the soul is dead"

Chapter Five

Worthy of Hallows
Courage in Arthur, Gawain, and Harry

J.R.R. Tolkien made a big statement in "On Fairy-Stories" about the place of King Arthur in the Cauldron of Story:

> It seems fairly plain that Arthur, once historical (but perhaps as such not of great importance), was also put in the Pot. There he was boiled for a long time, together with many other older figures and devices, of mythology and Faerie, and even some other stray bones of history ... until he emerged as a King of Faerie. (4)

As J.K. Rowling threw her ingredients into the Pot, she was perfectly aware of Arthur's presence there. As Tolkien wrote, "There are many things in the Cauldron, but the cooks do not dip the ladle in quite blindly. Their selection is important." ("On Fairy-Stories" 15). Rowling's selection of Arthurian ingredients is important, and she had many clever recipes in mind as she blended the existing ingredients with her own. In talking about J.K. Rowling's "totally bastard mythology," this cauldron in which British mythology is brewing, we do well to spend a good deal of time on Arthurian legend. While Tolkien sought to write his own mythology for England, he was invested in the study of Arthurian lore, as evidenced by his translations of the anonymous medieval texts "Sir Gawain and the Green Knight" and "Sir Orfeo;" the themes of worthiness and the flawed hero, so evident in Arthurian legend, are present in Tolkien's great work of fiction, *The Lord of the Rings*. Not only England, but France also is home to the most well-known versions of Arthurian legend; and, of course, Rowling's time studying French literature at Exeter and her year in France would have thoroughly familiarized her with French Arthurian lore.

Rowling borrows from Arthurian legend for names, story lines, and thematic elements of her series. If ever this was in doubt prior to the release of *Harry Potter and the Deathly Hallows,* Ron's plunge into the forest pool to retrieve the sword of Gryffindor put that doubt to rest. Ron ("Reginald"=King), son of Arthur, is a clear flawed hero in that instance, struggling with his own worth as well as with doubts about the loyalty and love of his two closest friends. In this moment, Ron is finally confronted with every doubt and struggle that the reader knew was lying under the surface through the course of the series, and the Riddle inside the Horcrux revealed them all: his fear that he was "least loved" by his mother, that Hermione truly loved Harry instead of him, and that Harry and Hermione thought him stupid and ridiculous. Nevertheless, he overcomes those fears, figuratively killing them in himself by literally killing the fear-producing Voldemort. At the heart of this is a battle with his own worthiness to be a hero, to defeat a Horcrux in the midst of a struggle with his greatest flaws.

The Wizarding World is an Arthurian world. The first thing to note is that Hogwarts, and the Wizarding World itself, is in a very medieval setting. Castles, knights, coats-of-arms, suits of armor, Latin, magical objects, quills and parchment, and ancient creatures all serve to set Harry in a world similar to Arthur's. The evidence of Arthurian influence is bountiful:

- Harry and Arthur were both orphaned, taken from their parents at an early age.

- Both became orphans as a result of some kind of prophecy.

- Both returned to their original "worlds" with no idea of their own special status, Harry as vanquisher of Voldemort, and Arthur as heir to the throne.

- Both were protected by a wise old wizard (Dumbledore/ Merlin).

- Dumbledore and Merlin were both very powerful and wise, but when they made mistakes, they made monumental ones.

- Accomplished wizards are given the "Order of Merlin."

- Arthur pulls the sword out of the stone (and is given Excalibur by the Lady of the Lake), and Harry pulls the Sword of Gryffindor out of the Sorting Hat. In both cases, it is their special status that allows them to be able to pull the sword (heir to throne and "a true Gryffindor"). Later, Ron would also pull the sword out of a small body of water, and Neville will pull the sword out of the hat.

• Both stories employ the symbolism of a gryffin as well as a white stag.

• Arthur marries Guinevere; Harry marries Ginny (Ginevra, an alternate spelling of Guinevere).

• The use of "Hallows" straight out of Arthurian legend (see below).

There is a particularly interesting parallel[1] that suggests Howard Pyle's version of the Arthur tales might be among Rowling's favorites, or at least ones by which she was influenced. The Court with the Round Table is described with a striking similarity to the Great Hall at Hogwarts:

And when the King and the Queen and the Court had entered in therat they were amazed at the beauty of that pavillion, for they perceived, as it were, a great space that appeared to be a marvellous land of Fay. For the walls were all richly guilded and were painted with very wonderful figures of saints and of angels, clad in ultramarine and crimson, and all those saints and angels were depicted playing upon various musical instruments that appeared to be made of gold.

And *overhead the roof of the pavillion was made to represent the sky,* being of cerulean blue sprinkled over with stars. And in the midst of that painted sky was an image, as it were, of the sun in his glory. And underfoot was a pavement all of marble stone, set in squares of black and white, and blue and red, and sundry other colors. (Pyle, *The Story of King Arthur and His Knights,* emphasis added)

The ceiling in Great Hall at Hogwarts was magically enchanted to reflect the sky – though that ceiling changed, because it reflected whatever was going on in the sky directly outside.

What all of this medieval, Arthurian imagery is meant to communicate is a certain view of virtue – particularly courage. Rowling believes courage is the most important virtue:

Well, I would want to be in Gryffindor and the reason I would
want to be in Gryffindor is because I do prize courage in all its
various ramifications. I value it more highly than any other virtue
and by that I mean not just physical courage and flashy courage,
but moral courage. ("Edinburgh 'cub reporter' press conference")

Is Rowling overstating the case here? Isn't love, after all, the most
important virtue? Isn't it love that ultimately defeats Voldemort? Many
virtues are celebrated in *Harry Potter:* love, mercy, loyalty to the good,
friendship, perseverance, and more. Why courage? Mark Eddy Smith
gives helpful insight here in his book, *Tolkien's Ordinary Virtues.* He
writes:

Courage seems to be made up of equal parts pity, wonder, love and
faithfulnesss, occasionally mixed with a liberal dollop of wrath. *It
is ordinary virtues pushed to the extreme.* (112, emphasis added)

That's a nice summary statement about courage: ordinary virtues
pushed to the extreme. It is well and good to be a loving and loyal person;
but when one's love and loyalty is tested, courage is required. Apart from
the courage to follow through with loving someone through a hard time, or
after being personally hurt by that person, love falls by the wayside. Apart
from the courage to be loyal to what is good when ridiculed for standing
for what is right, loyalty falls by the wayside. This is why Rowling believes
courage is most important; without courage, all the other virtues fail,
because they are not maintained during a time of testing. Tom Morris[2]
agrees: "Courage is a fundamental virtue ... without which none of the
other virtues could be exhibited properly in circumstances of perceived
personal risk" ("The Courageous Harry Potter" 13).

What does Rowling mean by courage? She seems to be utilizing an
Aristotelian definition of courage. Aristotle defines courage as a virtue by
placing it in between two extremes: cowardice and rashness (Morris 13).
This, Morris notes, is Aristotle's definition of courage from *Nicomachean
Ethics* (13). Morris writes,

We typically think of courage as the opposite of cowardice, but
it's just as different from rashness. A courageous person is not the
deed of a person insensible to danger, unaware of its presence, or
reckless in the face of it (13).

We already saw how cowardice is treated in the series in chapters
3 and 4, particularly with Pettigrew, whom Rowling said represented a

"shade of evil" stemming from cowardice. Harry's flaw, however, is the other extreme. His rashness got him into trouble in *Order of the Phoenix* and led, in part, to the death of Sirius. Dumbledore wisely gave Hermione *The Tales of Beedle the Bard* that made so much of Harry's quest difficult; "I was afraid that your hot head might dominate your good heart," Dumbledore told Harry (*Hallows* 720).

Harry Potter, then, is a story of the quest for the pursuit of virtue, particularly courage, and Rowling places Harry in a Arthurian context for this quest.

Chasing the White Stag: In Pursuit of Hallows and Virtue

In Harry's pursuit of virtue and worthiness, Rowling borrows from Arthurian symbolism – most notably in her use of the White Stag symbol and in the . The appearance of the stag in *Harry Potter and the Prisoner of Azkaban* is a compelling symbol, utilized powerfully in many fantasy fiction favorites. We see it in the Arthur stories as well as *Chronicles of Narnia* (see below). John Granger points us, via C.S. Lewis, to the use of the stag in medieval times as a Christ symbol. He explains that the antlers of the stag came to represent regeneration, in that they would "break off and grow back, tying the animal symbolically to the tree of life and the Resurrection" (*How Harry Cast* 103). Granger continues:

> Given this correspondence, it is no accident that when Harry
> first sees the stag Patronus who saves him from the dementor's
> kiss – the living, soulless death worse than death – he sees it "as a
> unicorn" [another symbol for Christ].

C.S. Lewis, a scholar of the Middle Ages, utilized the same imagery in the obviously Christian book, *The Lion, the Witch, and the Wardrobe*. It is the hunt for the "White Stag who would give you wishes if you caught him" that resulted in the Pevensies' return to their own world after becoming kings and queens in Narnia (Lewis, *Lion* 203).

Howard Pyle used the white stag imagery in his telling of the Arthurian Legends. In the final section of *The Story of King Arthur and His Knights*, an adventure ensues upon the hunting and killing of a white stag. This adventure threatens to take King Arthur's life, but he ends up defeating the evil sorcerer with help from an apparently old, ugly woman. The woman demands as thanks for her help that she be taken back and allowed to marry whichever of the knights of the Round Table that she chooses. Her choice is Gawaine, who willingly sacrifices himself for the King by marrying the old woman, bringing shame upon himself. After their wedding, the woman reveals herself as one of the immortal ladies of the lake who gives up her immortality in order to be with him. And as she reveals herself, she is quite beautiful, and not an old woman at all. (The symbol on Sir Gawaine's shield in Pyle's story, by the way, is a Gryffin.)

This is why the silver doe is such a symbolically important part of *Deathly Hallows,* for she is, of course, a female version of the white stag – in a sense, a female version of Harry's own white stag patronus, because Harry's mother, Lily, is the reason Snape's patronus took that form. The pursuit of the silver doe into the forest leads to the most Arthur-rich moment of the entire series: Ron's pulling of the sword of Gryffindor out of the pool, which points to his royal worthiness to possess the Hallow – his courage and chivalry – despite his glaring flaws.

Heroes and Hallows

Harry's dive into the freezing water was courageous, but his rashness made him foolish, as Ron noted – Harry failed to consider the locket Horcrux around his neck, and it almost led to his death. That Harry was rash, among other obvious flaws which could have led to failure in his quest, puts him once again in the Arthurian tradition. Rowling has taken up the Arthurian themes of the flawed hero and the battle for worthiness, and this is nowhere more evident than in her use of the Hallows of Arthurian legend, which are rooted in the concepts of the worthiness of the possessor of said Hallows.

First, we should examine the Hallows themselves. It's important to note that the three "Hallows" of Book 7 are qualified: they are *Deathly* Hallows. In reality, it could be argued that there are seven "Hallows" in the Harry Potter series, because a Hallow, or a "sacred thing," is a powerful, magical item created by an important and brilliant wizard. As such, it's best to say there are seven Hallows, three of which are "deathly." Though Rowling never specifically defines a "Hallow" in the story, defining "Hallows" in this way is not arbitrary or imposed; it is found in their deliberate parallels to Arthurian Hallow lore:

- **Gryffindor's Sword** parallels the "sword" Hallow, obviously. The "sword of Rhydderch," one of the 13 Hallows of Britain, would burst into flame if a "well-born man" drew it (Squire 339-340). Fire underscores the Gryffindor connection.

- **Hufflepuff's Cup** parallels the "cup" or perhaps the "cauldron" Hallow. According to legend, the cauldron, another one of the 13 Hallows of Britain, would heat food for a true hero but not a coward (Squire 339-340). One wonders if this was merely locked away in Bellatrix's vault because the coward Voldemort never unlocked its magical powers. There is also a Grail parallel here.

- **Slytherin's Locket** parallels the "pentacle" Hallow.

- **Ravenclaw's Diadem** parallels the "crown" Hallow.

- **The Elder Wand** parallels a Hallow called the "Spear of Lugh," the holder of which would be victorious in any fight: "No battle was ever sustained against it, or against the man who held it in his hand" (Gray 25).[3]

- **The Resurrection Stone** parallels the "stone" Hallow, perhaps the "Stone of Fal" or "Stone of Destiny" (O'Dubhain). Another intriguing option is one of the alternatives for the 13 Hallows, "The Stone and Ring of Eluned the Fortunate, which she gave to save Owain son of Urien, who was between the portcullis and the gate, in the contest with the Black Knight of the Fountain: it had a stone in it, and if the stone were hidden, the person who hid it was not seen at all" (Squire 339-340).

- **The Invisibility Cloak** parallels the "Mantle of Arthur," which made the wearer invisible, one of the 13 Hallows of Britain (Squire 339-340).

This schema for Hallow lore in *Harry Potter* is not borrowed directly from any one strain of Arthurian legend. In other words, these seven Hallows do not come whole cloth from either the "Thirteen Treasures of Britain," nor the Irish Hallows. They are transformed, taken out of the "compost pile" of Rowling's influences, and made to work in the context of the Wizarding World.

In Arthurian Hallow lore, one does not simply find a Hallow and use it. The hero must be worthy of the Hallow. As noted above, only a "well-born" man could unlock the power of the Sword of Rhydderch, and a coward could not use the Cauldron Hallow. In *Harry Potter*, unworthy people do possess and use Hallows – but neither well nor successfully. The Elder Wand is grasped by power-hungry wizard after power-hungry wizard, leading to their deaths, in most instances. The Resurrection Stone ended up haunting those who used it unworthily – including Albus

Dumbledore. Neither the Gaunts nor Voldemort ever understood, much less unlocked the Stone's power. Voldemort never successfully used the Elder Wand, and his misunderstanding and unworthiness to possess it was "the flaw in the plan" that became his downfall (*Hallows,* Chapter 37).

Harry and Gawain: Flawed Heroes

One of the most important "Sir Gawain"[4] stories, and indeed one of the most essential Arthurian stories, is "Sir Gawain and the Green Knight," anonymously written in the 14th century and later translated by Tolkien, among others. It is a story of the flawed hero, the hero who desires to be noble and virtuous above all, but who fails somewhere along the way. Sir Gawain's flaw seems a bit absurd to the modern reader. Having set out on a quest to find and fight the Green Knight, he ends up in a castle whose lord is the Green Knight himself, though Gawain does not know this. They make an arrangement during Gawain's stay: the castle's lord will go hunting, and Gawain will stay in the castle, and at the end of the day, each will give the other his winnings – the best thing he received during that day. On most days, the exchange is fairly simple: the lord's best catch of the day in exchange for a kiss, given to Gawain by the lord's wife. One day, however, he was handed a belt that would protect him from death at the hands of the Green Knight, and though he had agreed to give the lord of the castle his "winnings" for the day, he kept the belt. The Green Knight, after all, was a formidable opponent, having ridden into the Court of Arthur, been beheaded, and continued to live. Most of us, quite frankly, would do the same as Gawain. Gawain, however, saw it as a matter of honor, and though the flaw was laughed off both by the Green Knight (though he did give the minor punishment of a nick on the neck) and Arthur's court, Gawain knew he had done wrong in not keeping his word.

The temptation here is key, because it strongly parallels Harry's most important decision in the series: Gawain held onto a magical item that would protect him from death. This is the same temptation that gripped Grindelwald, Dumbledore, Voldemort, and Harry, and only one of those four overcame the temptation. Harry did, indeed, carry both the cloak and the ring into the forest with him, but he did not do so in order to avoid death; he did so in order to walk into its arms when the right time came, making the journey toward Voldemort under the cloak, and then revealing himself in order to stand and take Voldemort's killing curse. More than this, when the moment came in which Harry could have made himself Master of Death forever – possessing all three Hallows – he chose to return the Elder Wand to Dumbledore's grave and to leave the Resurrection Stone in the forest.

The Crux of Virtue: Courage

Setting Harry's story in the context of Arthurian Hallow lore establishes the need for Harry to be virtuous in order to accomplish his goal. The finding of a Hallow is a *quest* – it is something that one must do for oneself, and one must be worthy to find and possess it properly. Dumbledore makes the point when lamenting his failures in the King's Cross conversation:

> Maybe a man in a million could unite the Hallows, Harry. I was fit only to possess the meanest of them, the least extraordinary. I was fit to own the Elder Wand, and not to boast of it, and not to kill with it. I was permitted to tame and to use it, because I took it, not for gain, but to save others from it. (*Hallows* 720).

Notice the words Dumbledore uses: he was "fit" (or worthy) of one of the Hallows, but manifestly unworthy of the other two. He even speaks of the Elder Wand as though some higher power were giving it to him; he was "permitted to tame and to use it." It was a permission granted him, not something he accomplished of his own accord. How very different from Voldemort's approach to the same Hallow! Voldemort wanted it to kill, to rise to greater power, and to solidify his invincibility; Dumbledore wanted it to end forever the bloody trail of the Elder Wand.

One must be worthy of a Hallow, or the Hallow will not unlock the fullness of its power for the possessor; as noted previously, the Deathly Hallows *will* work for evil purposes, but they ultimately lead to the death of the evil possessor. The need for worthiness in order to possess a Hallow is the reason the story's heroes are primarily from Gryffindor. Rowling has repeatedly named courage as the most important virtue. Not only must one be courageous to be in Gryffindor, but one must be courageous to retrieve and *be able to properly use* a Hallow. This is nowhere more evident than in the appearances of the sword of Gryffindor.

When first Harry acquires the sword in the Chamber of Secrets, he demonstrates not only courage in the face of Voldemort and the basilisk, but extreme loyalty to Dumbledore. Only a "true Gryffindor" could have pulled the sword out of the hat, and by "true Gryffindor," Dumbledore means someone demonstrating true bravery. When the sword appears again, it is lying at the bottom of an ice-cold pool, and Harry did not, at first, know how to retrieve it. Then he thought:

> What was it, Harry asked himself (walking again), that Dumbledore had told him the last time he had retrieved the sword? *Only a true Gryffindor could have pulled* that *out of the hat.* And what were the qualities that defined a Gryffindor? A small voice inside Harry's head answered him: *Their daring, nerve, and chivalry set Gryffindors apart.*
>
> Harry stopped walking and let out a long sigh…. He knew what he had to do. (*Hallows* 368)

Why did it have to be so difficult? Why would Dumbledore and Snape have created a scenario in which Harry could potentially die? "Do not forget," Dumbledore's portrait says to Snape, "that it must be taken under conditions of need and valor" (*Hallows* 689). Dumbledore knows his Hallow lore: Hallows must be acquired by the virtuous for virtuous ends. As was already mentioned above, the "Sword of Rhydderech would only work for a "well-born man;" and the Sword of Gryffindor would only come to the brave at heart and chivalrous.

Harry does not succeed in retrieving the sword, for the locket Horcrux begins to choke him in his attempt. Ron's return saves the day, and his act of bravery in saving Harry and retrieving the sword makes *him*, not Harry, its rightful possessor for the task at hand: the destruction of the locket Horcrux.

> "No, you should do it."
>
> "Me?" said Ron, looking shocked. "Why?"
>
> "Because you got the sword out of the pool. I think it's supposed to be you."
>
> He was not being kind or generous. As certainly as he had known that the doe was benign, he knew that Ron had to be the one to wield the sword. Dumbledore had at least taught Harry something about certain kinds of magic, of the incalculable power of certain acts. (*Hallows* 374-75)

In the battle with the Horcrux, all of Ron's fears are laid bare. Voldemort's soul piece says that he has seen Ron's fears, and *"all that you dread is...possible"* (375). He calls him "least loved" of his family and digs at his fear that Harry and Hermione would prefer to be without him, and that Hermione loves Harry instead of Ron. In staring down all of his greatest fears, and then destroying the Horcrux, Ron accomplishes his act of bravery and demonstrates himself, twice within the span of a few minutes, to be "a true Gryffindor."

It is interesting to note here the difference between the virtuous possession and use of a Hallow and the use of another powerful object: the Mirror of Erised. In Book 1, when Ron stands in front of the mirror, he sees himself as Head Boy, a good-looking and accomplished student. Dumbledore explains that Ron saw this because he has always been in the shadow of his brothers; in short, his fears that was exposed by the Horcrux were present even at the age of 11 (*Stone* 211). The mirror, though, cannot show truth; people waste away before it. The mirror is a powerful symbol, because it represents vanity; instead of courageously facing fear, the one who stands before the Mirror of Erised sees what he thinks will relieve his fears. The mirror is a narcissistic thing, and dwelling on its dreams gives no one victory over his fears.

That Ron's ultimate vindication as a Gryffindor came through an act of courage at a pool, then, is symbolically appropriate. The mirror symbolism most definitely calls to mind Narcissus, who "wasted away" before the pool – thirsted to death, because he was unwilling to disturb his own reflection. As the mirror is a symbol of narcissism, so is a pool, quite obviously; that Ron won the victory over his fears – the ones the Mirror of Erised attempted to overcome – in an act of bravery at a pool demonstrates that it is not dreams based in deep-rooted fears that lead to victory over those fears, but acts of bravery in the face of one's greatest fears.

The final appearance of Gryffindor's sword is to Neville Longbottom, who had come into his own as a hero, leading the rebellion against Voldemort from inside Hogwarts. When Voldemort attempted to finally destroy Neville by placing the flaming Sorting Hat over his head, Neville's worthiness as a courageous hero and true Gryffindor became apparent as the sword fell once again from the hat, and Neville took up that Hallow to destroy the final Horcrux, Nagini. Neville proves his courage and worthiness in the midst of a literal fiery trial.

Remembering Dobby: Courage Unto Death

Hallows versus Horcruxes takes over the plotline after the trio's meeting with Xenophilius Lovegood, and while it seems to the reader a rather sudden turn of events, it is central to Harry's development as a hero. If one is seeking immortality, it is better to choose Hallows over Horcruxes, as Harry said to Dumbledore when they met in his mind at King's Cross at the climax of *Deathly Hallows*. But in Harry's attempt to defeat evil the great paradox is this: the only way Harry could possibly be worthy of the Hallows was for him to forget about them, and to choose to pursue and destroy the Horcruxes.

Harry did a good many brave and virtuous things throughout the course of the seven books, but the most transformative moment in the entire series was the moment of Dobby's death. It was in the digging of Dobby's grave that all his hot-headed, impatient impulses, and anger at Dumbledore dissipated, and were transformed into resolve and trust. Harry realized where the Elder Wand was in that moment in Dobby's grave. He was certain he was in the possession of two of the Hallows already; one more, and he would be invincible, true master of death. But that was not the plan Dumbledore had laid out. Harry realized, having watched the effects of Dobby's heroic and self-sacrificial death, and having been deeply moved and transformed by it, that even if he had to die, good would come.

It was in this moment that all of Dumbledore's lessons about love finally clicked and changed Harry. A year previous, Harry had scoffed at the idea that "love" was powerful enough to defeat Voldemort. He had spent lesson after lesson getting to know the younger Riddle, and in this final formal lesson, Dumbledore was to the point of agitation at trying to get Harry to realize that "love" was "the power the Dark Lord knows not." But here, at Dobby's grave, Harry abandoned magic; *that* was the real significance of Harry's choosing not to dig the grave magically. There was no "magic" that could defeat Voldemort. Only voluntary, self-sacrificial love could stop the evil of Voldemort. The contrast between "Magic is Might" and Harry's digging Dobby's grave with a spade could not be starker.

Harry's labor over Dobby's grave is described by Rowling: "He dug with a kind of fury, relishing the manual work, glorying in the non-magic of it, for every drop of his sweat and every blister felt like a gift to the elf who had saved their lives" (*Hallows* 478). It was in this moment that

Dumbledore's teaching about grief and love came into focus. It was in this moment that he finally mastered occlumency. It was in this moment, as he dug Dobby's grave and recalled Dumbledore's funeral, that he chose Dumbledore's plan – the pursuit of Horcruxes – over the Hallows, and in doing so made the choice that Dumbledore, even in his old age, could not make. When Dumbledore had the ring in his possession, he faced the same choice: Hallows vs. Horcruxes. Instead of destroying the Horcrux forthwith, he attempted to use the Resurrection Stone, and it resulted in his inevitable death.

Moments after digging Dobby's grave, one virtue shone through while being tested, because of courage. Harry's loyalty to the good was proven through his courage, for he recalled Dumbledore's promise that "help will always be given at Hogwarts to those who ask for it" (*Hallows* 483). Calling for help upon seeing the blue eye in the mirror had resulted in Dobby's arrival in the first place. The courage to be loyal to that which is right (the destruction of the Horcruxes) instead of taking the easy way out (the temptation of the Hallows) was finally made fully in Harry's mind. Hallows vs. Horcruxes was the ultimate test of the lesson Dumbledore taught just after Voldemort's rebirth and Cedric's death: choosing what is right over what is easy. Rowling always links these huge lessons with death; the most important lessons in life are learned in the midst of grief. Courage is required for the other virtues to stand in the midst of trial.

The Virtuous Exchange: Felicity for Fear

Peter Leithart makes a striking observation about *Sir Gawain and the Green Knight* in comparison to previous hero tales:

> Comparison with the heroes of antiquity is especially striking. For Achilles and other Homeric heroes, life affords a few passing moments during which the hero has a chance to achieve immortality. Every hero knows he will die, and soon, and knows too that the world of shades holds no attraction. If he is going to survive, he must live and die so as to achieve an eternal reputation. Man-killing Achilles, as Auden said, "will not live long," but if he leaves mountains of corpses on the battlefield during his brief life, at least his name will endure. Similarly, the worst fate that Odysseus can imagine is death, alone, without witnesses or glory, floating on a plank of his ship in the open sea. Lives of ancient heroes were infused with a palpable anxiety that life would not provide sufficient opportunity for immortality, and this heroic

mentality did not die with the last of the ancient warriors. The "cosmic resignation" (Paul Tillich) of the Stoic was ultimately a Socratic resignation before death, and the apparent joy of the Epicurean "eat, drink, and be merry" was a philosophy of life only because it was followed by "for tomorrow we die." Ancient warrior culture is a culture built on the fear of death. ("The Sport of Easter")

So, Harry finds himself in the midst of this passage from fear to faith, from death as something to be dreaded, to death that is something to be welcomed in its time, after the living of a noble life. Harry is Ignotus Peverell, willing to walk under the Invisibility Cloak, until that moment he must take it off and die honorably. And Harry is even greater than Ignotus, because he was asked to die young. Ignotus simply lived under the cloak to an old age and finally welcomed death at the end of a full life. Harry was willing to give up that long life for the sake of others.

It is this great exchange – Harry's willingness to give up fear of death for felicity in his association with the deceased who went before him in the battle against Voldemort – that makes Harry, despite his flaws, the truly virtuous person. Not only does it make him a good person, it makes him a person whom Dumbledore calls "the better man" (*Hallows* 713). Harry has eclipsed Dumbledore as the "epitome of goodness," and we can expect the same kind of patience, forgiveness, and tolerance from Harry throughout his life as we saw from Dumbledore. As cowardice in the face of fear, which we examined in Chapter Three, was the root of the evil we examined in Chapter Four, so the courage examined in this chapter leads to the self-sacrificial victory over evil, to which we presently turn.

Chapter 5 Notes

1   Credit must go to John Granger for pointing me toward the Pyle stories several years ago.

2   Morris makes a great observation after surveying the first five books: Every reference to fear by someone other than Harry is a physical description: shaking knees, gaping mouths, scared facial expressions. Harry's fear experiences, on the other hand, are always expressed as *feelings* in the mind, heart, and body. One obvious explanation for this is Rowling's third-person, limited omniscient technique of causing us to see the majority of the story through Harry. But in experiencing this fear with Harry, readers track with him on his journey to bravery.

3   Squire says of Lugh: "He also had a magic spear, which...he had no need to weild, himself;for it was alive, and thirsted so for blood that only by steeping its head in a sleeping-draught of pounded poppy leaves could it be kept at rest. When battle was near, it was drawn out; then it roared, and struggled against its thongs; fire flashed from it; and, once slipped from the leash, it tore through and through the ranks of the enemy, never tired of slaying" (Squire 63)

4   The reader will notice the shift in the spelling of the knight's name from "Gawaine" to "Gawain." This reflects the different spellings by Pyle and Tolkien.

Chapter Six

Christ in the Forest:
Aslan and Harry Walk to Their Deaths

> Rowling has never finished *The Lord of the Rings*. She hasn't even read all of C.S. Lewis' Narnia novels, which her books get compared to a lot. There's something about Lewis' sentimentality about children that gets on her nerves. "There comes a point where Susan, who was the older girl, is lost to Narnia because she becomes interested in lipstick. She's become irreligious basically because she found sex," Rowling says. "I have a big problem with that" (Grossman, "Hogwarts and All").

So reported Lev Grossman in *Time*, shortly after the release of *Half-Blood Prince*.

But Grossman hardly tells the whole story here, and one wonders about his rather deliberate attempt to distance Rowling from Lewis and Tolkien just when the Christian content of the series was becoming more evident. In any case, it's best to set the record straight about Rowling, Lewis, and Tolkien.

In 1998, de Bertodano reported Rowling's love for C.S. Lewis's books, including the direct Rowling quote, "Even now, if I was in a room with one of the Narnia books I would pick it up like a shot and re-read it" ("Harry Potter Charms a Nation"). Later in the same year, Rowling is quoted by Patricia Nicole: "C.S. Lewis is quite simply a genius and I'm not a genius" ("Boy wizard"). Lewis has consistently appeared on her lists of favorite authors of children's literature. In a Barnes and Noble interview in 1999, she called Eustace, from *Voyage of the Dawn Treader*, one of her favorite heroes and one of Lewis's "funniest characters." In both 2000 (eToys interview) and 2003 (Fry), she again called Lewis one of her favorite children's lit authors.

Not only has Rowling confessed such admiration for Lewis, she has admitted direct Lewisian influence on her *Harry Potter* stories, noting that "the wardrobe route into Narnia" was on her mind when creating the passage to King's Cross through the barrier (Renton). We've already noted that Rowling loves Lewis's imagery of the pools between worlds. It is unquestionable that Rowling both loves and has been influenced by Lewis.

There are a few distinct points of departure for Rowling. She notes that now that she's not a kid anymore, she sees Lewis as being a lot more "preachy" than she realized when she was young (Renton). She takes issue with her perception that Lewis's young characters never grew up, and along those same lines, she cites the Pullman complaint that Susan gets kept out of heaven because she "found sex" (Renton; Grossman, "Hogwarts and All"). The Susan issue will be taken up in the discussion about Ginny in Chapter Fourteen.

Quite frankly, this is not enough of a list to discard Lewisian influence. She's consistently argued that she's doing "something different" than Lewis, i.e., she's not intending to teach a morality lesson or create religious converts with her books. But we already established in Chapter One that the difference isn't quite as vast as it might appear. As "inevitably, morals are drawn," both Narnia and Hogwarts contain moral and religious lessons for readers – even if Lewis is a bit more deliberate than Rowling.

Examples of parallels between the two great authors could be enumerated, but one stands above them all: Both Aslan and Harry serve as a Christ symbol, albeit in different literary ways. Aslan is clearly a one-to-one Christ parallel. Harry is a flawed human who commits himself to a Christlike sacrifice. Both voluntarily take a painful walk through the forest to their deaths, and in their deaths and resurrections, secure victory over their respective Satan-figures, the White Witch Jadis, and the Dark Lord Voldemort. In fact, the two accounts highlight different aspects of the atonement of Christ, which we shall see.

Concerning Tolkien, there is less evidence that Rowling is any kind of avid Tolkien reader, but there are links that can easily be made between the two. There are, of course, the obvious differences, which Rowling herself enumerates:

> Well, I love *The Hobbit*, but I think, if you set aside the fact that the books overlap in terms of dragons & wands & wizards, the Harry Potter books are very different, especially in tone. Tolkien created a whole mythology, I don't think anyone could claim that I have done that. (AOL Live 2000)

> "I do admire him," Rowling admits ("Mother"). While we've noted that Tolkien is is not one of Rowling's favorite authors, admiration does lead to some influence, and there are a few similarities that have not gone unnoticed. We already saw the similarities between Dementors and Ringwraiths, as well as the parallels between the concept of a Horcrux and Sauron's Ring of

Power. Even if one argues that she did not borrow from Tolkien there, they both stand in the same tradition of storytelling that led them to similar creative concepts for their stories.

Again, the strongest parallel between the two comes in addressing the issue of death. Rowling admits as much in a rare moment of invoking Tolkien:

> Q: Solitude, death. We speak of dark things. At its best, literature comes from that.
>
> A: Well, I think it was Tolkien who said that all the important books are about death. And there's some truth in that because death is our destiny and we should face up to it. All that we have done in life had the intention of avoiding death. (Cruz)

The most likely candidate for the quote to which Rowling is here referring is Tolkien's statement about his story: "But I should say, if asked, the tale is not really about Power and Dominion: that only sets the wheels going; it is about Death and the desire for deathlessness. Which is hardly more than to say it is a tale written by a Man!" (Letter 203, 1957) That comment is equally true for *Harry Potter.* There is much commentary on Power and Dominion in the series, particularly through Voldemort, but Voldemort's quest for Power is ultimately rooted in his "desire for deathlessness." Tolkien and Rowling both counter the twisted desire for deathlessness as expressed through Sauron and Voldemort with self-sacrificial heroes.

From Christmas to Easter:
Liturgical Drama in Narnia, Middle-Earth and Hogwarts

There is an interesting similarity between Rowling, Lewis, and Tolkien in their depictions of Christ-like death: all three precede that event with a significant nod to Christmas. This is not a stretch in the least, for all three freely admit the Christian influence, character, or undertone to their story, and all three learned and lived their Christian faith in the context of the liturgical drama: Tolkien was a lifelong Catholic, and both Lewis and Rowling Anglicans.

Lewis's nod to Christmas is obvious (and the most controversial): Father Christmas, giving gifts to the Pevensies. Tolkien's is a matter of dating the journey of the Fellowship (see below). Rowling's is the simple technique, which she probably did not deliberately intend but is there nonetheless, of highlighting Christmas every year with crucial plot points, not least in *Deathly Hallows* (which uses explicit Christian imagery).

For Lewis, his particular reference to Christmas has been a matter of debate since he wrote it.[1] Michael Ward has convincingly argued, in *Planet Narnia,* that the medieval imagery of the seven heavens serves as the imaginative key to the *Narnia* series, and that Father Christmas's inclusion was important for his Jovial imagery (*The Lion* is the Jupiter book in the series) (73). Retelling the Christian story in a "supposition" was important to Lewis, but it was built on the foundation of the planetary imagery he used; supposing the 'Christ story' into *The Lion* was secondary and even subservient to the Jovial imagery of that book (73). It is secondary, but it is there, lurking in Lewis's subconscious as well as conscious decisions about that Jovial book.

Doris T. Myers makes an interesting statement about the meaning of Christmas in Narnia in her essay examining the influence of Anglican spirituality on Lewis's *Chronicles.* She writes, "A story about a young child's first awareness of Christianity needs Christmas as well as Easter" (477).[2] Lewis was putting the Christian story of redemption into Narnia, wanting to "cast Christianity into an imaginary world, stripping it of its stained-glass and Sunday School associations" (Ward 73). And in that story, Christmas precedes Easter.[3] Myers follows her statement with this important point: "Lewis's decision to include the episode must have been just as *intuitive*" (Myers 477, emphasis added). Indeed, Lewis believed that the entire worshiping context of the Christian life itself should be intuitive, arguing that the ordered, predictable structure of Anglican liturgy should be such that believers are not thinking about what is coming next, but focusing on God in a familiar pattern of events (*Letters to Malcolm* 4-5). Lewis thought of the Christian events that parallel Aslan's death and resurrection primarily in the context of a story – and even more so, a drama that is acted out each year by Anglican participants. He lived year-round in the rhythm of liturgical drama. Recall what was argued in chapter one: those influenced and shaped by Christian spirituality will find the Christ story smuggling itself into the pages of their work – including Philip Pullman!

Putting that observation into the conversation, Myers is correct to think that Lewis would not, intuitively, have been thinking about the Christ story apart from some expression of Christmas. The adult heart is moved by the Christmas-Good Friday-Easter progression, just as any child; or at least it *should* be, Lewis would probably argue. And if Lewis was right that *wonder* needs to be the foundation for genuine learning (Scott, Jr., Cagle, "A Cat Sat on a Mat" in *Past Watchful Dragons*, 2007), there are few better starting places than the mystery of Christmas. As theologian Eugene Peterson writes,

> Wonder is the only adequate launching pad for exploring this fullness, this wholeness, of human life. Once a year, each Christmas, for a few days at least, we and millions of our neighbors turn aside from our preoccupations with life reduced to biology or economics or psychology and join together in a community of wonder. The wonder keeps us open-eyed, expectant, alive to life that is always more than we can account for, that always exceeds our calculations, that is always beyond anything we can make.

Lewis captures this wonder in a brief moment in which Christmas comes, the spell breaks, and the revealing of Aslan is anticipated.

It would not be out of place to think that Lewis had the liturgical calendar subconsciously working on his mind when writing *The Lion, the Witch, and the Wardobe*. Even had he chosen to do so *deliberately*, it would not have been without precedent. After all, his good friend and colleague J.R.R. Tolkien, writing his pre-Christ mythology, rather deliberately made reference to two dates: December 25th was the day the fellowship departed from Rivendell, and March 25th was the day the Ring was destroyed and Sauron fell. Concerning the latter date, Tom Shippey writes that the

> 25th March remains a date deeply embedded in the Christian calendar. In old tradition, again, it is the date of the Annunciation and the conception of Christ—naturally, nine months exactly before Christmas, 25th December. It is also the date of the Fall of Adam and Eve, the *felix culpa* whose disastrous effects the Annunciation and the Crucifixion were to annul or repair. One might note that in the Calendar of dates which Tolkien so carefully wrote out in Appendix B, December 25th is the day on which the Fellowship sets out from Rivendell. *The main action of* The Lord of the Rings *takes place, then, in the mythic space between Christmas, Christ's birth, and the crucifixion, Christ's death.* (208-209, emphasis added)

Reflecting on Shippey's point in his article "Why Tolkien Says *The Lord of the Rings* is Catholic," Joseph Pearce writes[4],

A Catholic and an Oxford don, Tolkien was well aware of the significance of "the twenty-fifth of March." It signified the way in which God had "unmade" the Fall, which, like the Ring, had brought humanity under the sway of "the Shadow." If the ring that the hero wants "unmade" at the culmination of Tolkien's quest is the "one ring to rule them all ... and in the darkness bind them," the Fall was the "one sin to rule them all ... and in the darkness bind them." On March 25, the one sin, like the one ring, had been "unmade," destroying the power of the Dark Lord. (Pearce, "Why Tolkien Says")

Cleary, Tolkien found himself leaning on the liturgical drama in his own epic story.   This is no surprise, for Catholics and Anglicans both follow a very similar calendar. Shippey's commentary is profound: the time between Christmas and Easter is "mythic space." It is powerful and transformative.

J.K. Rowling grew up in the same ecclesiastical setting as Lewis: the Church of England. Indeed, she was the only member of her family who went to church (Runcie)! As such, she would also be intuitively aware of the rhythms of the liturgical calendar, and while it's likely she did not *deliberately* write a story[5] on the pattern of liturgical drama, the *Harry Potter* series contains a Christmas to Easter progression, not with Father Christmas, but with significant plot events happening to highlight the Christmas holiday – more so than any other holiday – in each novel. A brief look at each of the novels will demonstrate that major plot shifts occur each year at Christmas.

In *Philosopher's Stone*, the Invisibility Cloak and the Mirror of Erised are introduced, and Harry sees his parents for the first time. Christmas in *Chamber of Secrets* gives us our first glimpse at Polyjuice Potion as the trio attempts a covert operation to discover Slytherin's heir. In *Prisoner of Azkaban*, the Marauder's Map passes into Harry's hands, and he receives his Firebolt from Sirius Black. *Goblet of Fire's* Christmas sees the whole school staying at Hogwarts for the Yule Ball, and Rowling gives a specific reference to a Christian Christmas carol: a suit of armor is enchanted to sing "O Come All Ye Faithful." Christmas in *Order of the Phoenix* deepens the mystery of the connection between Harry and Voldemort, as Harry was able to see the snake attack on Arthur Weasley, and the holiday is spent at 12 Grimmauld Place while Arthur recovers. Christmas in *Half-Blood Prince* is spent at the Weasleys, where the mystery of the Prince's identity is explored and Scrimgeour's request of Harry to team up with the ministry is denied by "Dumbledore's man through and through." None of these are minor happenings; all contribute significantly to major shifts in the story.

The objections to all this are obvious enough. England is not as disinclined as the United States to use the Christian terms for the school holidays; winter and spring breaks are referred to, even by atheists, as Christmas and Easter holidays, and Christmas is celebrated with traditional religious carols. Christmas lends itself to exciting plot developments, because it's a holiday, a break from the regular rhythm of class attendance, and the school is in a much different state over that break.

These counter-arguments would stand and apply had *Deathly Hallows* not been written; but the final volume contains a deliberate recognition of the meaning of Christmas, that, especially in the overarching context of the story which leads to Harry's walk into the forest to sacrifice himself on behalf of the Wizarding World, indicates this Christmas-Easter story progression. The central actions of *Harry Potter and the Deathly Hallows* occur in that transformative "mythic space." In *Deathly Hallows*, Harry and Hermione enter Godric's Hollow, and Hermione suddenly realizes that it's Christmas Eve. The observation takes Harry, and also the reader, by surprise. We were used to the anticipation of the Christmas holidays, book by book; in this case, we have been mired in the misery of the unsuccessful Horcrux hunt and enveloped by the pain of Ron's departure. Harry and Hermione enter the graveyard in the light of the adjacent church and with the singing of Christmas carols in the air. As Harry continues to search for his parents' graves, and after having read the quotation from Jesus on the tombstone of Dumbledore's family – *Where your treasure is, there will your heart be also* – darkness and despair envelop him as the Christmas carols stop and the church lights are turned off. Immediately after the light goes out, Hermione finds the Potters' graves, on which another Scripture, this one from St. Paul, is found – *The last enemy that shall be defeated is death*. The words leave Harry cold, with no encouragement whatsoever, and he departs the graveyard in further despair, wishing he were under the ground with his parents.

Finding Bathilda Bagshot – that is, Bathilda's body inhabited magically by Nagini – they are led to her house, and Harry is led alone to the second floor, where Bathilda's body falls away and Voldemort's faithful snake attempts to hold him while Voldemort makes his way to Godric's Hollow. With Hermione's help, he escapes Nagini's clutches, the text says, "as the bells rang in Christmas Day" (*Hallows* 342). There is a fascinating parallel here, whether Rowling intended it or not, to the Christmas imagery of Revelation 12, in which the Serpent waits till Christmas Day for the Christ child to be born, only to fail in his attempt to kill him:

> Then I witnessed in heaven an event of great significance. I saw a woman clothed with the sun, with the moon beneath her feet, and a crown of twelve stars on her head. She was pregnant, and she cried out because of her labor pains and the agony of giving birth.
>
> Then I witnessed in heaven another significant event. I saw a large red dragon with seven heads and ten horns, with seven crowns on his heads. His tail swept away one-third of the stars in the sky, and he threw them to the earth. He stood in front of the woman as she was about to give birth, ready to devour her baby as soon as it was born.
>
> She gave birth to a son who was to rule all nations with an iron rod. And her child was snatched away from the dragon and was caught up to God and to his throne. And the woman fled into the wilderness, where God had prepared a place to care for her for 1,260 days. (NLT, Revelation 12:1-6)

This is an apocalyptic picture of the first Christmas, and the imagery chosen is that of the great, evil serpent (drawing on the Genesis-myth) who is prepared to devour the prophesied Messiah. Similarly, Harry, the prophesied vanquisher of Voldemort, escapes a serpent attack in his hometown just as Christmas dawns, and immediately afterward, Harry enters Voldemort's mind and lives through Voldemort's initial attack on Harry as a baby. Another interesting parallel, even if stretching just a bit, is the dragon's response to not being able to kill the Christ child is to make war on his mother's offspring; likewise, when Voldemort misses Harry time and time again, he draws him out by making war on all of Harry's loved ones at the Battle of Hogwarts.

The progression of each book then moves us toward a Good Friday-Easter experience, figuratively in the first six books, and literally in the seventh. John Granger has explained in detail the figurative death/resurrection pattern of each book, noting that in every novel, Harry is saved from death in the presence of some kind of Christ or resurrection symbol. Here is a quick book-by-book breakdown of that pattern:

Philosopher's Stone: Harry figuratively descends into the Underworld, passing by the three-headed dog Fluffy, a "comical

version of the three-headed dog Cerberus that guards the path
to the underworld in Greek myth" (Mills 3). In battle with
Quirrellmort, which can almost be seen as a figurative battle for
eternal life over the stone, Harry "knew all was lost, and fell into
blackness" (*Stone* 295). He awakes again in the hospital wing with
Dumbledore watching over him. When Harry asks how long he
has been out, Dumbledore replies, "Three days" (296).

Chamber of Secrets: Harry once again makes a descent, this time to do
battle with a great serpent, the basilisk. As Harry is succumbing to the
basilisk's poison, Riddle pronounces Harry's death. But he is saved by the
healing tears of the resurrection bird, Fawkes the phoenix, and once again
ascends victorious (321).

Prisoner of Azkaban: After a descent underground where Sirius'
identity is revealed and a return to the surface, Harry is on the edge of
death as the Dementor begins to perform its soul-sucking kiss on him.
The text holds two clear references to death prior to the kiss, and Harry
hears his mother's final screams as it begins; once again, he was saved, this
time by his own patronus charm, which appeared in the form of a stag
(*Prisoner* 384-85, 411). It is important to point out that in the absence of
the phoenix symbol, a stag is present. The stag is also a medieval Christ
symbol which represents new life because of its cycle of losing and re-
growing its antlers (Granger, *How Harry Cast His Spell* 103).

Goblet of Fire: The death/resurrection scene takes place, appropriately,
in a graveyard. After Voldemort is reborn, he "attacks Harry with a spell
that certainly is meant to call to mind the sacrifice of Jesus, the Cruciatus
Curse" (Grimes 113). As the subsequent duel ensues, and Voldemort
explains his intentions to kill Harry, his Avada Kedavra curse meets Harry's
expelliarmus charm, and the Priori Incantatem effect links the two phoenix-
core wands (*Goblet* 668). Harry hears the same phoenix song he had heard
when Fawkes came to his rescue two years prior in the Chamber of Secrets,
and he is saved from certain death in the presence of the phoenix symbol
(664-69).

Order of the Phoenix: Harry descends into the Ministry and has to
deal with the "very arbitrary and sudden death" of his godfather, Sirius
(Fry, "Royal Albert Hall"). Facing Voldemort's killing curse once again,
Harry, entirely unable to defend himself this time, is saved by Dumbledore
and Fawkes, the latter having to swallow a killing curse, burst into flames,
and be reborn from the ashes (*Order* 815).

Half-Blood Prince: Harry has forced Dumbledore to drink the green potion of fear and death, and is at the point of knowing for certain that he'll be dragged underwater to become another Inferius, when "red and gold flames" erupt around him. This is an obvious Dumbledore/Fawkes connection, and Harry rises from the underground having been saved from death.

In *Deathly Hallows,* there is no subtlety to the matter. It is masterfully done. Fawkes is gone, but she maintains her fire imagery in some interesting ways. For example, after Mad-Eye's death, everyone is looking around at each other suspiciously. Who's the sneak? Harry calls Dumbledore to mind, remembers the way he trusted, and then he takes a drink of *firewhisky* and immediately feels strength and courage (*Hallows* 80). We suddenly see a very decisive, very Dumbledore-like Harry in that moment, who simply will not let them be divided (80).

The death and resurrection scene, chapters 34-36, whatever else one thinks of *Deathly Hallows,* has secured this series a place in the list of classics. Plot details and contradictions will be forgiven in light of this masterfully written section of the story. Chapters 34-36 were the whole point of this series. Rowling wrote the previous 6.9 books for these three chapters, which serve as a set-up for the ultimate *eucatastrophe* of Book 7 and of the whole story comprised by the seven book series. The specific attention Rowling gives to Christmas book after book, simply by making so much happen during the Christmas holidays – and in *Deathly Hallows* invoking imagery reminiscent of Revelation 12 – prepares the reader for the Easter experience of each novel.

Aslan, Harry, and Christ

When J.K. Rowling began speaking of her Christian faith in interviews after the release of *Deathly Hallows,* one particular article of faith was mentioned: "life after death." From the MTV interview in which she first discussed her faith clearly:

> On any given moment if you asked me [if] I believe in life after death, I think if you polled me regularly through the week, I think I would come down on the side of yes — that I do believe in life after death. [But] it's something that I wrestle with a lot. It preoccupies me a lot, and I think that's very obvious within the books. (Adler 15 October 2007)

Indeed, it is quite evident within the books as Harry wrestles with his trust in Dumbledore, and it can even be seen in a certain vagueness that Rowling left in the text itself. For example, has Harry truly called his parents, Sirius, and Lupin from a real afterlife? There is room in the text for different interpretations: "We are part of you," said Sirus. "Invisible to everyone else" (*Hallows* 700). At the end of Harry's after death experience, Dumbledore assures Harry that what happened there was simultaneously "in his head" and "real."

Lewis is not as unsettled about the question in Narnia, writing its Armageddon and giving us an unambiguous picture of the afterlife in *The Last Battle*. In the places where Rowling *is* most confident in an afterlife, she sounds much like Lewis. "Death is the next great adventure," Dumbledore tells Harry in *Philosopher's Stone*. Aslan tells Prince Caspian's nurse that death is "the long journey" (*Prince Caspian* 217).

The most important parallels are the ones which are shared with the Christ story as well. There are at least three: the walk to death, the voluntary death, and the defeat of evil. We will narrow our focus on Aslan and Harry, but it would be well to briefly touch on Tolkien's death/resurrection narratives, for the following analysis could also include the three symbolic death/resurrection scenes in *The Lord of the Rings*, all of which have profound similarities to Rowling. The most literal death/resurrection, Gandalf's, occurs when the fellowship has descended underground, and Gandalf's battle with the demon takes him even further into the depths. Aragorn also "descends" into the Paths of the Dead, where he calls the dead up to pay their vow and atone for their sin. Frodo bears the Ring to Mordor, climbs a mountain, descends into it, and the Ring is destroyed on the 25th of March. There are, in all three obvious "descents" symbolizing death; there is willing self-sacrifice; and there is victory over evil as a result.

Aslan and Harry in the Forest

Both Aslan and Harry walk through a forest to get to their deaths. There is significance to the forest imagery, as John Granger has written: "Dante's journey through Inferno, Purgatorio, and Paradiso begins with his waking in the woods on Holy Friday in the year 1300" (Granger, *Lectures* 148):

> 1 Midway in the journey of our life
>
> 2 I came to myself in a dark wood,

3 for the straight way was lost.

4 Ah, how hard it is to tell

5 the nature of that wood, savage, dense and harsh –

6 the very thought of it renews my fear!

7 It is so bitter death is hardly more so.

8 But to set forth the good I found

9 I will recount the other things I saw.

(Inferno, Canto I, 1-9)

As Aslan begins the walk to his death in *The Lion, the Witch, and the Wardrobe*, Susan and Lucy see "the Lion slowly walking away from them into the wood" (163). The ensuing slow trod through the woods is painful and conjures images of the women who followed Christ, and even Christ stumbling under the weight of the cross when Aslan stumbles under the weight of his grief (164). Aslan seems very much to be in *need* of company, of comfort. As he approaches the Stone Table and commands Susan and Lucy to come no further (at which they cry "bitterly"), Lewis writes that the Stone Table was surrounded by all manner of villainous creatures carrying "torches which burned with evil-looking red flames and black smoke."

Harry's journey into the forest is, in J.K. Rowling's mind, the point of the whole series. "That is the chapter that I had planned for 17 years. That moment is the heart of all of the books" (Cruz). Harry reaches the forest much like Aslan – his strength is spent (so much so that he's unable to conjure a patronus), and he is terribly shaken at the prospect of death. Also like Aslan, the context of the horde of dementors sets the tone of sadness, but Harry is able to derive comfort from loved ones ("their presence was courage"). Dumbledore has designed the plan so that Harry will be able to walk to his death in the company of his departed parents, godfather Sirius, and mentor and friend, Lupin. When Harry arrives at the clearing in the forest, there is much the same imagery as Lewis describes: a burning fire, and a motley crew of baddies; and just as Aslan went silently without a struggle, so Harry stood and let the killing curse hit him.

A Voluntary Death

The voluntary death should not be overlooked, because it is the most potent part of the equation in the defeat over evil which each death affords.

Though Jesus was arrested by a violent mob, he is very clear that this was his purpose all along:

> For this reason the Father loves me, because I lay down my life that I may take it up again. No one takes it from me, but I lay it down of my own accord. I have authority to lay it down, and I have authority to take it up again. This charge I have received from my Father. (John 10:17-18, ESV)

Lewis emphasizes Aslan's willing submission to death: "Lucy and Susan held their breaths waiting for Aslan's roar and his spring upon his enemies. But it never came," and once again conjuring images of Calvary as well as the prophet Isaiah who spoke of the suffering servant who "opened not his mouth," "But [Aslan] made no noise, even when the enemies, straining and tugging, pulled the cords so tight that they cut into his flesh" (166). Aslan is shaved (again, harkening back to Isaiah – "as a sheep before its sheers is silent"), mocked, and then murdered by the White Witch.

As with Christ, it is Aslan's willingness that makes the difference: "[W]hen a willing victim who had committed no treachery was killed in a traitor's stead, the Table would crack and Death itself would start working backward" (*Lion* 197).

Rowling also underscores Harry's voluntary sacrifice:

> "Harry understood at last that he was never supposed to survive. His job was to walk calmly into Death's welcoming arms."

> "Dumbledore had known that Harry would not duck out, that he would keep going to the end, even though it was *his* end...." (*Hallows* 691, 693)

In fact, with *Harry Potter* more so than *Narnia*, the willingness is the central element, because there is a sense in which Harry did not *actually* die:

> "I didn't defend myself! I meant to let him kill me!"

> "And that," said Dumbledore, "will, I think, have made all the difference." (*Hallows* 708)

> "You won't be able to kill any of them ever again. Don't you get it? I was ready to die to stop you from hurting these people – I meant to, and that's what did it. I've done what my mother did. They're protected from you." (*Hallows* 738)

With their willing sacrifices, Harry and Aslan achieved Christ-like victories over death, and it is in those victories that some profound, classical Christian theology can be found.

Atonement: Theory and Magic

Aslan's and Harry's sacrifices accomplished, from a story standpoint, different things, but both are consistent with historical Christian theology. It would first be helpful to give a brief overview of Christian atonement theology; though, while we are wandering into the complicated realm of propositional atonement theology, we must remember that Lewis and Rowling wrote stories that reflect *the* Story, not Christian systematics. This can get a little complicated and sticky; know that on the other end of the next few paragraphs, we'll be back to the simplicity of the magical power of sacrificial love.

When using the word "atonement," we are referring to what Christ accomplished in his death and resurrection in order to reconcile human beings to God. "In the early church, the idea of Christ gaining a cosmic victory over sin, death, and Satan through his death and resurrection became very influential," writes theologian Alister E. McGrath (341). These early theological writings would later be placed under the banner of the *Christus Victor* theory of the atonement by Gustaf Aulen. Crucial to Irenaeus's thoughts on the atonement was the concept of "ransom," which refers to is the nonviolent redemption Christ achieved in winning back humanity from the dominion of Satan, under whose discipleship humanity had been since Adam's fall. This sets the cross-work on the cosmic plane – a battle between God and Satan over to whom humanity belongs. In the atonement, Satan's dominion is forever broken by a nonviolent act on the part of Christ.

Eleventh-century theologian Anselm set out the classic understanding of Christ's death as a substitutionary act in his work, *Cur Deus Homo* ("Why did God become man?"). He argued that the sin of humanity was too great a transgression to be satisfied by the work of a mere, sinful human; and infinite sin against an infinite God cannot be paid back by a finite, sinful creature. Therefore, only God can pay the debt. But God is not the one at fault; it's human sin, so humans *must* pay the debt. As Anselm wrote, "Nobody can make this satisfaction except God. And nobody ought to make it except man" (quoted in McGrath 340). Hence, Anselm argued, humanity needed a God-man. The key element is *substitution* – someone dying to pay the debt of another. Another medieval theologian, Abelard, emphasized the love of Christ in his sacrifice, stressing the transformative example he set for his followers.

Lewis's Aslan-Christ parallel is far stronger than Rowling's Harry-Christ parallel. Aslan is an *quasi-allegorical*⁶ Christ, whereas Harry accomplishes a Christ-*like* sacrifice. Nevertheless, both characters serve as Christ-*figures*, accomplishing with their deaths victories over evil that typify Christian atonement theology.

While Lewis demonstrated some hesitation with a substitutionary theory of atonement, writing in *Mere Christianity*, "this theory does not seem to me quite so immoral and silly as it used to," it's clearly an element in Aslan's death (57-58). Lewis's "deeper magic from before the dawn of time" looks like this: "When a willing victim who had committed no treachery was killed in a traitor's stead, the Table would crack and Death itself would start working backward" (*Lion* 179). The key words are *in a traitor's stead*.

There are differences between the details of Anselm's substitutionary atonement theory and Aslan's death and resurrection. In the first place, Aslan is not a human, and as we have already observed, there is no incarnation. (In Narnia, they never asked the question, "Why did God have to become a Lion?") Furthermore, Aslan is not dying for the sins of all of Narnia, for a fallen race; rather, he is offering himself up for one person. It might even be fair to say that Aslan was not the only one who could have made the sacrifice; the incantation says, "a willing victim who committed no treachery," which could apply to any number of characters in the story. So Lewis establishes a different set of historical circumstances which necessitate the sacrifice. But the substitution is obvious: *in a traitor's stead*. Aslan died as a substitute for Edmund.

There are also "ransom" theory notes in Lewis's narrative. The nonviolence of Aslan's response is highlighted. The reader is shown the majesty and power of Aslan, only to watch him nonviolently submit to Jadis. Furthermore, Aslan has to effectively buy Edmund back from the Witch's ownership with his own life. It cannot be said, however, that Aslan's death and resurrection themselves broke Jadis's power; her power began to break at Aslan's *coming*.

Harry's death, on the other hand, is a power-breaking death. It is not in substitution for someone's sin. He does not take the place of someone else who deserves punishment; rather, he dies for those who are under the tyrannical reign of Voldemort.

Abelard's emphasis on the exemplary love of Christ in his death is a profound theme of Rowling's work, particularly as it relates to Lily's death motivating Harry to do the same, and even preserving him as a good and self-sacrificial person. But what Harry's death accomplishes, in particular, is a victory over the tyrannical power of Voldemort:

> "I've done what my mother did. They're protected from you. Haven't you noticed that none of the spells you put on them are binding? You can't torture them. You can't touch them. You don't learn from your mistakes, Riddle, do you?" (*Hallows* 738)

While not cosmic in its scope, Harry accomplished a defeat of Voldemort's power over the Wizarding World with his "death" and return. It could even be argued that, in a sense, Voldemort had taken "ownership" of the Wizarding World. With complete control over the Ministry through Pius Thicknesse, Voldemort owned the Ministry, the Wizarding World's governmental body. Harry's death *on behalf of the Wizarding World* broke Voldemort's ability to bind them with magic. He could control and hurt them no longer. Not only would the silencing spell not work, by corollary, the unforgivable curses would not longer work, meaning that Voldemort could no longer co-opt their wills, torture them, or kill them. Harry's willing sacrifice accomplished a redemption from the power of Voldemort.

A Fresh Start

In a sense, this is exciting for the theologian but not so much for the normal reader (most theologians, after all, are far from *normal*). *Christus what*, now? Lewis wrestled with this himself, and he did what he does best: he got to the very heart of what all the theories were trying to communicate:

> The central Christian belief is that Christ's death has somehow put us right with God and given us a fresh start. Theories as to how it did this are another matter. A good many different theories have been held as to how it works; what all Christians are agreed on is that it does work. (*Mere Christianity* 57-58)

Or, perhaps put more simply, the Pevensies never sat around theorizing about what exactly Aslan accomplished at the Stone Table, nor did they squabble over different notions of that act. They accepted the very simple description: "Deeper magic." Or, as Rowling called it, "old magic." The magic is simultaneously simple and profound – simple in explanation, profound in accomplishment: a fresh start, where there was before no hope. It's an empty tomb on Sunday morning, a baby phoenix in the dark ashes, a joyful morning romp after a tragic night of sorrow, a new dawn rising over Hogwarts as the Dark Lord falls. It's not just a new beginning at the original starting place. It's a new beginning with old evil defeated and new hope ahead.

The mystery of it all is captured profoundly by M. Scott Peck in the conclusion to his book, *The People of the Lie.* It would be difficult to find a better commentary on what Harry accomplished with his willing submission to death:

> The healing of evil – scientifically or otherwise – can be accomplished only by the love of individuals. A willing sacrifice is required. The individual healer must allow his or her own soul to become the battleground. He or she must sacrificially absorb the evil.

> The what prevents the destruction of that soul? If one take's evil itself into one's heart, like a spear, how can one's goodness still survive? Even if the evil is vanquished thereby, will not the good be also? What will have been achieved beyond some meaningless trade-off?

> I cannot answer this in language other than mystical. I can say only that there is a mysterious alchemy whereby the victim becomes the victor. As C.S. Lewis wrote: "When a willing victim who had committed no treachery was killed in a traitor's stead, the Table would crack and Death itself would start working backwards."

> I do not know how this occurs. But I know that it does. I know that good people can deliberately allow themselves to be pierced by the evil of others – to be broken thereby yet somehow not broken – to even be killed in some sense and yet still survive and not succumb. Whenever this happens there is a slight shift in the balance of power in the world (269).

The Cauldron of Story

We began Part I by arguing that authors who "listen," who are servants to this Cauldron of Story, who are adding their ingredients to the ever-simmering soup, will end up telling the Great Story, the story of the sacrificial love of Christ. We need not be quite this mystical to make the point, however. Regardless of how much Rowling has intended to "do something different" than Lewis and Tolkien, they are all Christians whose faith has struggled and grown in the context of the liturgical drama, the Christian year. All three have unequivocally admitted the Christian influence on their novels.

The invitation of all three authors is not for us to be simple readers, turning the pages of their books for enjoyment alone. The invitation is for us to participate in our own worlds the same way that Gandalf, Aragorn, Frodo, Samwise, Aslan, the Pevensies, Harry, Ron, and Hermione participating in theirs. We are being called upon to imagine better, and to be personally transformed on the imaginative journey. To that journey we now turn.

Chapter 6 Notes

1 For those unfamiliar with the discussion: In the first place, as Tolkien himself complained, introducing mythological characters of other worlds without translating them into that world (as Lewis also did with Bacchus, Silenus, and Pomona) creates "an awkward mishmash of a world" (Miller). It would be like Rowling calling Fluffy, "Cerberus," as if the actual Greek guardian of the underworld had been placed directly in her magical world. Furthermore, "There is no Christ in Narnia — there is only Aslan, the lion who dies for the sins of others and returns in glorious triumph. So instead of Christmas, shouldn't the Narnians celebrate *Aslan*mas" (Miller)? In Narnia, there is no incarnation (Aslan appears from the start as a lion), and there is no baby lion cub born in a manger.

2 In other words, because Lewis was writing children's literature in particular, he needed to use the simplicity of Christmas in order to get his Christian point across. There is a weakness to the argument. Explaining Father Christmas simply in terms of its being appropriate for kids would not have been sufficient for Lewis, who wrote, "The only imaginative works we ought to grow out of are those which it would have been better not to have read at all" ("On Stories" 15), and, "I am almost inclined to set it up as a canon that a children's story which is enjoyed only by children is a bad children's story. The good ones last" (24). It might be argued that Lewis failed his own criterion, because the arrival of Father Christmas seems out of place to so many adults. On the other hand, it might be a failure of adult imagination that is at the heart of the problem; in either case, Ward has adequately explained Lewis's imaginative reasons for the inclusion.

3 Myers's point about Lewis's inclusion of Christmas being *intuitive* and my argument that Lewis's intuition comes from the Anglican context for his faith lead me to speculate that, at least intuitively, the major events of the liturgical drama finds expression in *The Lion, the Witch, and the Wardrobe.*

Placing Christmas as the breaking point of Jadis's wintry spell and just prior to Edmund's repentance and the Stone Table establishes a sequence that, whether Lewis did so deliberately or not, follows the Christian liturgical calendar progression, the drama of redemption. If Myers is correct that Lewis intuitively knew that Christmas needed to precede Easter, then his Anglican intuition might have also crept into the rest of the book. The liturgical drama seems evident throughout *The Lion, the Witch, and the Wardrobe:*

Advent: Under Jadis's spell, Narnia is "always winter and never Christmas." The darkness of this imagery recalls the Christian season of Advent, the remembrance of time in history when the world was in darkness prior to the incarnation of Christ.

Christmas: Father Christmas's arrival signals new hope as the spell is breaking. The giving of gifts reinforces the remembrance of the season, and the statement, "Aslan is on the move" instills courage and hope in the Pevensies.

Epiphany: When the three Pevensies meet Aslan for the first time, the emphasis is on his being *seen*, being revealed to the Pevensies (see Ford, "Aslan"). Epiphany is the day on the liturgical calendar in which the public revelation of the person of Christ is celebrated.

Lent: Immediately after the "Epiphany" of Aslan and Peter's first battle, Lewis takes us back to Edmund, who has finally begun to realize that he has made a terrible decision to follow the White Witch. We are taken through a period of regret and repentance on the part of Edmund, calling to mind the Lenten season of the Christian year, the period of repentance and fasting in preparation for Easter.

Good Friday: Without a doubt, the Stone Table scene is to remind the reader of the pain and suffering of Christ's passion on Good Friday.

Easter: The joy of Aslan's resurrection and celebration with Susan and Lucy is a strong parallel to the resurrection of the Christ and his revealing himself first to the women who had followed him to his cross.

4   Pearce, like Shippey, also notes that March 25 is the Feast of the Annunciation, "the celebration of the absolute center of all history as the moment when God himself became incarnate as man." This interesting combination of salvific events celebrated on the same day underscores the idea: Christmas, Good Friday, and Easter are all necessary ingredients in destroying the power of evil.

5   Again, it must be emphasized that the argument here is not that Lewis, Tolkien, or Rowling sat down with the singular intention of writing a story to mimic the liturgical drama. Rather, they have thrown their characters into the Cauldron, which ultimately tells the only story that satisfies "primordial human desires" – the story of Christ. As such, it is no surprise that the Christ drama can be *found* even where it was not intended.

6   Lewis himself balked at the term "allegory," calling it instead a "supposition." I have no problem letting Lewis's intention here be the proper way to look at Aslan, which is why I call it "almost" allegorical. Aslan *is* Christ in Narnia, but there is not direct parallel in every respect.

PART II

THE CREATIVE HERO

Chapter Seven

Harry Potter, the Phoenix
The Hero's Fiery Trial

For the past several generations we've forgotten what the psychologists call our *archaic understanding*, a willingness to know things in their deepest, most mythic sense. We're all born with archaic understanding, and I'd guess that the loss of it goes directly along with the loss of ourselves as creators.

~ Madeleine L'Engle, *Walking on Water*, pg. 98

L'Engle does not think it enough to read the works of creators; in some way or another, we're all *made* to be creators (or "subcreators," as Tolkien would say). "Creativity is a way of living life, no matter what our vocation or how we earn our living" (98). It is for this reason that it's not helpful to move straight from themes in the Wizarding World to themes in our own Muggle world. If a story is going to have any effect at all, it must start between the page and the reader, the text and the individual.[1] Joseph Campbell is the one who translated Jung's *universal consciousness* or, in L'Engle's terms, *archaic understanding*, into the realm of story, and a fundamental contribution of his work was mythological archetypes. In short, we learn about ourselves through archetypal character patterns – hero, shadow, mentor, anima/animus, great mother, shapeshifter, all of which will be explored in the next several chapters.

The most important archetypes in the *Harry Potter* series – hero, shadow, mentor, and shapeshifter – are given their own chapters in what follows. Other archetypes are explored within these four chapters. It's not easy to simply divide up archetypes and recite them for several reasons. In the first place, archetypes are all relational to the hero. Campbell wrote,

> "The only way one can become a human being is in relationships to other human beings." (*Pathways* 80)

So while Harry, Voldemort, Dumbledore, and Snape drive the story's plot more than anyone else, they do so in constant interaction with the other archetypes of the series: the herald, trickster, and anima/animus. (Reflections on the mother archetype will be delayed until chapter 14, because they are so important to the discussion on gender).

Another reason archetypes are not easy to pin down is because of the nature of Rowling's story itself. As with the fantasy/fairy tale genre, so with archetypes: to an extent, she's subverting them, or at least playing with them a lot. The trickster archetype is the mischief-causing, pride-cutting, comic relief of the story, who also turns out to create needed turning points in the plot. Sometimes, the shapeshifter (an enigma whose loyalties are a mystery) and the trickster are the same character (Shapeshifter-Trickster). Not only does Rowling write trickster characters (Fred and George – see below), but her whole series is comprised of what Alice Mills calls "trickster texts; they are far from simplistic in their treatment of (generally) formulaic material" (8). Not only are the characters more complex than their archetypes, but archetypes are frequently shifting. Dumbledore is both hero and mentor. Grindelwald, Voldemort, Umbridge, and Fudge all serve as shadows for Dumbledore, while Voldemort also serves as Harry's shadow, along with Draco. Not all the Great Mothers are women.

Why does Rowling do this? There are the obvious reasons that were mentioned in chapter 2: she's not writing strictly fantasy fiction; she's trying to "subvert the genre;" she's writing the story she wants to write. The more important reason, perhaps, is that despite all the brilliant plot complexities and twists and turns, Rowling's stories really come alive because of her characters. In fact, the only places where the story seems a bit forced is when an intriguing, multi-layered character has to be crammed into a plot line, Snape being the primary example of this. Snape drove the story for six books – more so from the end of Book 4 to the end of Book 6. When Rowling needed Snape to be the important but not-quite-as-prominent character in Book 7, everything about Snape that was intriguing was set aside until a jet tour through his memory in a chapter near the end of the book. Perhaps Harry's comment to Dumbledore about the Elder Wand plot works here as well: "That bit didn't work out." But, of course, despite it not working out, just like Dumbledore's plans for the Elder Wand, her overarching story still came through with brilliance and power.[2]

It's evident that Rowling is thinking according to archetypal patterns which are, to some extent, to be followed. Observe the following from the Anelli/Spartz interview in 2005:

> JKR: Yeah, well, I think if you take a step back, in the genre of writing that I'm working in, almost always the hero must go on alone. That's the way it is, we all know that, so the question is when and how, isn't it, if you know anything about the construction of that kind of plot.

ES: The wise old wizard with the beard always dies.

JKR: Well, that's basically what I'm saying, yes. (emphasis added)

She's clearly referring to mythological, archetype-driven literature here, as she makes reference to a particular genre in which she's writing. The hero must be taught by the mentor (the "wise old wizard"), but he must embrace the final battle alone, even surpassing his mentor. This Harry Potter does, as we will see in this chapter's conclusion.

The great themes of *Harry Potter* are not communicated through textbook, theoretical, propositional statements, but are embodied in the beliefs and actions of its characters. We have already looked at the virtues extolled by J.K. Rowling, as well as the vices condemned; now we turn to an examination of her incarnations of good and evil. Along the way, readers are being called to be creative heroes in their own worlds. It is through our being shaped as creative heroes that we learn creative solutions to the problems of evil that exist in our own spheres of influence.

The Forest Again

Chapter 6 was called "Christ in the Forest." The forest was not an accidental choice for Dante, Lewis, or Rowling. It turns out the "Forest" has potent mythological meaning; as George MacDonald wrote in Phantastes, "Everywhere in Fairy Land forests are the places where one may most certainly expect adventures" (Chapter 22). Campbell writes about the Arthurian quest for the Grail, noting that Gawain courageously proposed the quest, and then quotes the following:

> They thought it would be a disgrace to go forth in a group. Each entered the Forest Adventurous at that point which he himself had chosen, where it was darkest and there was no way or path (*Pathways* xxvi).

And then he follows this quote with this analysis:

> You enter the forest at the darkest point, where there is no path. Where there's a way or a path, it is someone else's path; each human being is a unique phenomenon (xxvi).

One could hardly find a more apt description of Rowling's anthropology or her purpose with the character of Harry Potter. The "Forest Adventurous" is the Perilous Realm, the world of Faerie, and each has his or her own quest to pursue through that land. This is why examining individual characters is of utmost importance. One might think we could move from the themes introduced in Part I straight into the reflections on building a better world in Part III. But two things prevent that. First, ideas do nothing unless they are believed in by individuals and communities; and second, ideas do nothing in the world until they've made a change in *us*. Rowling quoted Plutarch in her 2008 Harvard commencement speech: "What we achieve inwardly will change outer reality." Hence, we travel with Harry into the Forest, meeting sundry characters along the way, with the goal of inner transformation leading to the ability to create outer, societal transformation. In walking through the Forest with Harry, we learn about our own journey through the Forest.

Deathly Hallows revealed Harry to be a pioneer – perhaps a "creator" – of magic and of courage. His journey into the Forest was unique in magical history, and as Dumbledore so succinctly put it, Harry and Voldemort journeyed into realms of magic hitherto unexplored. Harry's final walk through the Forest eclipsed anything previously known in the Wizarding World, and he undoubtedly returned from the journey with the "Boon" needed to vanquish that world's most dangerous enemy. We need not rehash Harry's book-by-book "Hero's Journey" here; it has been done well elsewhere (see Granger, *Unlocking Harry Potter*). Rather, we will take an overarching look at Harry's development as a hero over the course of the series. The thesis is very simple: For three years, Harry was becoming a fairly standard but entirely wrong kind of fairy tale hero. In his fourth year, he began, more so than ever before, to be put through a refining process of dealing with grief, and through years five, six, and most of seven, he was being torn down and rebuilt into the hero the Wizarding World really needed.

Harry's Nursery Demon

Campbell gives a perfect starting point for understanding Harry's journey:

> The first work of the hero is to retreat from the world scene of secondary effects to those causal zones of the psyche where difficulties really reside, and there to clarify the difficulties, eradicate them in his own case (i.e., give battle to the nursery demons of his local culture) and break through to the undistorted, direct experience and assimilation of what C.G. Jung has called "the archetypal images." (Campbell, *Hero* 17-18).

J.K. Rowling gave Harry a quite literal "nursery demon," as the Dark Lord and demon of the Wizarding World attacked the young hero in his own crib at the age of one. The Dark Arts, and Voldemort himself, are the nursery demon of the entire culture – the thing young ones are taught to fear the most. Even Hogwarts students born after the fall of Voldemort are taught from the beginning not to say his name. Harry, on the other hand, says the name from the first time he hears it; right from the start, the story's hero has taken a braver stance towards the nursery demon than the majority of the Wizarding World.

Throughout the series, Harry enters into those "causal zones," the places where, in confronting Voldemort, he confronts himself and controls his shadow. As Voldemort represents Harry's shadow (see next chapter), his book by book victories are symbolic of the hero's defeat of his own darker side, that which Campbell says he must "eradicate." Indeed, the "nursery demon" is not merely a cultural fear embodied by a baddie in a children's tale for Harry, but a part of his very existence, since a piece of that demon's soul resided with him from the moment of Voldemort's attack on Halloween 1981.

In *Philosopher's Stone*, Harry is forced to confront the concept of power and morality, and two figures stand as the proverbial angel and demon on his shoulders: Dumbledore and Voldemort. Dumbledore had one primary reason for leaving Harry with the Dursleys instead of giving him to a magical family: it would be a more healthy development, despite the Dursleys' inevitable mistreatment, to grow away from the fame that would accompany being "the boy who lived." Dumbledore knows all too well the temptation of power, as *Deathly Hallows* revealed. It must have weighed heavily on his mind, both because of his own past failures which shaped him, and because it was the power-hungry Voldemort who had killed Harry's parents the previous night. It's likely Dumbledore started wondering and making guesses about Harry's scar that very night.

When Harry is sorted, he makes a choice of Gryffindor over Slytherin, though at the time he thinks he's simply gotten lucky. He learns almost two years later that in the moment, it was his choice that mattered, indeed, that revealed who he was, not the whim of the Hat. Harry's character is developed in important ways throughout these first three years, and the theme of choice is central to that development. In *Philosopher's Stone*, Harry chooses to go after the stone at great risk to himself, a choice that demonstrated his own selflessness as he looked in the Mirror of Erised and no longer saw his deceased family, but himself holding the stone. In

Chamber of Secrets, he chooses loyalty to Dumbledore in the face of young Voldemort, and that choice summons his salvation. In *Prisoner of Azkaban*, he chooses mercy in the face of temptation to great anger and revenge as he stares at his parents' betrayer and refuses to let him be murdered. All of these choices and all of this development is hugely significant, and one would hardly want to diminish them in any way.[3] But there was one problem: Harry, in the context of the fairy tale, was becoming a fairly stereotypical hero. Is anything wrong with this?

In a postmodern context, absolutely.

Book 4 to 5 Interlibrum

Divine providence smiled upon academia when it ordained a three year pause between *Goblet of Fire* and *Order of the Phoenix*. But the fullness of that blessing was not realized until *Order of the Phoenix* was read – and even more so when *Deathly Hallows* was completed. Between books 4 and 5, while eager fans were waiting with excitement, scholars were capitalizing on the series's wild popularity and the extra time to write and analyze provided by the three year pause.

The problem is, many of them got it all wrong, and the simple reason for this was that Rowling planned to change everything as Harry's fourth year transitioned into his fifth. Here is a typical complaint about Harry's hero-status, written post-*Goblet*, pre-*Order:*

> Harry's status is interesting. At first he appears to be an outsider and thus is neither dominant nor powerful. He is a skinny boy with tousled hair who is trying to find his place. And yet, as the stories progress, he obtains significant status. He becomes rich and famous. He has some of the best stuff such as a top quality broom and an Invisibility Cloak. He is also a school sports star able to get a date with one of the prettiest girls in the school. I think part of Harry's appeal comes from the fact that he is introduced to us as a skinny, orphaned outsider and yet he goes on to have success in every important venue of masculinity. (Heilman 231-32)

Heilman's statement is not too far off the mark as it relates to his identity in the Wizarding World (if not in the Muggle world); it could be noted, of course, that Harry is grappling to deal with his identity in two completely different worlds (as if it's not difficult enough to do so in just one!), and that in the Muggle world, he is an oppressed minority as a wizard. In the Wizarding World, however, he's a superstar upon arrival; but Harry doesn't stay on the same path he's been on in books 1-3. Year 4 is something of a transitional year, and it would have been hard for anyone to anticipate the importance of that year's transformative power in Harry's life until reading his experience through year 5. It turned out that instead of continuing on his seemingly upward rise to superhero status, he needed to be entirely torn down. Harry was becoming, by the end of his fourth year at Hogwarts, entirely the wrong type of hero; he was something of a cookie-cutter, standard fairy-tale hero. In a sense, the critics didn't get it *wrong*; Harry *was*, after all, an orphan boy who didn't become a hero until he suddenly reached a privileged status. From poverty to wealth, from insignificance to fame, from persecution to power, and from skinny-boy to sports star, Harry was becoming a very typical hero.

Then he stood before Voldemort; and the villain killed Cedric right in front of him. *"Kill the spare,"* he said (*Goblet* 638, emphasis in original). The spare. The extra. The unnecessary one; just kill him and get him out of the way. And for the first time, Harry had a vivid picture of what it was like when Voldemort struck down his parents and attempted to kill him as a baby – the cruelty, the lack of concern for life. *Goblet of Fire* was the first book of the *Harry Potter* series in which good did not prevail in the end. Year 5 would end with Harry's horrendous mistake, resulting in Sirius's death, and year 6 would end with the murder of Albus Dumbledore. With *Goblet*, Rowling shattered the pattern of good prevailing at the end of the year, and she shattered her hero in the process. The Harry Potter that we meet at the opening of *Order of the Phoenix* is not the likable, downtrodden kid-turned-hero that we had grown to love throughout the first four books. He was sarcastic, mean, angry, bitter, and HE SHOUTED A LOT. Ultimately what the critics didn't realize was that Rowling agreed with their critique, but she was planning to tear Harry down and rebuild him.

Baptized in Fire

The *Harry Potter* series is baptized in fire. The fire references throughout the series are many and sundry. There are multiple references to fireplaces and fires, and these become key magical elements in the Wizarding World both for communication and travel using the Floo Network. Then there are fire-based creatures like fire salamanders and fire crabs. Fireworks get multiple mentions throughout the series and play a prominent role in the Weasley twins' anti-Umbridge rebellion. Harry's broom is a Firebolt. Gryffindor's element is fire.

Then there are moments throughout the series when Rowling makes a reference to fire just prior to a significant choice or event – often a choice or event that occurs in the face of grief. Lupin had conjured fire just prior to Harry's first encounter with a Dementor. There was a reference to Trelawney's usual fire just prior to her giving the prophecy about the return of the servant of Lord Voldemort, and Voldemort's rebirth. Sirius said of his motivation to break out of Azkaban upon seeing Pettigrew in the picture of the Weasleys: "It was as if someone had lit a fire in my head, and the dementors couldn't destroy it.... It wasn't a happy feeling... it was an obsession... but it gave me strength, it cleared my mind" (*Prisoner* 372).

Rowling writes a few moments like this for Harry (apart from his Fawkes-related moments, which shall be examined below). In *Philosopher's Stone*, she mentions fire when Harry is told he is a wizard. The reference takes place not only in that context, but in the context of Harry's remembering all the times he'd been able to magically rise above being bullied and mistreated, which is phoenix-like and significant to his development (see below). Hagrid has magically created a fire in the cold cottage to which Vernon had tried to hide the family; as Harry tries to take in the news that he's a wizard,

> Harry looked into the fire. Now he came to think about it... every odd thing that had ever made his aunt and uncle furious with him had happened when he, Harry, had been upset or angry... chased by Dudley's gang, he had somehow found himself out of their reach... dreading going to school with that ridiculous haircut, he'd managed to make it grow back... and the very last time Dudley had hit him, hadn't he got his revenge, without even realizing he was doing it? Hadn't he set a boa constrictor on him? (*Stone* 58)

Then, the first time Harry encounters Voldemort, in the Forbidden Forest, Rowling describes his scar as being "on fire" (256). And, of course, in order to face Quirrell/Voldemort in the end, Harry has to pass through fire untouched.

In *Half-Blood Prince*, Dumbledore is adamant that Harry understand that the prophecy does not *make* Harry do anything, and he asks Harry in agitation what he would do even if he never knew about the prophecy.

He thought of his mother, his father, and Sirius. He thought of Cedric Diggory. He thought of all the terrible deeds he knew Lord Voldemort had done. A flame seemed to leap inside his chest, searing his throat (*Prince* 512).

So, then – a reference to a "flame" inside his chest, "searing his throat," and Harry concludes: "I'd want him finished...and I'd want to do it" (512)

Then, in *Deathly Hallows*, Harry is saved by fire in his first encounter with Voldemort in the skies after the departure from Privet Drive:

As the pain from Harry's scar forced his eyes shut, his wand acted of its own accord. He felt it drag his hand around like some great magnet, saw a spurt of golden fire through his half closed eyelids, heard a crack and a scream of fury. (*Hallows* 61)

Another interesting reference comes after the death of Mad-Eye Moody. Everyone is looking around at each other suspiciously. Who's the sneak? Who let Voldemort know the plan to get Harry from Privet Drive to the Burrow? Harry calls Dumbledore to mind, remembers the way he trusted, and then he takes a drink of *firewhisky* and immediately feels strength and courage:

The firewhisky seared Harry's throat. It seemed to burn feeling back into him, dispelling the numbness and sense of unreality firing him with something that was like courage. (*Hallows* 80).

After this, yet another reference to fire searing Harry's throat, we suddenly see a very decisive, very Dumbledore-like Harry, who simply will not let them be divided. He refuses to let them mistrust one another. This throat-searing imagery prior to decisive moments reflects a sort of purification, a doing away with fear so that Harry can speak courageously ("I'd want him finished...and I'd want to do it," above). It's a bit of a stretch, but it calls to mind the moment in the Old Testament when Yahweh's angel sears the quivering, fearful Isaiah's lips with a hot coal; when Yahweh then calls out for someone to go on his behalf, Isaiah is prepared to respond, "Here am I. Send me" (Isaiah 6:8). In this particular moment when Harry is rallying the Order, Dumbledore and Fawkes are still very much with him, and appropriately, his courage is summoned after a drink of firewhisky.

The Fire of Anima and Animus

Harry's most intimate relationships – his friendship with Ron and Hermione, and his relationship with Ginny, the two most clear-cut anima/animus archetypal sets in the series – are also baptized in fire imagery. Anima and Animus are perhaps the most complex archetypes, but for purposes here, we will make it as simple as possible: the anima is the "feminine side" of a man, and animus is the "masculine side" of a woman. We'll focus primarily on anima as an example, because Harry, our hero, is male. An anima can be a man's idealization of the feminine: everything that he thinks a woman should be. It plays out like this: Harry meets Cho, and she is pretty and appears to be everything that a man is supposed to like in a woman. So he dates Cho, but he simply cannot understand her, her feelings, or her struggles, and as she collapses into a mess of emotions, Harry jumps ship. He has projected his idealized version of the feminine onto Cho, but he has remained just the same person as he always was, without any inner transformation.

On the other hand, Harry begins to feel attraction toward red-headed Ginny. He has matured at this point, and though we know precious little about Ginny, we know this much: she is fiery, and she is powerful. These are things Harry needs, because he has a tendency toward passivity (how much of what happens to Harry in the first six books happens by chance, rather than by active pursuit?). Harry is a bit timid around girls. The whole Cho debacle was a mystifying experience for him. With Ginny, there's no tip-toeing around, no having to guess at what Ginny is feeling. She'll tell you, and she might punch you if she's angry. And she obviously has no problem showing affection and expressing her desires – Harry certainly got his chance to practice his "snogging" technique with Ginny as a girlfriend. The difference between Cho and Ginny is that Cho was a distant projection of the ideal feminine, whereas Ginny and Harry are reconciled to each other through intimate relationship, the drawing of each other toward the "androgyne" middle. They understood one another, and were changed into better people by one another.

The objection is that we barely see any of Harry and Ginny's interaction – so how do we know this? And further, if Ginny is Harry's anima, why did she not accompany Harry on his final quest in Book 7? The answer to these questions is alchemical, and it is explained in more detail in chapter 14. For now, let's turn to alchemical couples to get to the real point of the anima/animus pairing. This will be overly simplistic, and once again, I highly recommend John Granger's work for a full fleshing out of the alchemical foundation of the series.

The two most obvious alchemical couples (the "quarreling couple" of quicksilver and sulfur in which the Philosopher's Stone is made by the alchemist) are Bill and Fleur and Ron and Hermione. Bill and Fleur are an obvious anima and animus; as Granger writes, Bill and Fleur "are cartoons or caricatures of the archetypal studly man and drop-dead beautiful woman" (*Unlocking* 105). In the chemical wedding, these two meet and "die" (figuratively in their marriage union) to produce the Philosopher's Stone, the end product of alchemy – the purification of the soul.

Harry is the figurative Philosopher's Stone of the series, and his entire process of becoming that stone takes place in between the quarreling couple, the anima/animus pairing of Ron (red/sulfur/hot) and Hermione (quicksilver/mercury/cool). This is why Ron and Hermione fight all series long; and Harry becomes the hero, the Philosopher's Stone, in the midst of their bickering. This final "Red Stage" of alchemy in which the Philosopher's Stone is produced is fiery; the color is red because the heat is turned way up. It is no coincidence that Harry's final phoenix-like moment – his death/resurrection at the hands of Voldemort, is immediately preceded by the escape from the all-consuming fiendfyre and the romantic union (finally!) of Ron and Hermione, who embraced and kissed after the escape and Ron's call to save the house-elves. As Ron and Hermione, the quarreling couple, finally come together after almost seven full books of hints toward that end, and after a fiery escape, Harry is plunged straightway into a series of events (Fred's death; Snape's death; the "Prince's Tale;" the walk into the forest) that will bring him to his final heroic transformation: the willing embrace of death on behalf of the world.

Fawkes's Fire

Alongside these subtle-yet-potent fire-references is the obvious-yet-brilliant symbolism of Fawkes the phoenix. We should allow a slight distraction from Harry's character to examine the phoenix symbolism, because it is central to Harry's hero-development and to the meaning of the whole series. The best place to start when considering the phoenix is Rowling's own work, *Fantastic Beasts and Where to Find Them:*

> The phoenix is a magnificent, swan-sized, scarlet bird with a long golden tail, beak, and talons. It nests on mountain peaks and is found in Egypt, India, and China. The phoenix lives to an immense age as it can regenerate, bursting into flames when its body begins to fail and rising against from the ashes as a chick. The phoenix is a gentle creature that has never been known to kill and eats only herbs. Like the Diricrawl, it can disappear and reappear at will. Phoenix song is magical; it is reputed to increase the courage of the pure of heart and to strike fear into the hearts of the impure. Phoenix tears have powerful healing properties. (Scamander 32).

We see these characteristics clearly enough throughout the series. Harry first meets Fawkes on a Burning Day, so he becomes witness to a regeneration; this he sees again when the bird deliberately sacrifices itself for Dumbledore in the Ministry. The Phoenix song plays a powerful role in the series, twice frightening Voldemort (in *Chamber* and in *Goblet*) while simultaneously strengthening Harry. "One soft, wavering note" from Fawkes gave Harry the courage to tell the story of Cedric's death, while the lament gave the Order the ability to grieve after the loss of Dumbledore at the end of *Half-Blood Prince*. Twice in the series, Fawkes' tears healed Harry, once from certain death, the other time from the wound that led to Voldemort's rebirth.

Fantastic Beasts includes a footnote on the XXXX rating the Ministry gives the phoenix (Scamander 32). "XXXX" generally means that the beast is "dangerous" while needing a "specialist" and a "skilled wizard" to "handle" (Rowling, *Beasts* xxii). The footnote explains that while the "dangerous" part of the rating does not apply to the phoenix, but that "very few wizards have ever succeeded in domesticating it" (32). This, of course, says tremendous things about Dumbledore, the very skilled wizard and alchemist in charge of Harry's development throughout the series.

Fantastic Beasts claims that the phoenix lives in China, Egypt, and India. The reference to Egypt is important, due to Egyptian mythology's being the origin of the phoenix, in the form of the *Benu* bird, found in *The Book of the Dead* and "associated with the Egyptian sun-god Ra" (Lindermans, "Benu"). In Chinese mythology, the feng-huang is the phoenix parallel and represents "the primordial force of the heavens" (Lindermans, "Feng-huang").

The reference to India is of interest for the use of the phoenix in *Harry Potter*. While Arabia (the location of the phoenix in Greek mythology) is conspicuously absent, this connection to Hindu mythology sheds some light on Rowling's conception of Fawkes. This Hindu version of the phoenix, Garuda, "is one of the three principal animal deities in the Hindu Mythology that has evolved after the Vedic Period in Indian history" (Sanyal). Garuda is attached to an intriguing story about its opposition to snakes. The *Harry Potter* reader will find some striking parallels with the Garuda story. There's more to the story than this, but the significant details are these:

> Kashyap, Garuda's father, had two wives: Kadru, the elder, and Vinata, Garuda's mother, the younger. There was great rivalry between the two wives. They could not stand each other. Once, they had an argument over the color of the horse... produced ... just after the time of creation. Each chose a color and laid a wager on her own choice. The one who lost would become the other's slave. Kadru proved to be right and, as part of the agreement, imprisoned Vinata in the nether regions, Patala, where she was guarded by serpents. The serpents are, according to another myth, the sons of Kadru herself.
>
> Garuda, on hearing of his mother's imprisonment, descended to Patala and asked the serpents to release Vinata. They agreed to do so and demanded as ransom a cup of amrita (ambrosia). So Garuda set off for the celestial mountain where the amrita was kept. Before he could get to the amrita he had to overcome three hazards set up by the gods to guard the celestial drink. First, Garuda came upon a ring of flames fanned by high winds. They roared and leapt up to the sky but Garuda drank up several rivers and extinguished the flames. Next, Garuda came upon a circular doorway. A very rapidly spinning wheel with sharp spikes on the spokes guarded it. Garuda made himself very small and slipped through the turning spokes. Lastly, Garuda had to defeat two fire-spitting serpents guarding the amrita. He flapped his wings rapidly and blew dust into the eyes of the monsters and blinded them. Then he cut them to pieces with his sharp beak. So Garuda finally reached the amrita and started to fly back with it to the nether regions but the gods anticipated his purpose and gave chase. Indra, king of the gods, struck him with his thunderbolt but Garuda proved a superior warrior and defeated the gods and continued unscathed on his journey to Patala.
>
> When the serpents got the amrita they were overjoyed and released Vinata. Garuda got his mother back but he became an inveterate enemy of the serpents, the sons of his mother's rival Kadru. The serpents, the Nagas, symbolized evil and that automatically invoked Garuda's hatred. (Sanyal)

The phoenix vs. snake symbolism is clearly paralleled in *Harry Potter* in both the Fawkes/Basilisk battle at the climax of *Chamber of Secrets* and in the Dumbledore-Fawkes, Voldemort-Nagini parallel. Fawkes is an agent of healing, both physically (in the Chamber) and spiritually/emotionally (at Cedric's and Dumbledore's deaths); he honors life, and he honors the dead as well. Nagini, by contrast, is an agent of destruction – mistreating, tearing apart, using and devouring the bodies of those Voldemort has killed (Frank Bryce, Bathilda Bagshot, Snape).

The phoenix has been a powerful literary and religious symbol for thousands of years. Originally a crimson and gold bird of ancient mythologies of Egypt and Greece, the phoenix lived for 500 (or 1461) years, and as its death approached, it built itself a "nest of aromatic wood," set a fire, and "was consumed by the flames" (Lindermans, "Phoenix"). Out of the ashes, a new phoenix would rise, becoming a potent symbol of "immortality, resurrection, and life after death" (Lindermans, "Phoenix").

As such, it achieved some prominence as a religious symbol. "Judaic lore mentions that the phoenix achieved its unique status as an immortal bird because it refrained from bothering the overburdened Noah during the Flood voyage" (Lindermans, "Phoenix"). As early as 96 A.D., the Christian bishop Clement employed the phoenix as a Christ symbol, calling it a "remarkable token" of Jesus' resurrection as well as a future resurrection day (Clement 55). Subsequent Christian leaders followed this example, and by the Middle Ages the phoenix was referred to as a "resurrection bird" and "was used in heraldic devices and shields to represent the bearer's hope of eternal life in Christ" (Granger 94).

Fawkes: Grief and Purifying Fire

A fire-baptism can do one of two things to a person: it can consume him in judgment, or it can purify him. Harry's willingness and ability to be purified, to be "rebuilt," or "reborn" like a phoenix, becomes the key to his success as a hero. That *willingness* is key, as we noted in the last chapter; just as Fawkes willingly swallowed Voldemort's killing curse in the Ministry, so Harry must be willing to face death and be reborn, both figuratively and literally. Misty Hook argues in her essay, "What Harry and Fawkes Have in Common," that Harry's suffering throughout the series has been necessary, primarily because the character it produces in Harry makes him able to confront Voldemort.

In order to defeat Voldemort, Harry must show resolve and the determination to do what must be done no matter what the cost to himself. Thus, while Harry's humanity and capacity for love could have blossomed in the arms of loving parents and caretakers, it is only through Harry's multiple losses and his ability to be positively molded by his grief that he has discovered the toughness it will take to achieve victory over Voldemort. As such, Harry's grief is like a phoenix: it burns him up only to help him emerge a stronger, better person (Hook 92).

Harry's ability to love was created by multiple phoenix-like moments, beginning with the loss of his parents, continuing through mistreatment at the Dursley house, and being re-lived year after year as he progresses through trials, losses, and the figurative death and resurrection sequence of his journey.

Indeed, the grief that is so characteristic of Harry in book 5 turns out to be fundamental to his growth into a person who could face Voldemort. Hook makes the argument that despite the Dursley's mistreatment of Harry for 11 years, they end up playing a positive and necessary role in his life – not because they did anything right, but because Harry is resilient. The most important character trait Harry learned during his maltreatment at the hands of the Dursleys was what Hook calls "hardiness." "Hardiness is to believe that life has purpose, one can influence the outcome of events, and that growth can be achieved from both positive and negative experiences" (94). Harry's magical ability (unbeknownst to him, ironically) to escape bullies, grow his hair back, and set a python on Dudley all give Harry the internal belief that he has some say in what happens to him – whether or not certain negative things will happen at all, as well as whether or not he can bounce back from negative events.

This belief that both positive and negative events can shape a person's life is held by Albus Dumbledore, who, as will be argued in Chapter Twelve, has quite the penchant for letting people work through difficult situations on their own without intervention on his part. He seems to think it's an important part of life, and for Harry, he was completely correct. Dumbledore knew from his own experiences that grief plays a purifying role in one's life; when he chose Matthew 6:21, "Where your treasure is, there will your heart be also," he did so because *his* treasure had been in the wrong things (prestige, wizard dominance) and not with his family. The grief of losing his family changed all that. It is no coincidence that the two characters who best know the transformative power of grief are associated with the phoenix.

A Literal Goblet of Fire

Goblet of Fire seems a strange name for the fourth book, because it doesn't fit the pattern of significant names set by its predecessors. The *Philosopher's Stone* was the symbol that told the whole story of Book 1, and it set the stage for the alchemical pattern of the entire series. The *Chamber of Secrets* was the mystery to be solved in Book 2 and the final showdown between Harry and young Riddle. The *Prisoner of Azkaban* was Sirius Black, the perceived threat of the whole book and possibly Rowling's best surprise plot twist of the whole series. But the *Goblet of Fire?* It's just a magical cup that decides who gets into the Tri-Wizard Tournament; and the only real mystery to it is who put Harry's name in. It appears to have no real significance to the plot after the first few chapters.

This is true, unless we see the entire book, and Harry's fourth year, as a figurative Goblet of Fire – a crucible in which he is being tested, purified, transformed in a way he has not been in the previous books. Recall that this series is about death more than anything else. In *Goblet of Fire*, Harry first experiences and feels the weight of someone's death – Cedric Diggory. His parents' deaths had been tragic and life-shaping for Harry, but most of that was subconscious for him; he was so young, he never experienced the conscious grief of having lost loved ones. The death of Cedric, on the other hand – watching Voldemort kill someone just because he was there – wrecked him, plunged him into grief he had never known before. This is evident in the sudden, dark transformation we see in Harry in *Order of the Phoenix*. He's gone from our innocent, easily-lovable hero to a sarcastic, angry, impatient kid. He can see thestrals, which means he has fully experienced the pain of watching someone die. He isolates himself and snaps at those closest to him – a natural subconscious, survival-minded reaction to the realization that death can come at any moment, even to those closest to you.

The Dark Night of the Soul

J.K. Rowling doesn't make things easier on the poor boy. Instead of moving him from watching Cedric die and Voldemort return to a place of renewal and refreshment, she forces him to watch another death – that of his own beloved godfather. What makes this death all the worse is that it is, in part, Harry's fault for not heeding Dumbledore's advice to learn and practice Occlumency against Voldemort.

Wedged right in between Harry's experience of Cedric's death and his depression and anger in *Order of the Phoenix* is his first moment of learning how to deeply grieve; and that moment is only helped along by Fawkes the phoenix. Fawkes recognizes the pain of death that Harry felt, because Fawkes immediately "left his perch, [flew] across the room, and landed on Harry's knee" (*Goblet* 694). Harry absolutely does not want to talk about it, but Dumbledore wisely presses him:

> If I thought I could help you…by putting you into an enchanted sleep for a while…I would do it. But I know better. Numbing the pain for a while will only make it worse when you finally feel it (695).

As Harry realizes that he would have to tell the whole story of Cedric's death right then and there, the interplay between Dumbledore and Fawkes continues: Fawkes "let out one soft, quavering note" that warms and strengthens Harry for the story he is about to tell (695). With the combination of Dumbledore's words and Fawkes's song, Harry learns how to begin to grieve Cedric's death not by pushing it down, but by speaking and letting it all out. It's painful, but simultaneously a "relief" for Harry to relive the night's awful events (695).

Fast-forward, then, to the climax and denouement of *Order of the Phoenix*. In Dumbledore's battle with Voldemort in the atrium of the Ministry, there is a moment when Voldemort would have succeeded in killing Dumbledore had there not been a sudden "burst of flame in midair," Fawkes appearing and swooping down to swallow the killing curse, and then another burst into flames as he died and was reborn. After the battle, Harry is portkeyed back to Dumbledore's office, and when Dumbledore himself returns, Rowling writes:

> He did not look at Harry at first, but walked over to the perch beside the door and withdrew, from an inside pocket of his robes, the tiny, ugly, featherless Fawkes, whom he placed gently on the tray of soft ashes beneath the golden post where the full-grown Fawkes usually stood. (*Order* 822)

Fawkes stands as a symbol for Harry's grief in this passage, for this is precisely Harry's current emotional state. He is entirely diminished and feels destroyed inside, naked and exposed, powerless, and entirely removed from any glorious status of "hero" that he had achieved in the first four books. Instead of Fawkes being present to sing and internally warm and strengthen Harry as he grieves, Fawkes is a baby, completely external to Harry, and nothing warms him, strengthens him, gives him courage. He is numb and cold.

Fire turns against Harry in this moment. The fires of purification have become the fires of rage; "Harry felt white-hot anger lick his insides, blazing in the terrible emptiness, filling him with the desire to hurt Dumbledore for his calmness and his empty words" (*Phoenix* 823). What are those "empty" words? "[T]he fact that you can feel pain like this is your greatest strength" (823). Harry breaks into a rage at these words, and this is precisely where he proclaims he no longer wants to be human – a scary notion in light of the fact that Tom Riddle, Jr. became Voldemort precisely because, in the face of grief, he no longer wanted to be human (see next chapter). Harry leaves that meeting with Dumbledore not healed and whole (which would be an insult to the process of grieving loss), but hurt and more damaged than ever before. But Harry's love – Dumbledore called it his greatest strength – would cause him to rise out of this grief stronger than ever before.

We should pause for just a moment and reflect on what happened to Harry in his fifth year. John Granger, explaining the fifth book as the "Black Stage" of the alchemical process, succinctly summarizes this dark-night-of-the-soul period of Harry's life:

> Harry, literally and figuratively, is burnt up, broken down or dissolved, and bled until everything that he thought he was – Quidditch seeker, Ron and Hermione's superior, pet of Dumbledore, lover of Hogwarts, son and spitting image of a great man, victim of the Dursleys, valiant enemy of Snape, even his being the hero and man of action in time of crisis – are taken from him or revealed as falsehoods. The boundaries of his world collapse; the Dementors come to Little Whinging and Aunt Petunia knows about them. Privet Drive is no longer a sanctuary, however miserable, and Hogwarts is no longer edifying or any joy to him. The world is no longer separated into Good Guys, Muggles, and Death Eaters – and Harry has been reduced to his formless elements. (*Unlocking* 66)

He loses everything, most importantly, in order to become the phoenix-like hero, his status as superhero. His heroic endeavor to save his godfather turns out to be his biggest mistake yet, resulting in his Sirius's death.

Trickster Intervention

Harry is hardly a hero in *Order of the Phoenix*. His attempt at being the hero, his "saving-people thing," as Hermione called it, was an utter disaster. This was necessary for Harry, but in the meantime, somebody had to step into his shoes; the tricksters answered the call.

Tricksters are comical characters, but also serve the important role of challenging and toppling oppressive systems. They are full of antics and practical jokes, and they are sometimes perceived as being dumb; in reality, they are more clever than the rest and contribute something fundamental to the plot. The trickster became an important archetype in African American folk tales, for example, serving as challengers to slavery. The trickster defeats the oppressors by outwitting them. S/he is both funny and clever, and shows the oppressor to be a fool.

Fred and George are the series' tricksters, no doubt about it. They are comical through and through, but they are not mere comic relief. They are also thought to be not as intelligent as others, at least in the mind of Mrs. Weasley; compared to their older brothers, their grades are terrible, and they are always in trouble. It appears they are the classic slackers, caring more about having fun than getting a good education. It turns out that Mrs. Weasley and anyone else who thought that about the Weasley twins were wrong.

Their rebellion in *Order of the Phoenix* is classic trickster behavior. Until that moment, Umbridge's tyranny was unchallenged. No one had been able to break her control in the least. From the time of the twins' two-stage rebellion on, Umbridge entirely lost control. Even the teachers are beginning to revolt, as evidenced by Flitwick's amusing claim that he had to call Umbridge to deal with the Weasleys' magical fireworks in his classroom, because he didn't know if he "had the *authority*" (*Order* 634, emphasis in original). It's not a coincidence, given the fire theme, that while Harry is off-stage, as far as being the hero is concerned, wrestling with his shadow and in utter darkness and coldness in his soul (the "dark night" or "winter season" of the soul), the red-headed twins launch a rebellion starting with fireworks. They make Umbridge look a fool, and she never quite gains control again after the Weasley's effective revolution against her tyranny.

Becoming Dumbledore's Man

Half-Blood Prince would force Harry, finally, to rise out of the ashes of pain, grief, and death into the hero that must face Voldemort in the end. Dumbledore would have to die for this to happen, but before his death, a poignant fire-moment occurs in the cave. After Harry has forced Dumbledore to drink the green potion of fear and death, the Inferi have risen from the water and begin to drag Harry down. He is at the point of knowing for certain that he'll be dragged underwater to become another Inferius, when "red and gold flames" erupt around him, conjured by a vivified Dumbledore. Death is forced backward into the water (a clear symbolic reference to Gryffindor fire vanquishing Slytherin water). But a change has occurred at this point: it is no longer Dumbledore leading and supporting Harry, but Harry doing the same for Dumbledore. At the beginning of *Half-Blood Prince*, Dumbledore assures Harry he'll be safe from attack as they travel because, "You are with me" (*Prince* 58). Exiting the cave, Dumbledore assures Harry that he, Dumbledore, will be safe during their travel, because, "I am with you" (*Prince* 578). This stunning turnaround demonstrates the point: Harry is not only "Dumbledore's man through and through," but he has taken his place as the next great hero of the Wizarding World.

Dumbledore's death makes the point firmly. When Dumbledore died, Fawkes sang a "stricken lament of terrible beauty," and the song once again helped Harry to grieve; he felt that the song is came from within, turning his own grief "magically to song," and then the phoenix "left Hogwarts for good," just as his master had (*Prince* 614-15, 632). When Dumbledore's white tomb burst into flames at the funeral, Harry "thought...he saw a phoenix fly joyfully into the blue" (645). Misty Hook's analysis is once again helpful:

> Each time a death occurs he becomes a little more convinced until, with the death of Dumbledore, Harry realizes that the meaning for all of their deaths is that sometimes there are things worth dying for, and fighting evil is one of them (Hook 96).

Following Dumbledore's funeral ceremony, Harry is confronted by Scrimgeour for a second time, and Harry affirms again that he is "Dumbledore's man, through and through." This is a fundamental, pivotal moment for Harry's development as a Hero. Campbell writes of the challenges faced by the ego: "The society will give you a mask to wear. You are to identify with it completely, canceling out every creative thought" (*Pathways* 71). Scrimgeour, the most prominent voice of the Wizarding World, is giving to Harry the mask that society wants him to wear – poster boy for the Ministry. Harry refuses. He will not wear a mask that causes him to cancel every creative thought. He will be a creative Hero, like Dumbledore before him.

But the hero must not become simply like or equal to his mentor; he must surpass him. This is precisely what happens in *Deathly Hallows*.

Harry, the Phoenix

The Harry Potter of *Deathly Hallows* is a new and improved Harry – one who is capable of leading the courageous battle against Lord Voldemort. His moment of leadership after the swig of firewhisky following Moody's death is evidence of that. It's interesting, then, that Rowling does not give us Harry Potter, new leader of the Order of the Phoenix; instead, we get a Harry Potter who is wandering around in tents, with no clue how to accomplish his goals. Indeed, Harry still has more transformative grief to feel and from which to rise. Shortly after the firewhisky gives him the courage to unite the Order, Harry is feeling the grief of loss:

> But Dumbledore, like Mad-Eye, like Sirius, like his parents, like his poor owl, all were gone where Harry could never talk to them again. He felt a burning in his throat that had nothing to do with firewhisky. . . . (*Hallows* 84)

It would only get worse before it gets better. Prior to the beginning of their journey, however, firewhisky[4] makes one more subtle but significant appearance: when Ginny gives him his "birthday present," a long and passionate kiss, Harry thinks, "it was blissful oblivion better than firewhisky; she was the only real thing in the world" (*Hallows* 116). In other words, an instance of love releases Harry, just momentarily, from his burdens. One can hardly blame the young man for enjoying one beautiful moment before setting off for months of suffering, and it underscores Dumbledore's – and Rowling's – belief that even in difficult times, it's better if there is more love in the world. This was the argument that McGonagall made after Dumbledore died, when Lupin and Tonks were discussing their love for one another in the hospital wing (*Prince* 624).

Rather than becoming General of a military effort against Voldemort, Harry keeps his word to Dumbledore not to tell anyone about the Horcrux mission, and he leads the trio into months and months of frustration, doubt, and despair in a seemingly futile Horcrux hunt. Barely into their journey, Harry becomes obsessed with one problem: Dumbledore's history. And not too long after that, he's suddenly enslaved to another obsession: the Deathly Hallows. This take-charge leader who rallied the Order after Moody's death is suddenly back into his old tendency to be hot-headed and distracted by something other than what he's supposed to be doing (think Draco's plot, rather than Slughorn's memory in *Half-Blood Prince*). But the thing that snaps him back into focus, and indeed that completes Harry as a hero, is the death of Dobby, which was examined in detail in Chapter Five.

We noted Hook's observation above that at Dumbledore's death, Harry finally realized that "there are things worth dying for, and fighting evil is one of them." Harry says as much to Aberforth, just prior to the Battle of Hogwarts. Aberforth is arguing that if Albus had really loved Harry, he would have tried to keep him alive at all costs:

> "I don't believe it. Dumbledore loved Harry," said Hermione.
>
> "Why didn't he tell him to hide, then? shot back Aberforth. "Why didn't he say to him, 'Take care of yourself, here's how to survive' ?"
>
> "Because," said Harry before Hermione could answer, "sometimes you've *got* to think about more than your own safety! Sometimes you've *got* to think about the greater good! This is war!" (*Hallows* 568).

Aberforth is here defining love as protection by any means and at all costs. Harry, on the other hand, has truly come to believe what Hook argued he had come to believe after Dumbledore's death, and he does so by quoting Albus himself, arguing that he must risk his life "for the greater good." This is the opposite of what Albus meant when he was young, when he was prepared to sacrifice *others* for the greater good. Harry, like the older Albus just a year prior, was now prepared to sacrifice *himself* for the greater good.

It should be no surprise by this point that when Harry finally stood before Voldemort in the forest, not to fight back, but willingly to die, a fire was prominent on the scene. As Harry stepped "forward into the firelight" upon announcing his arrival to Voldemort, the summoned forms of his parents, Sirius, and Lupin disappeared. Alone now, Harry and Voldemort, there was "nothing but the fire between them" (*Hallows* 703). As the gaggle of baddies settle down, "the only things that moved were the flames and the snake," an obvious reference to Gryffindor/Slytherin (704). And then, Voldemort let loose his killing curse.

The Better Man

Harry moves beyond Dumbledore, rising above him in hero-status. The brilliant thing about the "Dumbledore denouement" of *Deathly Hallows* is that it occurs before, not after, the climax of the story. And in another odd twist, there is very little Dumbledore needs to precisely explain to Harry; Harry is able to come to most conclusions on his own. Not only this, but the tables turn, and it is Harry who is comforting and explaining things to Dumbledore. In other words, the tables have turned. Harry is no longer having something that happened to him explained by Dumbledore after the fact. Rather, Harry is comforting Dumbledore, while Dumbledore finally reveals himself fully and explains the choice Harry has still in front of him – a final duel with Voldemort. It will come as no surprise by this point that Rowling mentions fire also in this chapter. Dumbledore's pride in Harry's courage, and his revelation to Harry both that he is not dead and that his willing self-sacrifice "will have made all the difference" is followed by this description: "Happiness seemed to radiate from Dumbledore like light, like fire" (708).

Later in their conversation, as Dumbledore compares himself with Voldemort, saying, "Yet I too sought to conquer death, Harry," Harry will have none of it, and reminds Dumbledore, "Hallows, not Horcruxes" (*Hallows* 713). In other words, he's reminding Dumbledore that, despite his youthful failings, Dumbledore sought a virtuous path to immortality, not an evil one. But it is precisely the issue of the Hallows that solidifies Harry as the better man, as the phoenix who rose out of his grief not only to Dumbledore's status, but to a greater status:

> "Maybe a man in a million could unite the Hallows, Harry. I was fit only to possess the meanest of them, the least extraordinary. I was fit to own the Elder Wand, and not boast of it, and not to kill with it. I was permitted to tame and use it, because I took it, not for gain, but to save others from it.

> "But the Cloak, I took out of vain curiousity, and so it could never have worked for me as it works for you, its true owner. The stone I would have used in an attempt to drag back those who are at peace, rather than enable my self-sacrafice, as you did. You are the worthy possessor of the Hallows." (*Hallows* 720).

And perhaps more poignantly still, when Harry asks why Dumbledore made it so hard:

"I am afraid I counted on Miss Granger to slow you up, Harry. I was afraid that your hot head might dominate your good heart. I was scared that, if presented outright with the facts about those tempting objects, you might seize the Hallows as I did, at the wrong time, for the wrong reasons. If you laid hands on them, I wanted you to possess them safely. You are the true master of death, because the true master does not seek to run away from Death. He accepts that he must die, and understands that there are far, far worse things in the living world than dying." (*Hallows* 720-21)

In the end, nothing makes it more evident that Harry is the only one worthy of the Deathly Hallows than his willingness to give them up at the end. He will not be "Master of Death," because he has come to learn, like the phoenix, that though death is a painful tragedy, good can still come of it when it is face courageously, and with love. As Harry, pretending to be dead, is carried by Hagrid through the forest, they pass through the Dementors once again. Not an hour before, these same Dementors had created utter despair in Harry's heart. But "[t]hey would not affect him now. The fact of his own survival *burned* inside him, a talisman against them, as though his father's stag kept guardian in his heart" (728, emphasis added). The dark night of the soul and the depression of the dementors has been banished by the fires of his willing self-sacrifice. Those fires carry him through to the final duel with Voldemort, and the moment of Harry's final victory, when they cast their spells against each other, is described like this:

A red-gold glow burst suddenly across the enchanted sky above them as an edge of dazzling sun appeared over the sill of the nearest window. The light hit both of their faces at the same time, so that Voldemort's was suddenly a flaming blur. Harry heard the high voice shriek as he too yelled his best hope to the heavens, pointing Draco's wand:

"Avada Kedavra!"

"Expelliarmus!"

The bang was like a cannon blast, and the golden flames that erupted between them, at the dead center of the circle they had been treading, marked the point where the spells collided. Harry saw Voldemort's green jet meet his own spell, saw the Elder Wand fly high, dark against the sunrise, spinning across the enchanted ceiling like the head of Nagini, spinning through the air toward the master it would not kill, who had come to take full possession of it at last. (744)

The fiery sun rises, and the Dark Lord falls to the master of the Elder Wand, and the only remaining mark of the battle is a fire of "golden flames" caused by the meeting of the two spells. Harry had given himself up for his friends, and now he stood before the enemy of life and love in victory. A self-sacrificial, phoenix-like person, able to rise out of grief and win the battle against evil with love: this is the true definition of a Hero in *Harry Potter*.

Chapter 7 Notes

1   This is not to deny that every individual is part of a community, rather than an isolated, rational, objective mind. The "Hero" is only aware of himself or herself in relation to the other archetypes.

2   It should be noted here that I agree with John Granger's conclusion, based on his thorough research into and knowledge of alchemy, that Jung didn't "get" alchemy in the way it was intended. Granger, tracking with Titus Burkhardt, argues that Jung put the alchemical process into the subconscious, a thing we have to go down into ourselves to find; the alchemist puts the transformation "above...individual consciousness" (*Unlocking* 52). Why is this a necessary observation? Because alchemy is the transformational process through which Harry goes, and Jung took alchemy and turned it into "archetypes" and "collective unconscious," a change one accomplishes by going within oneself, which Joseph Campbell (and L'Engle, above) tapped into in their views of story. It might be argued, then, that I want to have my cake and eat it, too: I want the alchemical framework and the archetypes, when in reality the two are polar opposites. Though they do have meaningful differences, I don't think it follows that we throw archetypes out the window as a way of at fantasy fiction that utilizes literary alchemy. That Jung made some mistakes regarding alchemy in his formation of the archetypes doesn't negate the usefulness of archetypal studies of the characters encountered in Faerie. Whether from above or below, the archetypes are there to learn from; the existence of archetypal figures in literature is so evident that it is necessarily one of many windows through which we should view Harry Potter.

3   For an excellent treatment of "Choice" in the series, see Chapter 8 in John Granger, *How Harry Cast His Spell*. Tyndale, 2008. See also my own work and that of the other writers of the "Blogengamot" at http://thehogshead.org/categories/themes/fate-and-choice/

4   In the event that someone thinks I'm making a bit too much of this "firewhisky" business, note that Rowling is conscious enough of her decision to include firewhisky in that decisive moment after Mad-Eye's death to refer back to it later in the book. After their narrow escape at the Ministry and Ron's splinching, Hermione makes some hot tea for the trio, and she writes: "Harry found the hot drink as welcome as the firewhisky had been on the night that Mad-Eye had died; it seemed to burn away a little of the fear fluttering in his chest" (DH-14).

Chapter Eight

Harry's Shadow
Voldemort as Sociopath and Sinner

A threefold look at "the Dark Lord" demonstrates exactly how J.K. Rowling has succeeded in creating a villain who simultaneously serves as a symbol of evil as well a sort of bad guy next door – a representation of the evil that could potentially exist in every one of us. As the shadow archetype of the series, Voldemort is fullest expression of evil in the Wizarding World, and a symbol of all that could have gone wrong in Harry Potter's life had he chosen his darker impulses. As a "Sociopath," nine psychological criteria can be utilized to describe him as a Malignant Narcissist, a dangerously guileful character who has managed to put even his own supposed enemies in his pocket. As a "Sinner," Voldemort's wicked choices demonstrate why he is a morally culpable person who is the antithesis of Harry Potter.

Voldemort as Shadow

Carl Jung described the Shadow archetype in the following way:

> Unfortunately there can be no doubt that man is, on the whole, less good than he imagines himself or wants to be. Everyone carries a shadow, and the less it is embodied in the individual's conscious life, the...denser it is. If an inferiority is conscious, one always has a chance to correct it. Furthermore, it is constantly in contact with other interests, so that it is continually subjected to modifications. But if it is repressed and isolated from consciousness, it never gets corrected. (Jung, "Psychology and Religion" 131)

It is a frightening thought that man also has a shadow side to him, consisting not just of little weaknesses- and foibles, but of a positively demonic dynamism. The individual seldom knows anything of this. (Jung, "On the Psychology of the Unconscious" 35)

> What is so difficult for the layman to grasp is the fact that in most cases the patients themselves have no suspicion whatever of the ... war raging in their unconscious. If we remember that there are many people who understand nothing at all about themselves, we shall be less surprised at the realization that there are also people who are utterly unaware of their actual conflicts. (Jung, "New Paths in Psychology" 425)

Voldemort manifestly fits this archetypal pattern. He is utterly unaware of himself. He is not self-conscious in the least. Rather, he carries grandiose ideas of himself that completely blind him to the horrible truth.

As M. Scott Peck wrote, "The evil do not serenely bear the trial of being displeasing to themselves" (72).

The important point, of course, is that he is *Harry's* shadow. There are many similarities between Harry Potter and Tom Riddle, Jr. that are emphasized throughout the series. There is the matter of the wand cores, which isn't coincidence, because the phoenix-core wand *chose* them both. They're both orphans for whom Hogwarts is their first real home. They both speak parseltongue and possess qualities worthy of a Slytherin – as Dumbledore said, "resourcefulness, determination, a certain disregard for the rules" (*Chamber* 333). There is, of course, the way in which Rowling makes many of these differences occur: Harry is a horcrux. This is Rowling's literary way of getting at the Shadow idea. If Voldemort is simply Harry's external enemy, and Harry the superhero, no real progress is made in understanding the importance of defeating evil in oneself before defeating evil in the world. In placing a piece of Voldemort's soul inside Harry, Rowling has given us one of the most interesting examples of the shadow archetype since Dr. Jeckyll and Mr. Hyde.

Harry's "dark side" finds expression in multiple places throughout the series. Snape's frequent accusation that Harry is just like his father is not always off the mark. While James Potter was a good man, his arrogance was clear in "Snape's Worst Memory." There are two stunning moments in the series that highlight Harry's dark side more clearly than anything else.

In the denouement of *Order of the Phoenix*, as Harry rages against Dumbledore, the wise old man tries desperately to explain to Harry how natural, normal, and healthy his grief at losing Sirius is. It's all part of being human, Dumbledore explains.

"THEN – I – DON'T – WANT – TO – BE – HUMAN!" (824)

Harry's response is chilling, because this is exactly the desire of Lord Voldemort – to avoid pain, death, and to dehumanize himself in the process.

In Deathly Hallows, after Amycus Carrow spits in Professor McGonagall's face, Harry fires a successful Cruciatus curse at him (593). This is another shockingly out of character moment for our hero, who earlier in the very same book refused to throw a stunning spell at Stan Shunpike for fear he would fall to his death. Blowing people out of the way "just because they're there" is "Voldemort's job," Harry says (71).

So is torture, Harry.

We are not meant to see Harry's "Crucio!" as morally justified. While it was certainly motivated by his anger at the Carrow's frequent torture of students throughout the semester, Harry is supposed to be the hero who rises above Voldemort's tactics of fear and coercion. Yet at the end of his journey, after seven years' transformation, book by book, Harry fires off the cruelest spell he's ever cast. Shadow, indeed.

While there are many similarities between Harry and Voldemort, the primary difference lies in what Jung described as the remedy to the problem of the inner shadow:

> If you imagine someone who is brave enough to withdraw all his projections, then you get an individual who is conscious of a pretty thick shadow. Such a man has saddled himself with new problems and conflicts. He has become a serious problem to himself, as he is now unable to say that they do this or that, they are wrong, and they must be fought against. Such a man knows that whatever is wrong in the world is in himself, and if he only learns to deal with his own shadow he has done something real for the world. He has succeeded in shouldering at least an infinitesimal part of the gigantic, unsolved social problems of our day. (Jung, "Psychology and Religion" 140).

Starting with Book 5, Harry becomes "a serious problem to himself." Harry spent the first four books becoming the standard hero, but the wrong kind of hero. He was becoming the fairy tale hero, when he needed to become the postmodern Christian hero, the one who cannot do what he must do until he is stripped of everything.

The biblical figure of Moses an example of this. Moses made an attempt, while in power and good standing in Egypt, to begin to free the Israelites. It didn't work. The martyr Stephen's commentary on Moses in the book of Acts is that he was a man powerful in word. But 40 years later, when God finally calls Moses to be Egypt's Deliverer, he has been so transformed that he says to God, "I don't speak well. I can't be the Deliverer." Stripped of power, authority, status, and strong speech, after 40 years in the desert herding sheep, Moses is finally ready to be the Deliverer. As with Moses, so with Harry.

Harry's transformation is obvious after Voldemort is defeated, when he decides to leave the Resurrection Stone and abandon the Elder Wand. Having faced his own Shadow, and having overcome the darkness inside himself, he is able to resist temptation.

Voldemort serves not only as a shadow for Harry, but as a symbol of all the evil present in the Wizarding World, only in much more subtle ways. The blatant racism of Voldemort, for example, can be found in the institutionalized prejudices of the Wizarding World. What Harry must defeat both in himself and in Voldemort is a symbol of the defeat of all evil in the Wizarding World (even if it doesn't accomplish that all in one victory).

We noted in the last chapter that much of Harry's growth as an individual and as a hero was underscored by his phoenix-connections. In typical hero-shadow form, Voldemort has many of the same symbolic connections to grief and to the phoenix, but he does the wrong thing with these challenges every time. Voldemort's greatest weakness lies in his inability to love and to see that "there are things much worse than death" (*Order* 814; see also *Prince* 559, 566). Voldemort, the series' shadow archetype, is key to understanding what not to believe about death. The name Voldemort, taken on by the young Tom Riddle, Jr. can literally mean, "willing death, flight of death, or flight from death" (Granger, *How Harry Cast* 116). Both ideas apply perfectly: he is simultaneously attempting to flee from death and willing death upon anyone who gets in his way.

Voldemort so despises and fears death that he has "gone further than anybody along the path to immortality" through certain "experiments" (*Goblet* 653). "Experiments" is a rather scientific word, underscoring his position as a soul-discarding materialist even in a magical world. We learn in Book 6 that these experiments are Horcruxes, "wickedest of magical inventions" (*Prince* 381). They are so wicked because, in order to create them to keep one's self alive, one must commit murder, "the supreme act of evil," ripping one's soul apart and placing the soul fragment into an object (497-98). Slughorn explaines to young Riddle that "death would be preferable" to an existence reliant upon a Horcrux (497).

It is quite apparent that Riddle did not agree. Even at the age of 11, Tom was convinced that someone who knew magic would be able to prevent death (275). The rest of his life is spent in pursuit of this goal, firm in his belief that "[t]here is nothing worse than death" (*Order* 814). So determined was Voldemort to never die, that he was willing to live a "cursed life" by drinking unicorn's blood, become less and less human, and kill anyone in his path to achieve his goal (*Stone* 258).

It is also evident that Voldemort has nothing but disdain for sacrificial love. He called Lily Potter's sacrifice "foolish" and challenged Dumbledore directly on his belief that "love is more powerful than [Voldemort's] kind of magic" (*Goblet* 653; *Half-Blood* 444). Voldemort is so unconvinced of the power of love that he thinks his use of Harry's blood, in which the "old magic" that he had "forgotten" resides, for his rebirth will counter its power and give him victory over Harry (*Goblet* 652-53). The twinkle of victory in Dumbledore's eye is now understood. Lily's sacrifice of love for Harry, and Harry's willingness to sacrifice himself out of love for the rest of the world just like his mother did, was the key to Voldemort's downfall (696).

Since sacrificial love connects us to the theme of choice, we can also see Voldemort's weakness in this area. As Dumbledore explains, the prophecy need not have been acted upon, but Voldemort "created his worst enemy" out of fear, making a "grave error" in marking his equal and establishing his own vanquisher, the one with power he knew not (*Prince* 510). In other words, Voldemort believes the prophecy to be necessarily fulfilled, because of his own fear of death, and therefore chose to act upon it when, in reality, he could have walked away. Because he did not understand the power of choice, "he not only handpicked the man most likely the finish him, he handed him uniquely deadly weapons" (510). Voldemort's fear of death and inability to comprehend love was his own undoing.

There are a few connections we can establish between the phoenix and Voldemort which give us a symbol for the defeat of the one who wills and flees from death. Three times the phoenix symbol is present and active in the thwarting of Voldemort's plans: in the Chamber of Secrets, as a result of the *priori incantatem* effect, and in the Ministry in his attack on Dumbledore. These phoenix-connections highlight the fact that Voldemort faced many of the same choices as Harry, but he failed in those choices. Like Harry, Voldemort lost his parents as an infant, was raised by people who did not deeply care for and love him, discovered at the age of 11 that he was a wizard, and found Hogwarts to be his true home. But unlike Harry, rather than letting grief shape and reform him, he was buried by it and driven to madness.

Voldemort as Sociopath

It was argued above that Voldemort has no real knowledge of himself, but rather carries grandiose ideas of himself. To maintain that false vision of himself he scapegoats others, making "Mudbloods" and Muggles the "others," who are, in Voldemort's twisted view, the real problem with the world.

Maria Hsia Chang has pinpointed Voldemort's mental illness: he is a "Malignant Narcissist" ("A Study in Evil"). This is significant, because as Chang notes, "narcissists and especially malignant narcissists are particularly prone" to scapegoating; this is where Voldemort's Nazi-like tendencies come from. What he loathes in himself, indeed, his own shadow side, he projects onto others. The malignant narcissist is the one who is not only unaware of his shadow side (having deluded himself by self-aggrandizement), but who through charm and deception rises to power and scapegoats others, projecting what he hates in himself onto them, and creating a justification to eradicate them.

The Diagnostic and Statistical Manual of Mental Disorders (IV) explains the Narcissistic Personality Disorder. One normally has to show signs of 5 of the stated criteria in order to be diagnosed. Voldemort manages to fit all 9.

The DSM-IV explains the Narcissistic Personality Disorder this way:

> The essential feature of Narcissistic Personality Disorder is a pervasive pattern of grandiosity, need for admiration, and lack of empathy that begins by early adulthood and is present in a variety of contexts (685).

Using the nine criteria given by the DSM-IV (691), Voldemort clearly has a Narcissistic Personality Disorder. A person with Narcissistic Personality Disorder:

> *(1) has a grandiose sense of self-importance (e.g., exaggerates achievements and talents, expects to be recognized as superior without commensurate achievements)*

In *Goblet of Fire*, Voldemort boasts, "I am not a man.... I am much, much more than a man" (15). In *Half-Blood Prince*, Voldemort's expectation of recognition is obvious in the conversation he has with Dumbledore:

> "You call it 'greatness,' what you have been doing, do you?" asked Dumbledore delicately.
>
> "Certainly," said Voldemort, and his eyes seemed to burn red. "I have experimented; I have pushed the boundaries of magic further, perhaps, than they have ever been pushed —" (443).

Voldemort is quite enamored with himself, and despite his obvious fear of Dumbledore, he expects to be treated as the most superior wizard the world has ever know. To be treated as anything else is to incur his wrath, as evidenced by his murder of Grindelwald when mocked by him.

> *(2) is preoccupied with fantasies of unlimited success, power, brilliance, beauty, or ideal love*

I think we can take love and beauty off that list, but Voldemort is clearly obsessed with unlimited success, power, and brilliance. We've already observed his pushing the boundaries of magic. His quest for immortality is a clear illustration of "unlimited" success and power. Dumbledore, explaining Voldemort's request to be a teacher, notes how desire for "power and influence" motivates his request for a teaching post:

> As a teacher, he would have had great power and influence over young witches and wizards. Perhaps he had gained the idea from Professor Slughorn, the teacher with whom he was on best terms, who had demonstrated how influential a role a teacher can play. I do not imagine for an instant that Voldemort envisaged spending the rest of his life at Hogwarts, but I do think that he saw it as a useful recruiting ground, and a place where he might begin to build himself an army (431-432).

(3) believes that he or she is "special" and unique and can only be understood by, or should associate with, other special or high-status people (or institutions)

Voldemort hated his name, "Tom." "There are a lot of Toms," young Riddle said (*Prince* 275). Upon discovering that he was a wizard, he said, "I knew I was different. I knew I was special" (271). Dumbledore says that he showed contempt for anything that tied him to what was common, normal.

(4) requires excessive admiration

During the glimpse of the Slug Club from Horace's memory in *Half-Blood Prince*, all the boys and Slughorn himself are absolutely taken with young Riddle (370). He basks in this admiration, and more than that, he demands it. He "knew he was special," and he demands of all his followers that they treat him as such. Bellatrix is the closest to Voldemort because, more than anyone else, she is obsessed with him. He loves her obsession, even though he does not love her (for he does not love anyone).

(5) has a sense of entitlement, i.e., unreasonable expectations of especially favorable treatment or automatic compliance with his or her expectations

"Tell the truth!" Riddle demands of Dumbledore in their very first meeting (269). Rowling describes it this way:

He spoke [these] three words with a ringing force that was almost shocking. It was a command, and it sounded as though he had given it many times before (269-270).

Voldemort's request for a teaching post at Hogwarts also illustrates this. Though he knows full well Dumbledore would not approve of him as a teacher at Hogwarts, he still seems to expect compliance with the request (444-446).

(6) is interpersonally exploitative, i.e., takes advantage of others to achieve his or her own ends

"Careful flattery of the people who matter" is Voldemort's way, and Slughorn recognizes this, though he fails to wisely read deeper into it (370). When he wants information from Slughorn, he flatters his wizarding power. When he wants to know which relics old Hepzibah Smith has, he flatters her with charm and a sinister use of his sexuality. All of this is to get what he wants, and never because he cares about people.

(7) lacks empathy: is unwilling to recognize or identify with the feelings and needs of others

Rowling describes Voldemort as "devoid of the normal human responses to other people's suffering" (Rowling, "Rowling Thunder"). We also see in *Deathly Hallows* the way Harry describes Voldemort – as one who kills people for seemingly no reason whatsoever; they're just there (71). Harry tells Lupin that he's not going to blast people and kill them just because they're in the way. "That's Voldemort's job" (71). When Voldemort considers a young trick-or-treater, just because he's there, we get a picture of how little Voldemort cares for the feelings of others (343).

(8) is often envious of others or believes that others are envious of him or her

When confronted by Dumbledore about his practice of dark magic, Voldemort deflects the criticism with the following explanation: "Greatness inspires envy, envy engenders spite, spite spawns lies" (443).

(9) shows arrogant, haughty behavior or attitudes

Voldemort's arrogance is so obvious that Harry is able to find his weaknesses, including his foolish belief that he only had discovered the Room of Requirement (620).

In his work on the psychology of evil in *The People of the Lie*, M. Scott Peck wrote at length about "Malignant Narcissist." In an illustration early in the book, he tells the story of a man who had such a radical fear of death that, rather than dealing with the underlying issues, he "made a pact with the devil." After a long time working with the same client, he finally gave this criticism and advice:

> If you're willing to face the painful realities of your life – your terrorful childhood, your miserable marriage, your mortality, your own cowardice – I can be of some assistance. And I am sure that we will succeed. But if all you want is the easiest possible relief from pain, then I expect that you are the devil's man, and I don't see any way that psychotherapy can help you (Peck 33).

Voldemort is a man who is completely unwilling to face his pain and weakness head on. The absolute brilliance of Dumbledore's lessons with Harry throughout *Half-Blood Prince* is that he was giving Harry knowledge of Voldemort that even Voldemort himself didn't have. The great irony there is that Voldemort lived the experiences Harry witnessed and learned from in the Pensieve, but Harry knew more about them, because Voldemort is completely unwilling to look at himself critically.

Throughout *Half-Blood Prince*, Harry becomes "Dumbledore's man," all the while learning how and why Voldemort became "the devil's man."

Avoiding pain is a key element of Voldemort's psyche. It's the framework upon which he builds his entire structure of oppression. Avoiding pain and death is what he considers his greatest achievement. Causing pain is how he conquers his enemies and controls his Death Eaters. He's so convinced that physical pain is the worst thing that can happen to a person that his first line of defense in the protection of the locket horcrux was mandatory cutting and blood sacrifice (*Prince* 559).

Voldemort as Sinner

The difficult problem of Voldemort's moral culpability remains. Having spent all this time diagnosing him with a personality disorder, the obvious question is, "If he has a disorder, is he really evil? Is it his fault he's evil? Could he have been cured with psychotherapy?"

The answer to these things is complex. Rowling's theme of "choice" present in the books is key here, but even that is not as helpful as it might seem on the surface. Rowling has a much more nuanced view of the problems of evil and choice than are presented in the sound-byte quotes of Albus Dumbledore in *Chamber of Secrets* and *Goblet of Fire*, which are:

> "It is our choices Harry, that show what we truly are, far more than our abilities" (*Chamber* 333).

> "You fail to recognize that it matters not what someone is born, but what they grow up to be!" (*Goblet* 708)

These are admirable lessons, but even Dumbledore holds a more complex view of the matter than these two statements would seem to indicate. It's better to see these two statements as proverbs – little nuggets of wisdom that are generally true but have exceptions, than moral laws.

Merope Gaunt, for example, presents a particular challenge to the simple lesson that it doesn't matter what we were born, as long as we make the right choices. And if we have a problem with Merope Gaunt, we have a problem with Voldemort by association. Observe carefully this dialogue between Harry and Dumbledore from *Half-Blood Prince*:

> "So we know that, near the end of her pregnancy, Merope was alone in London and in desperate need of gold, desperate enough to sell her one and only valuable possession, the locket that was one of Marvolo's treasured family heirlooms."
>
> "But she could do magic!" said Harry impatiently. "She could have got food and everything for herself by magic, couldn't she?"
>
> "Ah," said Dumbledore, "perhaps she could. But it is my belief— I am guessing again, but I am sure I am right — that when her husband abandoned her, Merope stopped using magic. I do not think that she wanted to be a witch any longer. Of course, it is also possible that her unrequited love and the attendant despair sapped her of her powers; that can happen. In any case, as you are about to see, Merope refused to raise her wand even to save her own life."
>
> "She wouldn't even stay alive for her son?"
>
> Dumbledore raised his eyebrows. "Could you possibly be feeling sorry for Lord Voldemort?"
>
> "No," said Harry quickly, "but she had a choice, didn't she, not like my mother —"
>
> "Your mother had a choice too," said Dumbledore gently. "Yes, Merope Riddle chose death in spite of a son who needed her, but do not judge her too harshly, Harry. She was greatly weakened by long suffering and she never had your mother's courage." (262)

Dumbledore's question, "Could you possibly be feeling sorry for Lord Voldemort" makes it sound almost as if Dumbledore is prodding Harry to find some sympathy for Voldemort. While Voldemort is an unredeemable figure, Rowling has to include some element of humanity into Voldemort's story in order to maintain the literary use of Voldemort as Harry's shadow, as well as to continue the theme of choice. But the whole situation surrounding Merope complicates the matter, because Dumbledore is acutely aware that Merope did not have the same resources Lily did when it came time to make a choice about her son.

The key tension is this: While "choice" is presented as the primary difference between Harry and Voldemort, it is not as simple as just making the right choices, regardless of what you were born; it is possible that someone else can make choices for you – choices that permanently damage your own ability to choose. Merope was unable to summon Lily's courage, not because she had two equally available choices to her and made the wrong choice, but because she had been severely abused, and for that reason did not have the courage to use magic to stay alive.

We can even back this up further in the Slytherin line: we at least know that Marvolo and Morphin were mentally ill (and we can probably be certain that others in the line were such as well) due to inbreeding amongst Slytherin descendants; in other words, their ability to reason properly was affected by the choices their ancestors made which resulted in genetic distortions. That raises the same question: If past Slytherins made choices that resulted in a mentally ill prodigy (for physiological reasons), and if they too were raised in abusive (at least emotionally abusive) environments, to what extent were Marvolo and Morphin culpable?

We certainly don't want to say, "Not at all." But we do have evidence that Rowling herself sees a difference in the extent of moral culpability from one person to the next, depending on his or her personal history. Here is a very telling answer to a question from the oft-quoted Anelli/Spartz interview in 2005:

> Melissa Anelli: Has Snape ever been loved by anyone?
>
> Rowling: Yes, he has, which in some ways makes him more culpable even than Voldemort, who never has.

At the very least, we learn here that some choices are morally more consequential than others, not based on the options themselves (good vs. evil), but based on the person's own circumstances. The key to Rowling's answer is this: Because Snape has been loved and Voldemort has not, the option to choose good is more available to Snape than it is to Voldemort.

How, then, do we solve this problem? Is Voldemort morally culpable? Did he have the same options available to him as Harry? Does the question of choice really work here as the explanation of the difference between Harry and Voldemort?

The solution to the problem lies in a few different realms. In the first place, J.K. Rowling has a thing about underestimating children. Observe the dialogue from this interview in July 2000:

> Q: Do you believe in witchcraft and have you ever done any witchcraft?
>
> Rowling: No.
>
> Q: What are your feelings towards the people who say your books are to do with cults and telling people to become witches? (reader's question, didn't give name)

Rowling: Alfie [a young boy]. Over to you. Do you feel a burning desire to become a witch?

Alfie: No.

Rowling: I thought not. I think this is a case of people grossly underestimating children. Again. ("World Exclusive")

The addition of "again," as noted previously, is telling. It's obviously something that bothers Ms. Rowling. It's instructive to the present discussion because we have to remember that the first time we see young Tom Riddle, Jr., he's 11 years old and already a budding sociopath. We think, "Wow, at 11...he's already so evil! It's almost like it was programmed in him! That doesn't seem right." But we should remember that Rowling would have placed more value on the choices young Riddle made, pre-11 years old, than most of us would. The choices Tom made to harm those two children in the cave, or to hang Billy Stubbs's rabbit, for example, would be choices Tom made along the way to becoming as deranged as he already was at 11. There were certainly many other choices as well that we don't know about.

The path to evil lies in the consistent choosing of evil over good. Tom's choices started at an early age, and they continued consistently to be evil. Here is an extremely helpful quote from Eric Fromm, the man who coined the term, "Malignant Narcissist:"

> Our capacity to choose changes constantly with our practice of life. The longer we continue to make the wrong decisions, the more our heart hardens; the more we make the right decisions, the more our heart softens – or better perhaps, comes alive.... [E]ach act of surrender and cowardice weakens me, opens the path for more acts of surrender, and eventually freedom is lost (quoted in Peck 81).

Voldemort lost his freedom of choice long before Harry ever met him, by making evil choice after evil choice from childhood to manhood. That he was deprived of love there is no doubt and so, to some extent, he is to be pitied. But this does not make him any less evil, or any less irredeemable, or any less worthy of death at the hands of Harry Potter.

Voldemort was destined to be a character beyond redemption to serve literary purposes in the Harry Potter series. But he's a credible and culpable "beyond redemption" character. He made the choices that put him into his deranged state, and he made the choices that put himself beyond redemption.

Gerald Van wrote,

> "There can be a state of soul against which Love itself is powerless
> because it has hardened itself against Love" (quoted in Peck 73).

Horcrux-creation is Rowling's picture of this "state of soul."
Horcrux-making is perhaps the best answer to the choice problem, how
Voldemort can be simultaneously a morally culpable person and beyond
redemption. His choice to make them – a choice that was not programmed
– that sapped him of his humanity. In effect, he chose to become less than
human, to give up his own humanity – and therefore hope of "redemption"
– by creating horcruxes.

There were other options available to Voldemort, which we know from
Book 1 and now from Book 7. Had Voldemort been patient, he could have
considered a *Philosopher's Stone* or the *Deathly Hallows*. Certainly we're not
meant to see Nicholas Flamel as an evil character in the least. He and his
wife easily accept death when the time comes, but they could have gone
on living forever. While Dumbledore was tempted by power, to be sure,
Harry assures him with three simple words, "Hallows, not horcruxes"
(*Hallows* 713). Voldemort, eager for power and full of grandiose beliefs
about himself, pursued the soul-splitting, humanity-destroying practice
of horcrux-creation, and in making that choice, placed himself beyond
redemption. By putting Voldemort's horcrux-creation in proximity to
both Harry's and Dumbledore's temptation of the Deathly Hallows,
Rowling shows us the deliberate choice Voldemort made of which he is
eternally guilty.

The Consequences of Choices

Rowling's lesson in all this is the lesson of the Hero and Shadow:
There is evil in the world, but the first place we must look for it and
eradicate it is in ourselves. The way to do this is self-sacrifice, and the
reliance upon self-sacrificial love.

Harry would not have been the person that he was if it were not for
his mother's sacrifice. Ultimately, we might want to say that this series
is not first about the choices Harry and Voldemort made, but about the
choices Lily and Merope made. From the Bloomsbury web chat after the
release of Book 7:

Ravleen: How much does the fact that voldemort (sic) was conceived under a love potion have to do with his nonability (sic) to understand love?

J.K. Rowling: It was a symbolic way of showing that he came from a loveless union — but of course, everything would have changed if Merope had survived and raised him herself and loved him.

There is here yet another powerful lesson: not only do our choices affect ourselves, they can powerfully harm or transform the lives of those around us. Your choices and my choices can effectively destroy another person's free will. Our choices can take life or give life. This is the contrast between what is right and what is easy. Selfishness is easy. Escapism and scapegoating are easy. Self-sacrifice is not. Being willing to become conscious of your shadow side, and even to depend upon the self-sacrificial love of someone else for your own healing — this is not easy. But it is necessary.

Chapter Nine

The Life and Love of Albus Dumbledore
Wisdom from Failure and Forgiveness

One has only to know and trust,
and the ageless guardians will appear.

~ Joseph Campbell, *The Hero with a Thousand Faces*, pg. 72

The mentor archetype is not terribly difficult to understand. He is or she is, put simply, the one who trains up the hero, giving him or her wisdom, and sometimes magical objects, to accomplish the hero's quest. Heroes, once they have accepted their call, need guidance; this comes from the mentor, often represented as the "wise old man" or the "fairy godmother." This guide in the quest will "supply the amulets and advice that the hero will require" (Campbell, *Hero* 72).

If the mentor archetype is not complex, however, Harry Potter's mentor is. Albus Dumbledore, already a fascinating character prior to Book 7, became an intriguing, multi-layered mystery throughout the course and conclusion of the seventh novel. Dumbledore cannot possibly be treated completely in one chapter; a significant amount of Dumbledore analysis takes place in chapter twelve as well. For now, we concern ourselves with the following questions: what, as mentor, did Dumbledore need to teach Harry, and how did he teach it? Two primary lessons rose above the rest: the power of choice and of love.

Dumbledore and Trelawney: The Call and Its Keeper

Dumbledore is the keeper of Harry's call to the quest. The primary call on Harry's life is Trelawney's prophecy that he would be the Dark Lord's vanquisher; the only full record of it existed in the mind of Albus Dumbledore after it was smashed at the Ministry. Trelawney is the story's herald, the archetype whose call summons the hero to journey. This particular herald is no profound prophet or oracle; rather, she seems an utter fraud who appears to be suddenly possessed by a spirit of genuine prophecy only once every 15 years or so. She makes two prophecies that are of importance: the original one of which Snape heard half, reporting it to Voldemort and serving as the catalyst for the story's plot, and the prophecy that Voldemort's servant would return to him, helping Voldemort come to power again. These two prophecies are set in the context of a whole string of silliness from Trelawney, who seems to think a prophecy is only genuine if it contains dark portents and morbid predictions. Harry and Ron are able to get by in her class simply by making up a bunch of bad stuff that they say will happen.

This is significant to Dumbledore's message about choice. J.K. Rowling does not put much stock in prophecy or fate. Referring to Trelawney's original prophecy, she said:

> It's the "Macbeth" idea. I absolutely adore "Macbeth." It is possibly my favorite Shakespeare play. And that's the question isn't it? If Macbeth hadn't met the witches, would he have killed Duncan? Would any of it have happened? Is it fated or did he make it happen? I believe he made it happen. (Anelli and Spartz)

Rowling makes a clear choice here between fate and free will – choice is the key. MacBeth was not fated to kill Duncan; he did so only because he chose to act on the prophecy. Had he ignored the prophecy, none of it would ever have happened. This is her point about Voldemort, which she presses through Dumbledore: the prophecy is only significant because Voldemort made it so. John Granger gets the analysis spot on here:

> Believe it or not, I don't think Shakespeare wrote MacBeth as the postmodern answer to the fate and freewill question. Ms. Rowling's interpretation, though, is the self-actualizing understanding of choice within a destiny that we would expect from a postmodern reader. And her having Dumbledore come down as hard as he does for choice over destiny or providence marks him as a postmodern guru. (*Unlocking*, 173)

There is no space here for in-depth philosophical or theological argumentation about fate and freewill, but it should be noted that despite Rowling's interpretation, the mystery of fate and freewill remains in the story. C.S. Lewis's statement about literature that centers around fulfilled prophecy that was quoted in chapter one remains a solid analysis of the brilliance of *Harry Potter,* and Dumbledore's favoring choice over and against freewill does nothing to shatter that mystery. After all, where do these *real* prophecies come from? The text clearly indicates that Trelawney has made two accurate predictions; if it were only choice and not prophecy/destiny at all, why would there be any such thing as a real prophecy? Wouldn't all prophecies be frauds? And if this is the point Rowling is trying to make, what exactly is possessing Trelawney in those moments when she makes the "real" predictions? Even Dumbledore, who is the prophecy deconstructor and who is very skeptical of divination, believes there are real seers (*Order* 840).

The fate/free will debate is not settled philosophically by *Harry Potter*, though Rowling most certainly leans heavily, through Dumbledore, in the direction of free will (paired with a literal destruction of the Hall of Prophecy, no less). To say much more than that would be to risk attempting what Lewis said could not be done – create a theory that explains the relationship between destiny and freewill.[1]

Nevertheless, Rowling has her reasons for herald choice, which was the original point: Trelawney's silliness as context for the real prophecies underscores Rowling's overarching moral that it is choice that matters, not an individual's need to get some "guidance" from a mystical source in order to make decisions. Even "within a destiny" – very well-chosen words by Mr. Granger – it is the real choices of the individual that matter. And this is one of Albus Dumbledore's two primary lessons for Harry, the other being the power of love. He teaches Harry about both of these things in his final formal lesson with Harry in *Half-Blood Prince*. Harry struggles significantly with the lesson about love, not being able to imagine how love could be "the power the Dark Lord knows not." The lesson about choice, however, finally hits home:

> But he understood at last what Dumbledore had been trying to tell him. It was, he thought, the difference between being dragged into the arena to face a battle to the death and walking into the arena with your head held high. Some people, perhaps, would say that there was little to choose between the two ways, but Dumbledore knew — *and so do I*, thought Harry, with a rush of fierce pride, *and so did my parents* — that there was all the difference in the world. (*Prince* 512, emphasis in original)

It would be a while before the lesson about love would sink in; indeed, Harry had to be plunged into despair about Dumbledore himself before he truly learned about the magical force of love.

Dumbledore in *Deathly Hallows*: Dumbledore Deconstructed

Dumbledore's biography is inextricably linked with his lessons for Harry, because Harry learns as much about himself through wrestling with the deceased Dumbledore in *Deathly Hallows* as he does in all his lessons in the previous six years. It's not until after Dumbledore is gone that Harry learns most of the lessons Dumbledore taught him while he was present with him. It's in the fires of doubt about Dumbledore that Harry comes finally to be not only "Dumbledore's man, through and through" (*Prince* 649), but "the better man" (*Hallows* 713).

Elphias Doge's article in the Daily Prophet is what we might call hagiography. He was writing a perfect saint out of Dumbledore, when indeed the man was quite flawed. One cannot be too harsh on Doge: it was a memorial article in the newspaper, which is not the place to drag ancient secrets out of the closet to skewer the poor old man. But it's obvious that Doge was completely enamored with Dumbledore, to the point of ignoring his flaws and idolizing him. As Aberforth said, "He thought the sun shone out of my brother's every orifice" (*Hallows* 563).

Rita Skeeter, on the other hand, did her typical hatchet job on Dumbledore. While she uncovered some facts, her (un)trusty "Quick Quote Quill" spilled its spin onto the page, twisting facts and creating scandal, ready to ruin the reputation of a great man. While many of her facts were far more accurate that Doge's, her desire for hype and scandal overruled any sense of responsible journalism. It's a shame to see the life of Albus Dumbledore in the hands of "that cow."

The central crisis for Harry in *Deathly Hallows* was the character of Albus Dumbledore. If Harry had spent all of the previous year becoming "Dumbledore's man through and through," did he still want to be? The answer to this is significant, and it needs to guide our analysis of what Rowling was doing with Dumbledore. The answer to that question is: Yes, after learning everything about Dumbledore, at the end of the story, Harry wanted to remain Dumbledore's man through and through.

Harry wrestled throughout Book 7 with the question of Dumbledore, and the decisive moment came at Dobby's death. This is significant, because it was Dumbledore, back in Chapter 37 of *Order*, who insisted that house-elves have been mistreated by Wizards for centuries. The Kreacher and Dobby subplots in *Deathly Hallows* highlight the fact that Harry finally took this lesson to heart. It was while burying Dobby that Harry decided to go through with Dumbledore's plan, to see it through to the end, to trust Dumbledore.

Dumbledore did not remain, for the rest of his life, the same man he was as a young wizard. He did not maintain the same ideas of Wizard domination; indeed, he actively fought against them for the rest of his life. In the words of Bob Dylan, his "repentance is plain" ("Beyond the Horizon," *Modern Times*). There are several key indicators:

- He gave up his quest for the Hallows.

- Even at his old age, when faced with his worst memory, he had to relive the death of his sister.

- He avoided the position of Minister for the very purpose of staying as far away from his own sins as possible, to avoid the temptation to go there ever again.

Dumbledore remained a flawed man, and made many mistakes. His isolation was, in many ways, a problem: while he did trust people in their repentance and goodness, the brilliance of his own plans made it difficult, if not impossible, for him to trust others in the execution of those plans.[3] Even though he gave up his Hallows quest, when faced with the Resurrection Stone, he chose embracing Hallows over destroying Horcruxes, and it resulted in his death. Undoubtedly, Dumbledore was a flawed character, even to the end. But while the flaws remain, his repentance is still evident.

In fact, it was Dumbledore's self-awareness, his willingness to wrestle with and conquer his own shadows, that made him such an able mentor for teaching Harry how to do the same with Harry's shadows. Dumbledore has more shadows that one man should have, it seems. Prior to being Harry's shadow, Voldemort could easily have been considered Dumbledore's shadow, for Voldemort is the extreme end of all of Dumbledore's temptation to power. Dumbledore admits as much in *Deathly Hallows:*

"Master of death, Harry, master of Death! Was I better, ultimately, than Voldemort?"

"Of course you were," said Harry. "Of course – how can you ask that? You never killed if you could avoid it!"

"True, true," said Dumbledore, and he was like a child seeking reassurance. "Yet I too sought a way to conquer death, Harry."

"Not the way he did," said Harry. After all his anger at Dumbledore, how odd it was to sit here, beneath the high, vaulted ceiling, and defend Dumbledore from himself. "Hallows, not Horcruxes."

"Hallows," murmured Dumbledore, "not Horcruxes. Precisely."
(*Hallows* 713)

So, then, Dumbledore admits that within himself was the capacity
to be Voldemort. But an even more important shadow to Dumbledore is,
of course, Gellet Grindelwald. As young equals, Grindelwald introduced
Dumbledore to all the temptations to power with which he would struggle
for the rest of his life:

> "Grindelwald. You cannot imagine how his ideas caught me,
> Harry, inflamed me. Muggles forced into subservience. We wizards
> triumphant. Grindelwald and I, the glorious young leaders of the
> revolution.
>
> "Oh, I had a few scruples. I assuaged my conscience with empty
> words. It would all be for the greater good, and any harm done
> would be repaid a hundredfold in benefits for wizards. Did I know,
> in my heart of hearts, what Gellert Grindelwald was? I think I did,
> but I closed my eyes. If the plans we were making came to fruition,
> all my dreams would come true." (*Hallows* 716)

Those temptations lead to the death of his sister Ariana, and but
for that, the dangerous duo may well have become an invincible pair of
dark lords. Grindelwald is, in some ways, a more compelling baddie than
Voldemort. Grindelwald believed and acted upon all the justifications
for oppression that once tempted Dumbledore. Voldemort seems to have
been acting out of sheer narcissism, and his entire racial ideology was only
a justification for his own excessive arrogance and selfish will to power
and immortality.

It is necessary to take a moment to explore this point more, because
commentary from Rowling since the release of *Deathly Hallows* has
presented an interpretive challenge for understanding Dumbledore's
temptation on this point. Avoiding all the culture war trappings of
Rowling's pronouncement that she always thought of Dumbledore
as gay, what has been disappointing about that statement has been her
follow-up explanations that Dumbledore is sort of off the hook for his
mistakes because he made them because of love. Consider, for example,
PotterCast #130, Dec. 17, 2007 (text available at http://www.accio-quote.
org/articles/2007/1217-pottercast-anelli.html). Rowling said,

> Dumbledore, who was the great defender of Love, and who sincerely
> believed that Love was the greatest, most powerful, force in the
> universe, was himself made a fool of by Love. That to me was the

interesting point. That in his youth, he was-- he became infatuated with a man who was almost his dark twin. He was as brilliant, he was morally bankrupt, and Dumbledore lost his moral compass.

She follows this up with a statement about Dumbledore being brilliant and honestly believing Grindelwald had the right answer for the world, but she's already explained that his judgment was distorted by love. This is nowhere to be found in the text of *Deathly Hallows*. Dumbledore consistently says that it was the temptation to *power* that was his downfall, and he orchestrated the rest of his life to avoid that temptation, not least in his refusal to accept the position of Minister of Magic. What make this opinion of Rowling's disappointing is that Dumbledore, in the text itself, is the clearest example of someone who goes from being on the edge of the Dark Arts, embracing its ideology, to being its strongest opponent. In other words, Dumbledore is the text's clearest example of true repentance, true choice against the evil and for the good, because he himself was tempted by evil.

It can be argued that Rowling has problem with her portrayal of choice. As choice is a major theme of her books, one would expect to find many characters who moved entirely from the bad side to the good side, or vice versa. But examples of this are scarce, if they're there at all. Even Severus Snape is ambiguous. There's something static about Rowling's characters that almost undermines her theme of choice. Dumbledore is the best textual example of the power of choice, in that he moves from being a step or two away from becoming the next Dark Lord to becoming the wise mentor of the story's hero. It would be a shame to sabotage this one clear example of someone moving from strong temptation to the Dark Arts to rejecting them in full by adding, extra-textually, that it was "love" – of whatever orientation – that clouded his mind.

There are yet three more shadows for Albus Dumbledore: Delores Umbridge, Cornelius Fudge, and Rufus Scrimgeour. Umbridge is the shadow side of Dumbledore as headmaster. His headmastership will be explored in detail in chapter thirteen; suffice it to say that Umbridge is everything Dumbledore is not, but everything that he could have been had he let his temptation to power take hold of him as a headmaster. In other words: Umbridge took the politics that Dumbledore avoided straight into the school. Dumbledore had avoided those political entanglements because he did not trust himself with that kind of power; but what was to keep him from giving in to those temptations while a headmaster? Fudge and Scrimgeour are representations of errors Dumbledore could easily have made as a power-hungry Minister for Magic, a position he was offered three times. At King's Cross, Harry and Dumbledore discuss the Minister offer:

> "I, meanwhile, was offered the post of Minister of Magic, not once, but several times. Naturally, I refused. I had learned that I was not to be trusted with power."
>
> "But you'd have been better, much better, than Fudge or Scimgeour!" burst out Harry.
>
> "Would I?" asked Dumbledore heavily. "I am not so sure. I had proven, as a very young man, that power was my weakness and my temptation." (*Hallows* 717-18)

Dumbledore is a very complex character, but his shadows all have this in common: they desire and abuse power. This potential was very real for Dumbledore throughout his life. The Dumbledore-shadows all prepared him for his role as Harry's mentor. Had Dumbledore not come to terms with his own shadows, he would have had little to offer Harry in battling Voldemort.

The most significant result of Dumbledore's repentance is his ability to forgive others and to hope for and believe in their transformation. "He who has been forgiven much, loves much," Jesus said. Why did Dumbledore trust Snape? Because he knew, from his own experience, that it is possible to go from having very foolish, very dark, very evil ideas to a place of repentance and restoration.

"Know and Trust"

This is Harry's deepest struggle throughout *Deathly Hallows*: did Dumbledore love him, care for him? Or was Harry nothing more than a pawn in Albus's chess game?

> "Look what he asked of me, Hermione! Risk your life, Harry! And again! And again! And don't expect me to explain everything, just trust me blindly, trust that I know what I'm doing, trust me even though I don't trust you! Never the whole truth! Never!'"
>
> "I don't know who he loved, Hermione, but it was never me. This isn't love, the mess he's left me in"....
>
> He closed his eyes at her touch, and hated himself for wishing that what she said was true: that Dumbledore had really cared (362).

Harry came to the conclusion, eventually, that Dumbledore did care for him, and that he may have known Harry better than Harry knew himself. But with the knowledge of what Dumbledore knew years before, it is easy for the reader to trace Dumbledore's deep concern for Harry throughout the previous books, which is perhaps nowhere more evident than in the "gleam of triumph" in *Goblet of Fire*. Dumbledore was resigned to the fate that was thrust upon Harry by Voldemort's actions. Dumbledore cared very, very deeply for Harry, and saw nothing but tragedy ahead for the poor boy. For 14 years, Dumbledore had been watching over the boy whom he knew would one day have to face Voldemort. For at least two years, he'd known that in order to defeat Voldemort, Harry would have to die. Harry returned from the tragic rebirth of the Dark Lord, and he explained the manner of the blood transfer.

Hope rose in Dumbledore's heart. All was not lost: Harry may not have to die! Or, more accurately, death would not have a hold on him. After two years of carrying the burden of the knowledge that this innocent, suffering boy will have to die in order to rid the world of Voldemort, he now knew that the distinct possibility, even probability, existed that Harry will survive. Gleam of triumph, indeed!

Harry, of course, did not know this, and his internal struggle in *Deathly Hallows* is to know and trust Dumbledore. "One had only to know and trust, and the ageless guardians will appear," Campbell wrote (*Hero* 72). This is a nice summary statement for *Deathly Hallows*. Dumbledore was gone, dead – but Harry still needed his guidance. He did not fully receive Dumbledore's guidance until, standing over the grave of Dobby and learning about the power of self-sacrificial love one more time, reflecting on all the bits of Dumbledore's plan that had come together in ways Harry couldn't have imagined, he decided to trust Dumbledore. That decision led to his "death" and finally to the conversation with Dumbledore that would confirm for Harry that he would be able to finally defeat the Dark Lord.

"Got To"

Harry's decision to trust Dumbledore would not going unchallenged, even after that moment at Dobby's grave. Albus's critics in *Harry Potter* fandom are going to be big fans of Aberforth, who seems to be the only one willing to give straight talk about Albus and the Dumbledore family: "Secrets and lies, that's how we grew up, and Albus…he was a natural"

(562). Indeed, our faults continue to tempt us and haunt us throughout our lives. Albus is good at lying when he needs to. He's also brilliantly trustworthy if you have a secret that would destroy you. It is difficult to criticize Albus for keeping secrets about Snape from Harry. For example: it was the right thing to do because he had given Snape his word. Furthermore, one suspects Albus was *correct* in his belief that Harry might not have been able to handle the truth before that final moment in *Deathly Hallows*, which was his justification for keeping that secret.

Is Aberforth correct that Dumbledore is nothing more than a master manipulator? The problem with Aberforth is that after all those years, he continued to hold his grudge against Albus. Aberforth was correct about the awful things Albus did that resulted in Ariana's death. But Albus knew it, too, and as demonstrated above, was repentant. Aberforth's inability to forgive – his refusal to recognize Albus's repentance – is troubling. Bitterness causes despair, and it will destroy a person from the inside. This is what has happened to Aberforth, as evidenced by his attitude: "The Order of the Phoenix is finished. You-Know-Who's won, it's over, and anyone who's pretending different's kidding themselves" (562).

In the Hog's Head Inn before the Battle of Hogwarts, Aberforth sets the record straight about Ariana, contradicting Doge's silence and Skeeter's spin. But Harry steps in and confronts Aberforth's bitterness and what it's done to him, arguing that Dumbledore was "never free" of guilt over Ariana's death, and pushing Aberforth's bitter pessimism right back in his face (567). It is manifestly true that Albus was never free. In fact, it was his guilt over the death of Ariana that ultimately killed him. When finally faced with the Resurrection Stone, a moment of weakness took over, and he wanted to see his parents and sister again. It was his deep remorse for what had happened that killed Albus Dumbledore that day he put the ring Horcrux on his finger and took its curse. It was a good thing Severus was nearby.

The lasting difference between Albus and Aberforth is that Albus learned from his grievous sins, repented, and learned how to love and forgive others as a result, and Aberforth was reduced to bitterness over being sinned against. Albus learned that "love covers a multitude of sins" (1 Peter 4:8). It is better to say, "The Life and Love of Albus Dumbledore," instead of "The Life and Lies." Love covered the lies.

When Albus and Aberforth were young lads, despite Albus's prolific magical talent, Aberforth was the better man. Albus's heart was not with his family. The death of Ariana rattled everything for both of them. For Albus, watching his friend cruciate his brother and (probably) kill his sister wrecked him for good. When Albus chose Matthew 6:21 for his mother's and sister's grave, it was an act of repentance. He knew his "treasure" had been the Hallows, causing his heart to be away from his family and instead invested in visions of power. Aberforth criticized Albus for being upstairs "counting his prizes" and not spending time with the family, and noted that there were "no prizes" for watching and caring for Ariana. Albus's prize had not been his family; it has been his selfish ambition. He was acting the Slytherin, when he should have been acting like a Gryffindor. All this would change for Albus, but too late to save his sister.

Aberforth, despite being the better man as a youth, could never have orchestrated the downfall of Voldemort, not simply because Albus was smarter and more gifted, but because only the love of Albus was able to mold Harry Potter. Aberforth's lasting bitterness would have prevented him from ever teaching Harry the kind of transformational, world-changing love that Albus demonstrated.

Rowling uses a parallel two-word phrase in Harry's conversations with Albus and Aberforth which gets this point across: "Got to." From *Half-Blood Prince*:

> "But, sir," said Harry, making valiant efforts not to sound argumentative, "it all comes to the same thing, doesn't it? I've got to try and kill him, or -'"
>
> "*Got to?*" said Dumbledore. "*Of course you've got to*! But not because of the prophecy! Because you, yourself, will never rest until you've tried! We both know it! Imagine, please, just for a moment, that you had never heard that prophecy! How would you feel about Voldemort now? Think!"
>
> Harry watched Dumbledore striding up and down in front of him, and thought. He thought of his mother, his father, and Sirius. He thought of Cedric Diggory. He thought of all the terrible deeds he knew Lord Voldemort had done. A flame seemed to leap inside his chest, searing his throat.
>
> "I'd want him finished," said Harry quietly. "And I'd want to do it."
>
> "Of course you would!" cried Dumbledore. "You see, the prophecy does not mean you have to do anything!" (*Prince* 511-12)

Albus is exceedingly agitated, and we never see him get this way. The point is absolutely crucial. Of course Harry's got to, but it's because of his love for his family and the knowledge that Voldemort had and would continue to tear loved ones apart. It was a decisive moment for Harry.

Now, fast forward to another moment of decision for Harry. He has chosen his path; he would follow Albus's plan, even if he didn't know what was to come. Harry has told a cynical Aberforth that Albus left him a job to do, and this following dialogue ensues:

> "I-it's not easy, no," said Harry. "But I've got to – "
>
> "'*Got to*'? Why '*got to*'? He's dead, isn't he?" said Aberforth. "Let it go, boy, before you follow him! Save yourself!"
>
> "I can't."
>
> "Why not?"
>
> "I — " Harry felt overwhelmed; he could not explain, so he took the offensive instead. "But you're fighting too, your in the Order of the Phoenix – "
>
> "I was," said Aberforth. "The Order of the Phoenix is finished. You-Know-Who's won, it's over, and anyone who's pretending different's kidding themselves." (*Hallows* 561-62, emphasis in original)

Aberforth, now old and jaded by years of bitterness, has all but given up and tells Harry to save himself and forget everyone else. He even goes so far as to define love as telling Harry to hide. "Why didn't [Albus] tell [Harry] to hide, then? Why didn't he say to him, 'Take care of yourself, here's how to survive'?" Harry replies:

> "Because…sometimes you've *got* to think about more than your own safety! Sometimes you've *got* to think about the greater good! This is war!" (*Hallows* 568, emphasis in original)

"Got to," indeed. Thankfully, Albus learned from his youthful foolishness and became the forgiving and loving man that mentors Harry. Thankfully, Harry had been shaped by and put his trust in Albus before meeting Aberforth. And thankfully, we begin to see a transformation in Aberforth as well, who joins the Battle of Hogwarts.

"Amulets and Advice"

Along with teaching the hero wisdom he'll need for the quest, the mentor also frequently gives amulets to the hero, magical items which will help him along the way (Campbell, *Hero* 72). Dumbledore does this as well.

The Invisibility Cloak is the first of these, and he gives this to Harry in the very first book (and returns it to him). Harry is told to "use it well," and "using it well" turns out to involve the lesson at the Mirror of Erised ("it does not do to dwell on dreams and forget to live," [*Stone* 214]) and the showdown with Quirrellmort at the book's climax, leading to Harry's first lesson about love and death ("Your mother died to save you;" "To the well-organized mind, death is the next great adventure") (*Stone* 297-99).

Fawkes, the Sorting Hat, and the sword of Gryffindor were all gifts from Dumbledore in the Chamber of Secrets, and these gifts taught Harry about the power of loyalty-to-the-good, courage, and choice when, post-Diary-crux defeat, Dumbledore explained that only loyalty to him could have called Fawkes; that only a "true Gryffindor" (read: brave person) could have pulled the sword out of the hat; and that Harry's choice was what demonstrated who he truly was.

In *Deathly Hallows*, Dumbledore leaves four gifts, two for Harry, and one each for Ron and Hermione. All four were meant to aid Harry in his hero's quest. Ron's Deluminator came through in two situations: Ron's return, leading to the saving of Harry's life, recovery of Gryffindor's sword, and the destruction of the locket Horcrux; and the ability to have light during their temporary imprisonment in Malfoy Manor. Dumbledore's gift of *The Tales of Beedle the Bard* to Hermione was meant, among other things, to keep Harry's hot-headedness in check; Dumbledore was "counting on Miss Granger" to slow him down (*Hallows* 720). Dumbledore and Harry were both tempted wizards, and Dumbledore's failures prepared him to be able to teach and guide Harry. The two are different, to be sure. Harry was never tempted in the same way Dumbledore was, or at least to that extent; but it was mentioned a few times by Dumbledore that the potential was there (*Hallows* 713, 720). It was Dumbledore's knowledge of the temptations of all three that led to his gift choices.

This is just as true with Harry's final two gifts: the sword of Gryffindor, and the snitch, containing the Resurrection Stone. Dumbledore was probably correct to think that had he not been mysterious about these gifts, had he just told Harry what they were for, it's likely Harry would have made some very early errors, particularly with the Resurrection Stone. The two gifts are precisely what Harry needs: the sword to destroy all the Horcruxes, and the Stone to give him the strength to walk to his death.

The Resurrection Stone in particular was the Deathly Hallow that killed Dumbledore. His temptation to use it to see his family again resulted in his going "on" to where his family was much quicker than he'd anticipated. Once the curse began spreading and Snape had informed Dumbledore of his year to live, Dumbledore replied, "Well, really, this makes matters much more straightforward" and then constructed his plot to save Draco (*Hallows* 681). Even after giving in to the Stone's temptation, Dumbledore demonstrated himself to be one who was willing to walk to death when the time came. As with Dumbledore, so with Harry, except that for Harry, the Stone did not cause his death; it strengthened him to choose it.

The Stone also symbolizes trust in Dumbledore; "I open at the close" made no sense whatsoever, but as Harry chose to follow Dumbledore's plan, he finally came to the realization that Dumbledore had provided exactly what Harry needed for that final walk into the Forest. This issue of "faith" became central to *Deathly Hallows*.

Dumbledore and Faith

Since the release of *Deathly Hallows*, Rowling has been much more candid about her faith than in previous interviews. Sadly, the candidness has not produced any change in tone and rhetoric from the fundamentalist camp, because Rowling commits spiritual faux pas – she has major struggles with unbelief.

> "The truth is that, like Graham Greene, my faith is sometimes that my faith will return. It's something I struggle with a lot," she revealed. "On any given moment if you asked me [if] I believe in life after death, I think if you polled me regularly through the week, I think I would come down on the side of yes — that I do believe in life after death. [But] it's something that I wrestle with a lot. It preoccupies me a lot, and I think that's very obvious within the books." (Adler)

This struggle with faith is nowhere more evident than in Harry's difficulty believing in his mentor, whose entire life is deconstructed before Harry's eyes throughout the course of *Deathly Hallows*. John Granger has argued that Harry's relationship with Dumbledore as reflected in *Deathly Hallows* is most likely a picture of a Christian believer's struggle with faith in spiritual authority – the Church, or a spiritual mentor – which acts, in a way, as mediators of faith, the ones who hold the authoritative teachings of the faith ("Christian Content"). Dumbledore and Harry are not as much a God/Jesus parallel as they are a Church/Believer parallel, and this makes it a powerful parable for a doubter. Which believer has not question his or her faith as a result of something their church or spiritual authority has done against the faith?

This is precisely what Harry wrestles with in the story – faith in Dumbledore, in his plan, and in his love for Harry, in the face of all of Albus's failures. If Rowling is trying to teach us that Dumbledore is ultimately a conniving, manipulative guy, she's lead us entirely in the wrong direction, because the choice she brings Harry to – which is the *right choice* – is this: trust Dumbledore. Indeed, Hermione's words in *Order of the Phoenix* and Lupin's words in *Half-Blood Prince* prove prophetic:

> "If we can't trust Dumbledore, who can we trust?" (Hermione)

> "It comes down to whether or not you trust Dumbledore's judgment. I do; therefore, I trust Severus." (Lupin)

Tolkien wrote very wisely of the struggle with faith, particular when doubting spiritual authority, and the advice could be applied directly to Harry's battle with doubting Dumbledore. In a letter to his son Michael, November 1, 1963, he wrote:

> You speak of 'sagging faith' ... In the last resort faith is an act of the will, inspired by love. Our love may be chilled and our will eroded by the spectacle of shortcomings, folly, and even sins of the Church and its ministers, but I do not think that one who has once had faith goes back over the line for these reasons.... 'Scandal' at most is an occasion of temptation.... It is convenient because it turns our eyes away from ourselves and our own faults to find a scape-goat ... The temptation to 'unbelief' ... is always there within us. (quoted in Pearce, *Man and Myth* 192)

Despite scandal, Harry, standing in Dobby's grave, grasps at that "last resort of faith...an act of the will, inspired by love." The love, of course, is the self-sacrifice of Dobby, and the act of the will is the belief that Dumbledore had the right plan all along, despite the things he withheld from him, and the old scandal of Dumbledore's family. It's important to observe that as Harry witnesses Dobby's death and while he is digging his grave, he thinks of Dumbledore's death and his funeral. It struck him, finally, the depth to which Dumbledore knew Harry, and the depth to which Dumbledore willingly sacrificed himself. Aberforth makes the bitter charge that those whom Dumbledore "cared about very much ended up in a worse state than if he'd left 'em well alone" (*Hallows* 563). But the glaring flaw in this statement is that Dumbledore himself ended up in a "worse state;" he was not a war master, sending his puppets off to die while he sat in a cozy armchair. He was in the midst of the battle, and he died doing his work against Voldemort. And not only was he fighting evil when he died, he was fighting to save the life of Draco, who was intending to kill him, and that deserves significant examination, for it is on that tower that Dumbledore's greatness is most evident.

A Lesson in Love

Before looking at the specifics of that night on the Astronomy Tower, it would be helpful to discuss exactly what Dumbledore taught Harry about love. His private lessons with Harry throughout *Half-Blood Prince* were fundamental to Harry's ability to defeat Voldemort, though Harry hardly realized it at the time. He was simultaneously getting to know his enemy and learning the potential evil within himself. The time came for Harry to find the final Horcruxes, and he knew precisely how Voldemort would act: both Gringotts and Hogwarts would be attractive hiding places. Even more than any of this, however, were the lessons about choice and love. It was Harry's *choice*, far more than any prophetic utterance, that made the difference in Harry's quest to defeat Voldemort. And though Harry would not figure it out until he was digging Dobby's grave, it was only his ability to *love* that could cause the defeat of Voldemort in the end.

Love remains a mystery, and that's as it should be. There is never any mechanical explanation for how Lily's love saved Harry, nor how Harry's love saved the rest of the Wizarding World. But neither does Rowling give us a Hallmark-card explanation for the salvific power of love. Love is a room in the Department of Mysteries. But in everyday life, it is worked out through grief, pain, suffering, tears, turning to hope, joy, faith, and courage. Hours and hours of complex defensive magic lessons with Dumbledore would have done Harry no good at all against Voldemort; only self-sacrifial love could defeat Voldemort. How did Dumbledore know love would conquer Voldemort? Voldemort himself gave it away in the Ministry atrium in *Order of the Phoenix*. Dumbledore, speaking to Snape of the Harry-Voldemort connection, says,

"Voldemort fears that connection," said Dumbledore. "Not so long ago he had one small taste of what truly sharing Harry's mind means to him. It was pain such as he has never experienced. He will not try to possess Harry again, I am sure of it. Not in that way."

"Lord Voldemort's soul, maimed as it is, cannot bear close contact with a soul like Harry's. Like a tongue on frozen steel, like flesh in flame – " (*Hallows* 684-85)

Though a much younger Voldemort, in Dumbledore's office, had told him that he saw "no evidence" that love was more powerful than his own "kind of magic" (*Prince* 444), Voldemort himself experienced that evidence several times in the following years: In his attempt to kill baby Harry, in his attempt to kill Harry again while possessing Quirrell, in his attempt to possess Harry in the Ministry atrium, and in the final showdown. Despite Voldemort's complaint that Harry always got away from him by luck and chance, it was love that consistently thwarted Voldemort. This is the real meaning of his mistake in the graveyard after he was resurrected. Voldemort thought it was a magical device he needed – Lily's blood. Instead, it was love itself. Dumbledore knew this, and it was his highest priority to teach Harry that. Ultimately, he taught Harry this by example, which we will see below.

Dumbledore's Mercy: Why Draco Couldn't Pull the Trigger

The scene that unfolds upon the Astronomy Tower is one of the most intense and well-written passages of the *Harry Potter* novels, and the dialogue between Dumbledore and Draco is a key element in that. Why couldn't Draco kill Dumbledore? Why didn't he even attempt to on that tower?

The most chilling part of the conversation comes right at its climax, after the "ways and means" have been discussed, and just prior to the break-in of the Death Eaters:

'But I got this far, didn't I?' he [Draco] said slowly. 'They thought I'd die in the attempt, but I'm here ... and you're in my power ... I'm the one with the wand ... you're at my mercy ...'

'No, Draco,' said Dumbledore quietly. 'It is my mercy, and not yours, that matters now.' (*Prince* 592)

What did Dumbledore mean?

Based on what we know of Dumbledore's tremendous power, a weakened, wandless, dying Albus Dumbledore is still more magically powerful than an armed, 16-year-old Draco Malfoy. Had it come right down to it, it's likely that Dumbledore, even without a wand, could have conjured up enough magic to prevent Draco's attempting a killing curse. But it doesn't seem Dumbledore even wants to prevent him by use of force, this is hardly the meaning behind Dumbledore's statement about mercy. A wizard like Dumbledore most certainly doesn't need to inform a young boy that he has more sheer magical powerful. Dumbledore has a different view of what's powerful in the first place; he does nothing to disarm or stop Draco, because he believes in the power of mercy to change Draco's *choice* in that moment.

It is Dumbledore's mercy that matters, because both he and Draco know that the Dark Lord has put Draco into this position because of his anger with Lucius for his Diary-crux and Prophecy blunders. Dumbledore is plain with Malfoy: Voldemort sent Draco on this task expecting Draco to die in the attempt; Snape's the backup plan, and whether Draco succeeds or fails doesn't matter. In Voldemort's mind, both Draco and Dumbledore will be dead in the end, whichever way it plays out. And this is where Dumbledore's mercy becomes so very profound and important. Dumbledore, staring at his would-be killer, offers freedom from Voldemort's wrath and tyranny – not only for Draco, but for the whole family. Dumbledore has to know that the Malfoys are having regrets about their service to Voldemort, as he surely knows about Narcissa's visit to Snape. Consider, then, the depth of this mercy: it was Lucius who was behind the re-opening of the Chamber of Secrets, putting the Hogwarts students in danger. Dumbledore's patience very rarely exceeds its limits, but Harry managed to cross that line when he implied that Dumbledore would leave his students in danger:

> "I … they're up to something!" said Harry and his hands curled into fists as he said it. "Professor Trelawney was just in the Room of Requirement, trying to hide her sherry bottles, and she heard Malfoy whooping, celebrating! He's trying to mend something dangerous in there and if you ask me he's fixed it at last and you're about to just walk out of school without -"
>
> "Enough," said Dumbledore. He said it quite calmly, and yet Harry fell silent at once; he knew that he had finally crossed some invisible line. "Do you think that I have once left the school unprotected during my absences this year? I have not. Tonight, when I leave,

there will again be additional protection in place. Please do not suggest that I do not take the safety of my students seriously, Harry."

"I didn't -" mumbled Harry, a little abashed, but Dumbledore cut across him.

"I do not wish to discuss the matter any further." (*Prince* 550)

But now, on the tower, just hours after Dumbledore made these statements, he stands ready to forgive and protect Draco, who put students in grave danger by his reckless attempts on Dumbledore's life, and his father Lucius, whose Diary-crux scheme threatened the lives of all the muggleborns in the school. Mercy is at its greatest when one is willing to overlook the greatest personal injury, the offense that most "hits home," and offer forgiveness to the offender. This is the case with Dumbledore's offer to Draco.

As the conversation between Dumbledore and Draco progresses, Dumbledore repeatedly affirms to Draco that he is "not a killer" (585-92):

- "Draco, Draco, you are not a killer."

- "You have been trying, with increasing desperation, to kill me all year. Forgive me, Draco, but they have been feeble attempts … so feeble, to be honest, that I wonder whether your heart has been really in it…"

- "I don't think you will kill me, Draco. Killing is not nearly as easy as the innocent believe…"

- "But as for being about to kill me, Draco, you have had several long minutes now. We are quite alone. I am more defenseless than you can have dreamed of finding me, and still you have not acted …"

- "'My options!' said Malfoy loudly. 'I'm standing here with a wand – I'm about to kill you -'"   "My dear boy, let us have no more pretence about that. If you were going to kill me, you would have done it when you first disarmed me, you would not have stopped for this pleasant chat about ways and means.'"

- "…come over to the right side, Draco … you are not a killer …"

But is Dumbledore saying that Draco is innately not a killer, as if he doesn't even have within him the capacity to do so? We can probably agree with Dumbledore that Draco's heart really isn't in this. He can talk a big talk in front of fellow Slytherins about his "job," but his crying sessions with Moaning Myrtle and the constant faltering in his conversation with Dumbledore demonstrate plainly enough that, as Dumbledore said, killing someone is not as easy as one might think. And yet two things suggest, though we know Draco was not going to pull the trigger on the Astronomy Tower that night, that he was very capable of doing it; the potential was there.

In the first place, the emphasis on "choice" in the series indicates that the choice truly was before Draco to attempt to kill Albus Dumbledore. Dumbledore's adamant assertion to Fudge that "it matters not what someone is born, but what they grow to be" (*Goblet* 708) suggests that Dumbledore was not saying that Draco didn't even have within himself the capacity to kill, for the choice was very much before him, as choices are before everyone, regardless of "what someone is born." In the second place, though Draco's heart was not in it, he nevertheless executed two plans that had every possibility in the world of succeeding on someone. It is by sheer luck that Draco was "not a killer" by the time he stood face to face with Dumbledore.

With that in mind, it's best to think of Dumbledore's statement, "You are not a killer," in this way: "Draco, you are not a killer; you have not killed anyone yet, and you don't have to. The choice is before you. Choose the right side." And instead of magically warding Draco off (which would have ensured his death by Voldemort) or allowing Harry to interfere (which would have had the same result), Dumbledore attempted to save Draco, both from the soul-scarring act of murder and the wrath of the Dark Lord.

Ultimately, at the moment of choice, Draco was unable to pull the trigger on Dumbledore, because standing before him at wandpoint was a man offering mercy that he simply could not comprehend and could not overcome. It was Dumbledore's mercy that caused him to falter, and even at one point to "bizzarely draw courage and comfort from his praise" (*Prince* 587)!

It might be argued that Draco was afraid of Dumbledore, and that is why he wouldn't cast the curse. Dumbledore even suggested that Draco was afraid to act until he had some support. But two caveats must be added: (1) Draco was ultimately more afraid of Voldemort than he was Dumbledore, for when Dumbledore offered sanctuary for him and his family, Draco spluttered on about Voldemort's threats to kill them all and would not accept his help, and (2) when the Death Eaters arrived, Draco still didn't pull the trigger. It wasn't fear of Dumbledore that stopped Draco from killing him; rather, it was Dumbledore's love for Draco. Draco, raised in the severely prejudiced and self-serving Malfoy family had never stood face to face with self-sacrificial love before. When Dumbledore offered Draco help and protection, he was offering redemption from evil for the entire Malfoy family – a family that had been a bit of a bane for Dumbledore for decades.

Consider again the lessons from *Half-Blood Prince*, in which the wise old man is preparing the hero to go it alone. In the climax of these lessons, the revelation about Horcruxes, as noted above already, a discussion ensues concerning the prophecy, and the ever-patient Dumbledore gets agitated in his attempts to convince Harry of two things: (1) Not to set too much store by the prophecy; it is choice that matters, and (2) Harry is "protected, in short, by [his] ability to love;" indeed, love is "the power the Dark Lord knows not" (*Prince* 509-11). By the end of this lesson, Harry gets lesson #1; in fact, he realizes it "makes all the difference in the world." But lesson #2 is not as clear. In fact, as far as Harry's ability to love is concerned, a sarcastic "Big deal" is about all the response he can muster. How in the world is "love" the power that will vanquish the Dark Lord?

While that was Dumbledore's last formal lesson with Harry, the teaching does not end there. There is a sense in which Dumbledore is teaching Harry straight through the entire trip to the cave. But on the Astronomy Tower, Harry silently witnesses Dumbledore's final lesson: Love is indeed powerful – powerful enough to stop death; powerful enough to make one willing to die for his own enemies.

Dumbledore's love for Draco must have astounded Harry; how could he offer Draco, and even worse, Lucius, protection? Had the old man really gone mad? But then, Draco didn't pull the trigger, did he? And why did Dumbledore do nothing to defend himself? Had he done so, Draco's mission would have failed, and Voldemort's wrath would have been expended on Draco and his family. Instead, Dumbledore submitted to his death at the hands of Snape (which was Dumbledore's plan all along), saved Draco from the Dark Lord's anger, and left him in the hands of his most trusted ally: Severus himself. Indeed, as Dumbledore submitted to his death on the Tower, his sacrificial love thwarted Voldemort's own plan: to kill Draco Malfoy as revenge for Lucius's failures.

Loving Lupin

Not only for Draco, but for all the "others" of the Wizarding World, Dumbledore shows tremendous compassion and love. Commenting on the place of the werewolf (and other evil creatures) in history and literature, Siamak Tundry Nacify offers the following observation:

> Throughout history, we have attributed onto others what we viewed as undesirable in ourselves, finding scapegoats upon which we could pin our notions of fault and blame and whose sacrificial death then could bring atonement. In this way, we put our sins upon the wolf and then put the wolf, instead of ourselves, to death – in literature, in folklore, in myth, in films, and, unfortunately too often, in real life. (Nacify 210).

We create evil beings that are really a representation of our own evil, and then make sure they get killed in our stories (we, of course, are the heroes who do the killing). In doing so, we believe we purge the evil from ourselves by taking the side of the good. This is at the center of the postmodern critique of metanarratives: making an evil out of the "other" in order to appease our own consciences and identify with the "good."

Not only do we create werewolves to kill, we ostracize the perceived abnormal and the diseased in order to have a place to point the finger, to make assumptions, and to say to ourselves, "At least I'm not like that." It happened in the past with lepers; it happens today with victims of HIV/ AIDS. Nacify notes that "there is a high cost in social interactions with diseased others," making it socially important to "quickly...identify sick individuals and to avoid interacting with them" (214).

The problem is that human evil still runs rampant both across the earth and in each one of us. Despite the many times we've slain werewolves, vampires, and dragons in our daydreams and stories, it is not so easy to separate ourselves from our darker sides. Despite all the times we've attempted to avoid the "diseased others" in our society, we find ourselves excluded by somebody, and greatly offended because of it – making us hypocrites. Rowling knows this, and while her use of the werewolf Lupin illustrates our folly in scapegoating, she also offers a substantive solution to the problem: self-sacrifice, instead of the sacrifice of others.

Lupin serves the roles of scapegoat and diseased others, fitting the psychological desire for a person to blame as well as the "diseased other," having been contaminated in his blood by a bite from another diseased other. And if there was ever a bad guy to be avoided, it's Fenrir Greyback! But this shows how easy it is to make false assumptions about someone like Lupin. While Remus is nothing at all like Fenrir, it is more than likely that most people in the Wizarding World, upon learning Lupin's secret, would be much more likely to impute the evil character of Greyback upon his name, rather than the good character of Dumbledore.

In place of stigmatization, Rowling offers us the self-sacrificial character of Dumbledore. The radical difference is this: while the rest of the Wizarding World points the finger at assumed evil – werewolves are evil, kill them! – in order to purge itself of its own guilt, Dumbledore looks into the face of his would-be killer, the racist Slytherin Draco Malfoy, and offers him redemption and protection before dying for him. Instead of saying, "Let's sacrifice werewolves, Death Eaters, Slytherins, etc., for the cause of good," Dumbledore says, "I am willing to die. I'll be the one to be sacrificed." It is the willing sacrifice of the one who does not deserve it that has transformative power, the power to destroy evil with good.

Not only is Dumbledore willing to die for others, to be the sacrifice, he does not shun the "diseased others." One of the most powerful aspects of Dumbledore's character is his willingness to graciously accept anyone. Who but Dumbledore would have the mercy to forgive Severus Snape and take him on as a confidante? Who besides Dumbledore would have actually clapped, out of courtesy and respect, at the end of Delores Umbridge's start-of-year speech in *Order*, and then, after all she did throughout the year, march into the forest to rescue her from the centaurs? Who but Dumbledore would think it appropriate to show manners to Death Eaters, standing before him on the tower, mocking him? Who else would be trusting of werewolves, half-giants, centaurs, mer-people, and every other magical being that the Ministry has ostracized?

Harry, Dumbledore's apprentice, learned this accepting and self-sacrificing attitude. He learned it from his mother's sacrifice. He learned it by watching Dumbledore. He learned it in the yearly figurative death-resurrection pattern of each volume of the series. And finally, he learned it in *Deathly Hallows*, whereby he saved the world. He most certainly showed a willingness to die for the right cause book by book. He befriended the social outcasts: Lupin, Hagrid, Luna, Neville. He is an "odd wizard," as we noted in the last chapter. Much of this came from his willingness to be "Dumbledore's man, through and through." The most challenging of all for Harry was Snape; during the latter part of Snape's life, Dumbledore was the only man who could conjure and love for poor Severus. As Pharr writes of Harry and Snape, "Their relationship as a whole implies that unrequited tolerance is a much more difficult skill to acquire than is proficiency with a wand" (59). Dumbledore had this tolerance, and Harry finally learned it, after Snape's death. This is evidenced by two powerful words: "Albus Severus" (*Hallows* 758).

As Rowling is influenced by the Christian story, it should be no surprise that this theme fits perfectly with the person of Jesus. While Dumbledore and Harry are not "Christ figures" in the direct way the Aslan was to Narnia (both Dumbledore and Harry are deeply flawed human beings), they are conduits for the Christ-message, the proclamation of sacrificial love's victory over evil and death. Jesus is the epitome of these themes. He touched lepers. He ate with prostitutes, corrupt tax collectors, and the worst sinners of society. He was not afraid of diseased others; in fact, he seemed to prefer their company to that of the finger-pointing Pharisees. And ultimately, his entire life was a rush toward the evil-defeating, death-destroying, self-sacrificial love of the cross on behalf of his own enemies.

He demanded that people put down their accusatory stones and pick up their own crosses, and this is the message Rowling is communicating so powerfully through Dumbledore and Harry. It works its way into Rowling's social vision, as we shall see in Part III.

Conclusion

In the end, Harry tells Dumbledore that as far as teachers go, he was "the best" (*Hallows* 718). Why? Because Dumbledore had the very unique ability to teach Harry everything he needed to know while letting Harry come to all the conclusions by himself. That's tremendous pedagogy. Snape could never do that; he lectured and bullied and ridiculed. None of the other teachers could do it either, save perhaps Lupin. All the others saw themselves as the experts, and the students as minds into which they must impart knowledge. Dumbledore saw them as whole people; he appreciated their processes, their strengths and weaknesses.

Dumbledore was the perfect mentor for Harry. They both, after all, saw the same thing in the Mirror of Erised, didn't they (*Hallows* 719)? Whole, healed families. While neither of them could achieve that dream while living, both, in the end, learned how to walk to death, as Ignotus Peverell, embracing it as an old friend. There was no greater lesson Dumbledore could have taught Harry.

Chapter 9 Notes

1   Sadly, this is what Rowling has done in her interpretation of *MacBeth*.

2   I do think we can find plenty of good reasons, however, that Dumbledore withheld information from certain people...but the lack of an "equal," as Rowling said, is what ultimately led to his "old man's mistakes" regarding his underestimation of Harry as young boy, which eventually resulted in Sirius's death.

Chapter Ten

The Sacking of Snape, the Shapeshifter
Examining the Cult of Snape

"I don't really see [Snape] as a hero."
~ J.K. Rowling, July 26, 2007

"Do I think he's a hero? To a point, I do."
~ J.K. Rowling, July 26, 2007

Severus Snape is such a complex character, his own author can't seem to make up her mind about him. The interview from which those two contradictory comments were taken was given within the week following the release of *Harry Potter and the Deathly Hallows;* just four days after that interview, when asked whether Snape was a hero, she promptly responded, "Yes, I do." These antithetical quotes from the author herself sum up the entire conversation about Snape, in a way. Leading up to the release of the seventh book, there was no question more hotly debated in Harry Potter fandom than the loyalties of Snape. And speaking of loyalty, there were hardly any fans more loyal to their hero than Snape fans. Many of those fans were not thrilled in the least with Snape's turnout in the final installment of the series.

The editing of that particular interview for two different shows (*Today Show* and *Dateline*) make it exceedingly difficult to parse out exactly when she made each comment concerning Snape, but it appears that they both took place within the same portion of the discussion. It seems that interviewer Meredith Viera brought up the Snape question first, referring to him as a "hero;" the transcript at *Accio Quote!* for the July 26 airing notes that Rowling took "a sharp intake of breath" at the mention of Snape as a "hero." She responded: "*Is* he a hero? You see I don't really see him as a hero." Viera pressed her: "Really?" And the apparently edited response for that particular airing (*Today Show*, July 26, 2007) went like this: "Yeh. He's spiteful. He's a bully. All these things are still true of Snape, even at the end of this book. But was he brave? Yes, immensely." When she, in modern political parlance, did a "flip-flop" and called him a "hero, to a point," it appears to have been in this very context. The full quote, given in the *Dateline* episode a few days later, reads like this:

> I knew from the beginning what Snape was. Do I think he's a hero?
> To a point, I do, but he's not an unequivocally good character.
> Snape is a complicated man. He's bitter. He's ... spiteful. He's a
> bully. All these things are still true of Snape, even at the end of this
> book. But was he brave? Yes, immensely. Was he capable of love?
> Very definitely. So he's-- he's a very-- he was a flawed human being,
> like all of us. Harry forgives him--- as we know, from the epilogue,
> Harry-- Harry really sees the good in Snape ultimately. I wanted
> there to be redemption and I wanted there to be forgiveness. And
> Harry forgives, even knowing that until the end Snape loathed him
> unjustifiably. It's totally, totally unfair that he loathes him so much.
> (Vieira, "Harry Potter: The Final Chapter" 29 July 2007.)

That was sort of a false start, as far as giving Snape a break goes. She
started to move towards saying nice things about him, but quickly returned
to his nasty character. She is prepared much better for the question about
Snape's heroics a few days later, and now it appears the "flip-flop" is
complete. This is from the Bloomsbury web chat, July 30:

> **Lechicaneuronline:** Do you think Snape is a hero?
>
> **J.K. Rowling**: Yes, I do; though a very flawed hero. An anti-hero,
> perhaps. He is not a particularly likeable man in many ways. He
> remains rather cruel, a bully, riddled with bitterness and insecurity
> — and yet he loved, and showed loyalty to that love and, ultimately,
> laid down his life because of it. That's pretty heroic!
>
> She seems to soften on Snape a bit in each passing interview. Here
> she is a few months later: "Snape is vindictive, he's cruel. He's not a
> big man. [...] But he loves. I like him, but I'd also like to slap him
> hard." (Adler, 15 October, 2007)

J.K. Rowling seems to be struggling deeply with her own creation.
In one instance, she claims, "It's fun to write about Snape because he's a
deeply horrible person." (Abel, 1999). In another place, she calls him "a gift
of a character." In fact, it's in that place – at the Edinburgh Book Festival
in 2004, that some really interesting Snape-thoughts from Rowling come
out:

> You always see a lot of Snape, because he is a gift of a character.
> I hesitate to say that I love him. [Audience member: I do]. You
> do? This is a very worrying thing. Are you thinking about Alan
> Rickman or about Snape? [Laughter]. Isn't this life, though? I

make this hero—Harry, obviously—and there he is on the screen, the perfect Harry, because Dan is very much as I imagine Harry, but who does every girl under the age of 15 fall in love with? Tom Felton as Draco Malfoy. Girls, stop going for the bad guy. Go for a nice man in the first place. It took me 35 years to learn that, but I am giving you that nugget free, right now, at the beginning of your love lives. (Edinburgh Book Festival, Sunday, August 15, 2004. http://www.accio-quote.org/articles/204/0804-ebf.htm)

There's much to unpack here. First, she hesitates to say she "loves him." This is telling; Snape comes from some portion of Rowling's mind and experience in which dislike is present, some character flaw which causes her to struggle to love someone if he possesses it. There's something she's invested in the character of Snape that she personally loathes in people. Well, there are probably many to which we could point, but the best candidate, as far as we know from Rowling herself, is his mistreatment of children. In *Telling Tales: An Interview with J.K. Rowling*, she makes reference to a bullying teacher she had as a kid upon whom she loosely built Snape, and says that the "worst, shabbiest thing you can do" is to bully children (21).

The second thing to note is her reference to Alan Rickman. There can be no doubt that in fandom, Rickman's portrayal of Snape has had an impact on his celebrity. Joyce Millman documents how Rickman's Snape has played a role in Snape-obsession in fandom, with particular influence on the fan fiction.[1] Millman, a careful student of pop culture, notes that Rickman is "well established as 'the thinking woman's sex symbol'" and that his "feline movements and mellifluous voice give the Potions Master a sensuality absent from the page;" he's clearly far more attractive than Rowling's description of the greasy git, and "no attempt is made to ugly [Rickman] up" (43). Whether Rickman provides the Snape that many fans were already reading into Rowling's character or readers are reading Rickman into the text is a mystery that will probably never be solved.

Finally, we should note that Rowling is really quite disturbed by Snape fans. This is evident in her answer to a follow-up question at the same conference in which she seems absolutely exasperated by Snape-lovers. I include the question and answer in full so you can see how this develops:

> Question: Apart from Harry, Snape is my favourite character because he is so complex and I just love him. Can he see the Thestrals, and if so, why? Also, is he a pure blood wizard?

J. K. Rowling: Snape's ancestry is hinted at. He was a Death Eater, so clearly he is no Muggle born, because Muggle borns are not allowed to be Death Eaters, except in rare circumstances. You have some information about his ancestry there. He can see Thestrals, but in my imagination most of the older people at Hogwarts would be able to see them because, obviously, as you go through life you do lose people and understand what death is. But you must not forget that Snape was a Death Eater. He will have seen things that... Why do you love him? Why do people love Snape? I do not understand this. Again, it's bad boy syndrome, isn't it? It's very depressing. [Laughter]. One of my best friends watched the film and she said, "You know who's really attractive?" I said, "Who?" She said, "Lucius Malfoy!"

She can't even get through her answer to the question without blurting out her frustration. She's clearly having fun here as well with the quip about her friend and Malfoy, but it can hardly be questioned that she thinks this "bad boy syndrome" applies to Snape's fans and is dangerous. What is this "bad boy syndrome" that causes such an attraction to Snape? It's the anti-hero, the Gothic villain-hero archetype. Joyce Millman gives a succinct history of this villain-hero:

> A funny thing happened to the Gothic villain – readers loved him. According to Thorslev, when Gothic novels like those of Radcliffe and Horace Walpole...were adapted for the stage near the end of the eighteenth century. the Gothic villain "became gradually more sympathetic, until he appeared as half-villain, half-hero in sensibility." (42)

Severus Snape is such a character. Millman points to two literary comparisons, written by the Bronte sisters – Mr. Rochester in *Jane Eyre*, Heathcliffe in *Wuthering Heights* – and then quotes the Rowling statements about girls trying to love bad-boys out of their badness (42). This, Millman argues, is why so much fanfiction turns Snape into the romantic hero. This is part of the attraction of Snape, and Rowling thinks it's an awful thing, to be sure. Draco and Snape are not capable of being loved into redemption, it seems, and it is foolish and dangerous for girls to try. It's an interesting belief for Rowling to hold, as it appears that Dumbledore's entire approach to Snape and Draco is that loving them will result in their redemption. Perhaps Rowling is saying something about the unconditional love of a friend versus romantic love; after all, Snape was capable of the latter, but never showed the former, until the very end (maybe).

So, then, in the context of this one interview, she's called this Snape obsession "very worrying" and "depressing." Something happened in fandom that she did not intend in her books. The factors involved are probably more complex than the character of Snape himself, and there is no way to cover them all here. Suffice it to say that the cult of Snape is nothing short of a sociological phenomenon that deserves careful attention and analysis.

But why is Snape seemingly a mystery even to his own creator? It might just be in the nature of the character himself. Severus Snape is a shapeshifter. The shapeshifter archetype is something of a mystery to the hero and provides the hero his greatest challenge in the journey, potentially more even than the shadow. The shapeshifter's loyalties are in question throughout, and often the truth of his loyalties end up the turning point of the entire story.

There are many shapeshifters in *Harry Potter* – mostly literal ones! Lupin is both a literal and figurative shapeshifter – literal, because he is a werewolf, and figurative, because there is a significant moment in *Prisoner of Azkaban* when it suddenly appears that Rowling has once again fooled us, and the new DADA teacher is really the bad guy. This is not the case, and we learn this from yet another shapeshifter, Sirius Black, who can turn into a dog, and whose real identity is a mystery throughout most of the Shrieking Shack scene. Animagi, also including Pettigrew and McGonagall (and Dumbledore?[2]) are potent symbols of the shapeshifting characters and texts of the *Harry Potter* stories.

Shapeshifters teach the hero that things are not as they seem. Quirrell didn't actually have a stutter, nor was he afraid of the Dark Arts. The big black dog wasn't really a Grim. The insane murderer who broke out of Azkaban turned out to have been the only person in Azkaban who kept his sanity, precisely because he knew he was innocent. Ron's rat was a traitor and a servant of Voldemort. Mad-Eye Moody was Barty Crouch, Jr. Voldemort did not have Sirius at the Ministry. Dumbledore was not perfect. But Dumbledore had left them a plan. Snape loved Lily.

Shapeshifters are there to destroy prejudice. Perhaps the most poignant symbol of this is the Marauders. Apart from the voluntary shapeshifters, Lupin would have remained everything for which a werewolf is ostracized (at least, until wolfsbane potion was invented): a danger to humans, a savage, uncontrollable murderer. When James, Sirius, and Peter voluntary became literal shapeshifters, a paradox was immediately introduced: a tame werewolf. Suddenly, this werewolf is not as he seems. The shapeshifter challenges the hero's preconceived notions and categories of people.

Severus Snape is a very effective shapeshifter; there was no more heated discussion in fandom between books 6 and 7 than his loyalties. Borders Books and Music geared its entire advertising campaign around the question of Snape. Blogs, books, and forums went over and over the evidence, and crafted new and increasingly complex theories about just what Snape was doing during *Half-Blood Prince* and before. What made Snape so intriguing as a character? Orson Scott Card wrote an essay on Snape in the interlibrum, and he made some poignant observations about the way a character develops. Using Tolkien's Strider and Gollum as examples, he notes that authors often encounter a character that comes out of their own brains, but that intrigues even them, because they come from the deep recesses of the subconscious – the things that the author believes without even realizing he believes them.

Tolkien described Strider as this type of character; the plot was just sort of mapped out, and Tolkien was plunking through the outline when he suddenly met Strider at Bree. Card notes:

> Then, as Tolkien famously explained, he got to the inn at Bree and met a character named Strider. Strider intrigued him -- an unconscious, visceral response -- and in figuring out who Strider was and what he was doing, Tolkien found the real story of *Lord of the Rings*.

Notice the way Tolkien had to operate: he created the character, but once he "met" him, he had to "figure out" who he was. Not only this, but while the rest of the plot leading up to Strider was mechanically followed according to outline, Tolkien made one alteration:

> He had Gandalf tell Frodo the story of the original finding of the Ring by Deagol and Smeagol -- and told of how Smeagol became Gollum. In other words, the only change in that opening sequence that was required to make the novel satisfy that inner, unconscious logic, was to move Gollum to the center of the tale. He was not the hero; nor was he the monster. Instead, he was the center of moral ambiguity, the character who, seeming evil, might also serve the good. Other, lesser characters might also show moral ambiguity (one thinks of Saruman, Theoden, and Denethor), but none is as central to the story as Gollum.

This fascinated Card, as it fascinated us all, because Snape had taken on a life of his own during the series. He was very much a Gollum-like character; Gollum's loyalties were always in question. Was he Slinker or Stinker? Would he help the hobbits in the end, or betray them? Gollum was a classic shapeshifter.

Snape was just as much of a mystery. He was a nasty, awful bully, formerly a Death Eater, and he hated the story's hero with whom we most closely identified. On the other hand, Dumbledore trusted him implicitly, and there was clearly a story we weren't hearing. Rowling's narrative misdirection – the Harry filter which made us think we knew the whole story but caused us to miss all the most important off-stage action – was not just a clever technique; it was the driving force of the whole story and the genius behind Snape's status as shapeshifter. As this character took on his own life and energy within the story, both and and off stage, the questions began to arise: What had Snape been doing, and what was Snape going to do? To an extent, we wondered whether even Rowling knew the answers. Commenting on the extent of Rowling's planning, Card speculated, "It is even possible that her 'outline' for the final volume was, in its entirety, 'Harry has it out with Voldemort.'" The point behind the comment is: Snape had the potential to take Rowling places in the final book that she had not planned to go.

Of course, Card was wrong about this. Rowling stuck faithfully to her plan, and she had planned it from the very beginning of the 17 year period over which she wrote *Harry Potter*. Asked about how closely her final Book 7 product followed her original plan, she answer, "The last third of the book is...as I always planned it" (Vieria, "One-on-One" 2007). That last third would include both the "Sacking of Severus Snape" and "The Prince's Tale," all the main action of Snape in the final book. Ultimately, that choice by Rowling might have been the undoing of Snape – or at least the reason many Snape fans did not care for *Deathly Hallows*. That's a strong statement, so let's examine it.

Rowling called Snape a "gift of a character," which is evident in everything we've just discussed; he's a character that took on a brilliant story-driving energy, just like Strider or Gollum. It's a pity she gave the gift back in *Deathly Hallows*. It might be possible to say that Snape, in a sense, got away from Rowling as a character by the end of *Half-Blood Prince*; he even shapeshifted on his own creator! When the time came to write the book she'd been longing to write for 17 years, her plot needs swallowed the Snape of the previous six books. It's one of the rare places in an otherwise character-driven story where Rowling's plot demands trumped a character's action.

Or perhaps it wasn't that Snape was really *changed* by Rowling from books 6 to 7; it's just that he didn't play as prominent a role as we had expected. For many of us, the revelations of "The Prince's Tale" were simply no surprise at all; Rowling even noted that someone had guessed Snape's love for Lily as early as Book 3 (*La Gazette du Sorcier*, April 2, 2008). This was supposed to be Rowling's *Emma* moment – her shocking twist at the end. But John Granger, myself, and many others were together hashing out the implications of Snape's "stoppering" Dumbledore's death and the Lily-Snape connection just weeks after the release of *Half-Blood Prince*. Dumbledore's request of Snape to kill him was already guessed. For many readers, there was simply no surprise there. It's likely Rowling never really had the chance to pull off an *Emma*-like surprise. After all, Jane Austen was able to pull off her surprise in that story because it happened over the course of one book. There weren't fan communities stopping every couple of chapters, taking a few years to work through and theorize about the evidence given thus far, and then turning to the next few chapters to find out if they were right. Rowling *had* to drop enough hints to make the surprise believable, with veiled precedent. Plainly put, Potter devotees had too much time to speculate.

One should be very, very hesitant to criticize a writer as talented as J.K. Rowling, especially when one has not, nor will ever, do what she has done. But it seems she would have done well to have written some form of a Harry/Snape showdown prior to that quick moment before he died. She had set it all up beautifully. In the final chapter of *Half-Blood Prince*, Harry vowed:

> "I've got to track down the rest of the Horcruxes, haven't I? … I've got to find them and destroy them and then I've got to go after the seventh bit of Voldemort's soul, the bit that's still in his body, and I'm the one who's going to kill him. And if I meet Severus Snape along the way,' he added, 'so much the better for me, so much the worse for him." (*Prince* 651)

And then in Rowling's first major interview after *Half-Blood Prince*, she said: "Harry-Snape is now as personal, if not more so, than Harry-Voldemort" (Anelli/Spartz). There it is! She realized something about her character that fans had caught on to – Snape had become the most "personal" villain for Harry. Voldemort remained distant, that brooding presence in the background. Snape was up close and very personal, the deconstructor of the father-hero in Harry's imagination, and the constant antagonist. Snape irrationally loathed Harry, yet he sought to protect him out of his strange, incessant dedication to Lily Evans. Whatever else can be said about Snape, this much is true: Harry vs. Snape was "more personal" both for Harry and for the readers.

It is for this reason that Rowling may have missed a great opportunity in *Deathly Hallows* to provide an emotional catharsis by having some form of a Snape/Harry showdown. It would be rather a shame to steal from Dobby Harry's final moment of commitment to Dumbledore's plan. More than this, to have Snape reveal the whole plot to Harry at some point prior to "The Prince's Tale" would have destroyed the entire message about Harry's need to trust in the midst of doubt and seemingly contradictory evidence. Yet it remains true that the reader never had the moment of Harry/Snape resolution, either before "The Prince's Tale" or in the events that followed. Snape is almost entirely absent from the remainder of the plot after Harry's trip into the pensieve, apart from a seemingly trite (though most definitely not so) "Poor Severus" from Dumbledore. Nineteen years later, Harry has moved through his own personal resolution in the matter, naming his second son "Albus Severus" and calling Snape "the bravest man I ever knew." These are monumental moments. But while Harry was able to process the shock of Snape off the page during a 19-year gap, the reader is left with no such resolution. There's no mention of an insistence that Snape's body be honored like Moody's was. There's no moment of clarification, in which Harry sets the record straight for others about this tremendously brave and self-sacrificial man. All of these things undoubtedly happened, but they happened off the page, which means they didn't happen as the reader experienced the story!

Rowling is under no obligation to satisfy all the desires of fandom, including its need for some sort of Snape-vindication heralded throughout Hogwarts. There's something quite disturbing about the almost religious dedication to Snape present in some realms of fandom. That Rowling missed opportunities with Snape seems hardly a reason to abandon the series and loathe it for the rest of one's life. Rowling didn't have to appease fandom in her final portrayal of Snape. But making more of his vindication just might have been the right thing to do, anyway.

Just as the Hogwarts teachers sacked Snape from the school, so Rowling sacked much of the Snape-intrigue that characterized him in the first six books by removing him, on the whole, from Book 7. "The Prince's

Tale" was crucial, there is no doubt, and it will be analyzed below. But there was something emotionally unsatisfying about his absence from the rest of the novel. Snape was a shapeshifter in the reader's experience, too, because we are feeling things along with Harry. Whatever each reader believed about Snape, it was held passionately, because readers were all twisted in knots about this shapeshifting mystery. It's likely that many, many people, for whom Snape had become "very personal," were let down, having never had the cathartic moment needed to resolve the Snape dilemma. Harry had 19 years off-stage to process and move on; readers, on the other hand, were left all alone.

"The Prince's Tale"

Even if Snape's loyalties were possible to deduce, given the amount of evidence we had from seven books and the amount of time we had to analyze it, Rowling's story line surrounding Snape is an intriguing one. In the end, when Snape was fully revealed, he was shown to be every bit as conflicted a character as his enigma-status seemed to us throughout the entire series; he was a shapeshifter from start to finish. It is difficult, even after all Snape had done for Dumbledore, to see him as actually *repentant* from his days as a Death Eater. When he approached Dumbledore with the message that Voldemort was going after the Potters, it was his second attempt at ensuring that Lily not die – in the first attempt, he had requested of Voldemort that Lily be spared when he killed James and Harry, prompting Dumbledore's rightful reply, "You disgust me" (*Hallows* 677). Not trusting that Voldemort would keep his word, he finally submitted to Dumbledore's terms, that all three Potters would be protected.

Then, after years of loyal service to Dumbledore, protecting Harry, the time finally came for Dumbledore to tell Snape the whole story:

> "You have kept him alive so that he can die at the right moment?"
>
> "Don't be shocked, Severus. How many men and women have you watched die?"
>
> "Lately, only those whom I could not save," said Snape. He stood up. "You have used me."
>
> "Meaning?"
>
> "I have spied for you and lied for you, put myself in mortal danger for you. Everything was supposed to be to keep Lily Potter's son safe. Now you tell me you have been raising him like a pig for slaughter – "

"But this is touching, Severus," said Dumbledore seriously. "Have you grown to care for the boy, after all?"

"For *him?*" shouted Snape. "*Expecto Patronum!*" (*Hallows* 687, emphasis in original)

Out came the silver doe, and we learn that even after all these years, it is still his intense love for Lily that motivated his actions. He's angry, but one wonders why, for one can hardly imagine Lily not coming to terms with what her son must do; indeed, when Harry calls her from the stone, the first thing she comments on in his bravery (*Hallows* 699). In other words, loving Lily never taught Snape to love anyone else, including her son; more than that, loving Lily did not teach him to love *as Lily loved*, at least up until that point. It could be argued that in the final decision, Snape did learn to love as she did, or at the very least, to be willing to die as she did. His love for Lily and his knowledge of her love might have been what motivated that final action on his part – his willingness to die while following Dumbledore's orders, even after Dumbledore's death and with the knowledge that Harry must die. Yet, Snape was certainly not aware he was walking to his death when summoned to the Shack by Voldemort; he didn't walk to his death as Harry did, so we have no true gauge of Snape in that moment. He remains ambiguous, even in his death.

One can imagine Snape weighing his options after feeling "used" by Dumbledore; if it never really was about protecting Harry, why continue this dangerous life? Why not run? Ultimately, however, it may have been revenge; in the end, he wanted to get back at Voldemort for killing Lily. And so, after all we have learned about Snape now that the series is complete, he's still a mystery, a shapeshifter. Was his sacrifice motivated by love for Lily, revenge, neither, or both? Snape remains the greatest challenge and enigma in the series, but for all his faults, he is forgiven by Harry. And that is the greatest lesson Harry needed to learn; indeed, it's the lesson that made him not just "the better man" than Dumbledore, but a better man than his own father.

In Hope of Redemption

A final note about Snape that might explain some of the attraction to his character; for this, we must return to the discussion of Snape as gothic villain, or antihero. Rowling is not alone in holding a disdain for the antihero. Madeleine L'Engle wrote strongly about this archetype in

Walking on Water:

> Children don't like antiheroes. Neither do I. I don't think many
> people do, despite the proliferation of novels in the past few decades
> with antiheroes for protagonists. I think we all want to be able to
> identify with a major character in a book – to live, suffer, dream,
> and grow through vicarious experience. I need to be able to admire
> the protagonist despite his faults and so be given a glimpse of my
> own potential. There have been a few young-adult novels written
> recently with antiheroes; from all reports they are not the books
> that are read and reread. We don't want to feel *less* when we have
> finished a book; we want to feel that new possibilities of being have
> been opened to us. We don't want to close a book with a sense that
> life is totally unfair and that there is no light in the darkness; we
> want to feel that we have been given illumination. (132-33)

Those are some fairly strong words, and it's hard to respond with
exceeding thoroughness, because L'Engle does not define her terms. What
does she mean by "antihero?" Perhaps she refers to a nasty guy whose flaws
are justified in light of the fact that he did something great; it's difficult to
know. Snape, of course, is not the series' protagonist, so the *Harry Potter*
stories would not likely fit the category of young adult literature to which
L'Engle is referring. Nevertheless if Snape fits her description of the
antihero, one could imagine L'Engle being just as perplexed by the Snape
phenomenon as Rowling has been; Snape defies L'Engle's statement that
people don't like antiheroes.

There may be, after all, a good explanation for the love of antiheroes
besides "bad boy syndrome." Snape's work for the side of good points
to the hope of redemption, despite having lived an abysmal, sinful life.
Snape is tragic; it can be debated, as argued above, whether or not he ever
truly repented. He is a shapeshifter in death as he was in life. Yet there is
hope that in all of Snape's penitential sacrifice, he began to turn his heart
toward the good. That means there is hope for any of us to go from being
a wretched person like Snape to becoming brave and being honored for
one's sacrifice. It might just be that some cling to Snape not out of some
weird obsession, but out of hope of redemption; and it's hard to fault a
Snape fan for that.

Chapter 10 Notes

1   If you can handle analysis of fan fiction – the adult, sometimes sexual kind – Millman's essay, "To Sir, With Love" in *Mapping the World of Harry Potter* is helpful.

2   I offer the suggestion only as a matter of interest and speculation, not as a claim. It would seem odd indeed that Albus would not have been an animagus, since he was the Transfiguration teacher prior to McGonagall, and he was a far more powerful wizard. His name would not have come up on the registry for Animagi that Hermione checked, because given his age, he may have learned to become one more than a century prior (except that because of *Deathly Hallows*, we now have a dating problem with Dumbledoore's age; he seems to have gone from 150+, as Rowling said in interviews, to about same age as Auntie Muriel, who was 107).

PART III

A POLITICAL FAIRY TALE

Chapter Eleven

The Postmodern Potions Master
Brewing a Story that Changes Culture

In his book *Unlocking Harry Potter*, John Granger enumerated the evidence that J.K. Rowling has incorporated many postmodern elements into the *Harry Potter* series. Granger writes:

> Is Ms. Rowling...a "Postmodern Writer"? ... The common sense of the idea is, of course, what else could she be? A time traveler? Ms. Rowling lives in the here and now of the 21st century, breathing the air and shaped by the ideas of our postmodern times. (144)

The postmodern element of the books is one of the many things that causes it to resonate so deeply with readers. But what exactly is postmodernism? It is by no means an easy concept to wrap one's mind around, and pop expressions of postmodernism do its complexity no justice whatsoever. One tires quickly of hearing things like, "Postmodernism just means everything is relative and that there's no absolute truth." The best way to begin thinking about this subject is to start with the definition of postmodernism as given by Jean-Francois Lyotard in *The Postmodern Condition*:

> I will use the term modern to designate any science that legitimates itself with reference to a metadiscourse and making an explicit appeal to some grand narrative, such as the dialectics of Spirit, the hermeneutics of meaning, the emancipation of the rational or working subject, or the creation of wealth. For example, the rule of consensus between the sender and the addressee of a statement with truth-value is deemed acceptable if it is cast in terms of a possible unanimity between rational minds: this is the Enlightenment narrative, in which the hero knowledge works toward a good ethico-

political end- universal peace…Simplifying to the extreme, I define postmodern as incredulity toward metanarratives (xxiii-xxiv).

It is crucial to understand what Lyotard is and is not saying about metanarratives here. The metanarratives against which postmoderns argue are not any and all grand, large-scale stories. They are stories that legitimate themselves autonomously. Justin Holcomb, editor of *Christian Theologies of Scripture* (NYU Press, 2006), `helpfully clarified the definition of "metanarrative" in an article at Common Grounds Online (http://commongroundsonline.typepad.com):

> Metanarratives are over-arching meanings and beliefs, but for the purpose of legitimizing autonomous humanity, validating the modernist "views from no where" and supporting the "myth of neutrality." When we use meaning to legitimize ourselves, our desires, and our autonomy [we] have constructed a metanarrative.

It's the myth of objectivity, that one rational human being can come to the right conclusion for all humankind, bringing the hero-knowledge to the people for their salvation – but based on nothing other than the human's own supposed objectivity. And it turns out we're not all as objective as we think we are; we're really justifying ourselves according to this "view from nowhere."

The Enlightenment Project is the foundation for this. In the interest of human universal peace and prosperity, the Enlightenment Project seeks the rational answers found in human science and philosophical discourse which will lead us to a proper human morality; Lyotard, Foucault, Derrida, and other postmodern thinkers don't buy this motive, because the whole project turns out to be self-serving. What happens when rational minds can't come to agreement on the best ways to achieve universal human peace? Even more so, how does one define "rational" apart from assuming that one's own ideas define what is truly rational? To get to the crux of the matter:

> Nobody who ever fought to separate people into superiors and inferiors ever came up with the novel idea of categorizing their own into the ranks of the inferiors. (Castro 121)

In other words, postmodernists have noted that in the inevitable event that communities and people disagree on the way the world is and should be, those who have the most power get the final say, and the ones without the power get oppressed. Since all the language is centered in the quest for world peace and prosperity, the people in power deceive themselves into thinking that the oppression of anything that gets in the way of their own methodology of attaining said peace is justified, because the cause is noble. The justification for the oppression is inherently built into the lofty language of the stated goals.

A troubling example of a grand narrative in Western culture is the misuse of the idea of the so-called "American Dream," the belief that anyone in America can do anything they want as long as they're not lazy. To come right out and ask a challenging question: why is there such widespread economic disparity between races in America? Too frequently, we hear a very simple response to this: in America, anything is possible; as long as you work hard enough and continue to believe in your dream, it will come true.

The problem with this is that the logic behind it results in the following faulty conclusion: anyone who has not succeeded in America has not done so because he or she has not worked hard enough. This, in turn, leads to racist conclusions: black people are lazy (or black culture is lazy). It fails to take into account systemic oppression as well as systemic privilege of the dominant culture, both past and present, and therefore maintains, on the basis of the "American Dream" metanarrative, a "system of advantage based on race" (Wellman, quoted in Tatum 7). Note that the ideal behind the American Dream is a good one: hard work leads to freedom and prosperity. But it doesn't work out quite that simply. It's difficult to argue the point, however, because as stated above: the justification for oppression is built into the lofty language of the stated goals.

This is precisely the trap into which Albus Dumbledore fell as a youth. His letter to Gellert Grindelwald is the epitome of modernity:

> Gellert –
>
> Your point about Wizard dominance being FOR THE MUGGLES' OWN GOOD -- this, I think, is the crucial point. Yes, we have been given power and yes, that power gives us the right to rule, but it also gives us responsibilities over the ruled. We must stress this point, it will be the foundation upon which we build. Where we are opposed, as we surely will be, this must be the basis of all our counterarguments. We seize control FOR THE GREATER GOOD. And from this it follows that where we meet resistance, we must use only the force that is necessary and no more. (*Hallows* 357)

Albus is doing precisely what the Enlightenment Project encouraged: those philosophers who "knew best," who understood by "common sense" and "rational thought" what the world was like and how it should be, were under obligation (responsibility) either to convert those who disagreed or to oppose them, by force if necessary. After all, they were simply trying to make it a better world. Albus's entire viewpoint came crashing down when this justification for the use of force resulted in the death of his own sister.

Clearly, as Granger has explained, and as we've just seen by definition, we're dealing to some extent with literature that is carrying postmodern themes. The whole series opens with the cartoonish Dursleys, sad caricatures of the consequences of strictly rationalistic and materialistic thinking. Harry's dream about the flying motorcycle is met with outrage, because the idea of "anything acting in a way that it shouldn't" angered the rationalistic Dursleys (*Stone* 26). As Hermione said later in the same book, "A lot of the greatest wizards haven't got an ounce of logic," which makes them a bad fit for an Enlightenment metanarrative (285). It was intolerance toward the magical powers of the Wizarding World and their unique perspective on the world that drove them into hiding. But strangely, the postmodern critique of modernism is, at least at first, on the periphery of the Harry Potter series. We only see glimpses of it. Instead, Rowling has focused on "another idea." Observe the following from an interview in 2000:

> Bigotry is probably the thing I detest most. All forms of intolerance, the whole idea of "that which is different from me is necessary evil." I really like to explore the idea that difference is equal and good. But there's another idea that I like to explore, too. Oppressed groups are not, generally speaking, people who stand firmly together -- no, sadly, they kind of subdivide among themselves and fight like hell. That's human nature, so that's what you see here. This world of wizards and witches, they're already ostracized, and then within themselves, they've formed a loathsome pecking order (Jensen).

So what we have with *Harry Potter* is much more a critique of institutionalized racism and prejudice, which happens within a community that has already experienced its own oppression from others.

This may be an interesting critique of postmodernism in itself. While postmodernism lays the blame on the structuralist thinking of modernism, Rowling lays the blame at the feet of human beings themselves, no matter what the philosophical paradigm. She creates for us a magical world – by no means a rationalistic, modern, Enlightenment world – that contains the same types of prejudice and racism present in our own.

In the following chapters, we will examine in detail the Wizarding World's "loathsome pecking order." But before that, we have to ask why it all matters. If there are conversations to be had about weighty matters in our own world, why pass through the Wizarding World in order to have them? This is the point where much of what has been laid out in Parts I & II come together: we live by our stories. If there's one thing postmodernism has taught us above all other things, it's that we each have our own story, and each story is the context for how we think about life; not only this, but we live according to our story, unable to wholly overcome it (to reach some undiluted "objective" status), and we often force others to fit into our own way of looking at the world. Yet, if there are injustices in society, the surprising truth might just be that a story can change things.

Culture-Shaping Stories

University of Tennessee Professor of Law Benjamin Barton makes this striking claim about the Harry Potter books: "Rowling may do more for libertarianism than anyone since John Stuart Mill" (Barton 1526). The point about libertarianism itself will be addressed in the next chapter. The belief behind the point is what's shocking: that a series of so-called "children's books," set in a fantasy sub-world, made up of pretend magic, flying brooms, and imaginary creatures may do more to promote a certain political philosophy than all the lengthy, academic defenses published in the last century and a half (Mill died in 1873). Why would someone say something so silly?

Part I argued that fairy tales and mythologies can do more to teach us about meaning and truth than bare scientific facts. Part II tapped into mythology as well, arguing that finding our place as "hero," naming and controlling our shadow side, and being encouraged along the way by our supportive community (wise old man, great mother, etc.) teaches us how to make sense of reality and our place within it. Now, we put these together by considering how our stories shape and define who we are and where we're going. Umberto Eco, reflecting on literature, wrote:

> By helping to create language, literature creates a sense of identity and community. I spoke initially of Dante, but we might also think

of what Greek civilization would have been like without Homer, German identity without Luther's translation of the Bible, the Russian language without Pushkin, or Indian civilization without its foundation epics (Eco 3).

Harry Potter is an international phenomenon. Its impact on culture cannot yet be fully measured, and it will be a generation or so before we can even begin to make concrete conclusions. One thing is certain: it *will* have a widespread influence on culture. It might just be, as John Granger has suggested, that as the Great Books canon has served as a set of "shared texts" for moderns, *Harry Potter* is potentially the most widely recognized shared text of postmodernism (essay in *Touchstone Magazine*, Dec. 2008). In the remaining chapters, we'll be looking at many areas of culture that are specifically addressed by the *Harry Potter* series. These are significant sociocultural issues which *Harry Potter* addresses, and it has the potential to start vital conversations about our own world. But first, we must examine a bit more closely how story shapes culture.

Story and Hope for the Helpless

Madeleine L'Engle, ruminating on abuse of power within an ostensibly free society, remarked that neither philosophy nor theology are terribly helpful to her in answering the problem of hopelessness caused by oppression. Rather, for L'Engle:

> The painters and the writers who see the abuse and misuse of freedom and cry out for justice for the helpless poor, the defenseless old, give me more hope; as long as anybody cares, all is not lost. As long as anybody cares, it may be possible for something to be done about it; there are still choices open to us; all doors are not closed. As long as anybody cares it is an icon of God's caring, and we know that the light is stronger than the dark. (*Walking* 117).

It was noted in the Introduction that this book comes from a distinctly Christian perspective, and this is for two reasons: its author is a Christian (so to pretend otherwise would be dishonest), and the author of the series it analyzes is a Christian. Rowling has been more than a little cagey about her faith, even after Book 7, but there is one particular statement she made that deserves attention:

> There was a Christian commentator who said that Harry Potter had been the Christian church's biggest missed opportunity.

And I thought, there's someone who actually has their eyes open. (Amini)

"Missed opportunity" for what? For a bunch of people to "get saved" through reading *Harry Potter*? It's highly unlikely that is what Rowling had in mind.

Rowling has, on the other hand, called the series "an extended argument for tolerance." It's far more likely, since *Harry Potter* is by no means a salvation tract, that the "missed opportunity" to which Rowling was referring is the potential and power for Christian action for social change.

Some Christians will be disappointed in this conclusion, wanting *Harry Potter* to be a method of evangelism, or a movie to show their friends and then have an altar call. This is not the case at all, and while there will quite possibly be a flurry of books and church programs to that end, this will have missed the point of *Harry Potter*. Neither Harry nor Dumbledore are Jesus. The *Harry Potter* series does not seek to answer the cosmic questions: Why are we here? What went wrong with the world? How can we be saved from whatever went wrong? While the series of books gives hints here and there toward those questions, it answers instead the very simple question: How, then, shall we live? How do people convinced of the power self-sacrificial love live in the world and work for its betterment? That, I think, is the "missed opportunity" to which J.K. Rowling is referring. Once again, L'Engle is helpful:

> It is not easy for me to be a Christian, to believe twenty-four hours a day all that I want to believe. I stray, and then my stories pull me back if I listen to them carefully. I have often been asked if my Christianity affects my stories, and surely it is the other way around; my stories affect my Christianity, restore me, shake me by the scruff of the neck, and pull this straying sinner into an awed faith. (*Walking* 119)

The similarity between Rowling and L'Engle on this point should not be missed. Rowling has freely admitted to struggling with her faith, and that she was working this out in the *Harry Potter* stories:

> The truth is that, like Graham Greene, my faith is sometimes that my faith will return. It's something I struggle with a lot.... It preoccupies me a lot, and I think that's very obvious within the books. (Adler, October 17, 2007)

So, then, it seems that Rowling believes very much as L'Engle does: fairy tales like *Harry Potter* are an opportunity to reflect again on faith, to be restored, for faith to "come back," and for that faith to make a significant difference in the world. The *Harry Potter* stories, like the art and writing L'Engle mentioned, "cry out for justice." For the Christians Rowling mentioned above, it is a "missed opportunity" to remember that there was once a man accused of sorcery who walked through towns, healing the sick, raising the dead, forcing the darkness to flee, hanging out with outcasts of every variety – prostitutes, thieves, drunkards, adulterers, lepers, in L'Engle's words, "the helpless poor" – and that he told his followers to "go and do likewise," rather than to pass by on the other side like the religious snobs (Luke 10).

While the Church has failed miserably in its task at times throughout its history, there have been many – William Wilberforce, Lord Shaftesbury, Ashley Cooper, Samuel Hopkins, Florence Nightingale, Martin Luther King, Jr., to name just a few of the innumerable – who have taken Jesus' message of justice and compassion to oppressive powers and won significant victories resulting in lasting social change.

When J.K. Rowling wrote the 800 word prequel to the *Harry Potter* series for charity, most dismissed it as a cute little story about James and Sirius with little or no relevance. After 10 years of analyzing the writing of Ms. Rowling, readers should have known better! Can there possibly be anything close to a social commentary in just 800 words about two rebellious teens? Well, yes, there can. The first seemingly random name Sirius mentions is "Wilberforce," which is a very recognizable surname. William Wilberforce was a member of British Parliament in the late 18th and early 19th centuries whose Christian faith inspired him to fight for the abolition of the slave trade in England. His efforts were ultimately successful (his story has been recently told in the film *Amazing Grace*). Rowling would know all about Wilberforce, because she attended St. Michael's Primary School, which was founded by Wilberforce and Hannah More.

What is the significance? William Wilberforce was a Christian involved in social action whose work significantly altered history for the better. Not only that, but after his conversion, he struggled with whether or not to continue in Parliament, considering ordained ministry instead. Both John Newton (author of the famous hymn, "Amazing Grace") and William Pitt the Younger (Prime Minister and friend) counseled him to remain in politics, Pitt writing in a letter, "Surely the principles of Christianity lead to action as well as meditation." It is this kind of Christian action that Rowling sees as the church's "missed opportunity." Undoubtedly, there is a radical message of love, compassion, and acceptance in the story of Jesus – which Tolkien called a fairy tale (!) – who became friends with outcasts and excluded only the pompous elite.[1] The use of the name "Wilberforce" in the 800 word prequel is a one-word summary of Rowling's Christian social vision laid out in *Harry Potter*.

The significance of all this should not be missed: this observation turns the conversation, as it's been happening for the last 10 years, entirely on its head. Since Rowling's books were first challenged by culture-war Christians, the conversation has been a debate about how, or indeed if, Rowling's Christian faith influenced her stories. That debate is settled, even if there's still much to learn from the *how*. From this point forward, and in the chapters that follow, we will be asking the opposite question: does Rowling's work have anything to say to Christians, and indeed, to society as a whole? In doing this, we will see if there really is a "missed opportunity," and that as for both L'Engle and Rowling, a story can play a role in crying out for justice and restoring us. Analyzing the sociological issues of our time that pertain to tolerance – race, class, gender, disability, and governmental abuse of power – as well as asking whether Rowling fails in any of these areas is non-negotiable. If we pass that up, we miss the opportunity as well.

History and Myth

Tolkien wrote in "On Fairy-Stories" that "History often resembles 'Myth,' because they are both ultimately of the same stuff." Taking it a step further, we need the creative imaginations of Myth, because sometimes the recorders of history get it wrong. If we are going to ask the question about *Harry Potter*'s impact on society, we have to discuss it in a sociohistorical and cultural context, but this is in itself a difficult enough task. Reading history textbooks often prevents us from knowing the real or entire story of history, because so much is not told. It is assumed that a history book records facts and dates – accurate reporting of what happened. This is hardly the case. The fundamental problem with Professor Binns's view of history is that it ignores its meaning, favoring so-called "facts" instead. "History," according to Binns, is neither "myth" nor "legend," but " solid, believable, verifiable *fact!" (Chamber* 152). Rowling mercilessly ridicules Binns' view of history:

> History of Magic was the dullest subject on their schedule. Professor
> Binns, who taught it, was their only ghost teacher, and the most
> exciting thing that ever happened in his classes was his entering the
> room through the blackboard. Ancient and shriveled, many people
> said he hadn't noticed he was dead. He had simply got up to teach
> one day and left his body behind him in an armchair in front of
> the staff room fire; his routine had not varied in the slightest since.
> (*Chamber* 148)

Binns' view of history is the modern "myth of objectivity" (ironic that
the word "myth" is so commonly chosen for that phrase), or the positivist
way of thinking: There is a set of simple facts – names, dates, happenings
– and these are "objective." No meaning is given to them by the reciter
of said facts. But the postmodern critique is that all of these "facts" *do*
have meaning (and that some very important facts are omitted, thereby
shaping meaning as the historical editor sees fit). Not only do they have
meaning, but that meaning differs, depending on to whom one speaks.
The conversation between Griphook and the trio in *Deathly Hallows* about
historical wizard-goblin relations proves the point, and will be treated
in detail in the next chapter. If ever there were a concrete postmodern
claim, it is this: History is recorded by the winners. Once again, the
creative power of a fairy tale might just jar our minds enough to get us
to rethink the discourses of history, become aware of social injustice, and
work toward a more just society.

Fairy tales are not about "escaping" the "real world," but seeing it
more clearly, as has already been argued in Part I. Jack Zipes argues
that fairy tale "plays upon the imagination not to open it up to escape
into a never-never land but to make greater contact with reality" (quoted
in Ostry 89). Gallardo-C. and Smith tie in the "Between Two Worlds"
concept central to the argument of this book: "The liminal magical world,
then, exists to parallel the Muggle world and inside of it, so that like most
fantasy and science fiction it both mirrors reality and offers alternatives to
it by displacing controversial issues onto other Others." (201)

If the goal of postmodernism is to deconstruct Grand-Story power
plays, we would expect to find that in Rowling's work; and indeed, we
do. In one particularly clever twist, Rowling conducts a sort of critical
literacy experiment with the genre of the fairy tale itself (this is one of the
ways in which she "subverts the genre" – see chapter 2). Traditionally evil
and scary characters like werewolves, giants, and goblins are scapegoated
by the Wizarding World, and they serve in *Harry Potter* as examples of
the plight of the oppressed rather than creatures who really need to be

feared and killed. Through these characters and other discourses in the Wizarding World, Rowling offers criticism regarding social justice issues such as race, gender, class and disability throughout her story. The former two are analyzed in the follow two chapters. The latter two we shall look at presently to illustrate the point.

Class is an issue in *Harry Potter* as evidenced by the Draco-Ron confrontations. Both are pureblood wizards, and as such, you'd expect Draco to think of him favorably. But the Weasleys commit two sins in Draco's eyes: they are "blood traitors" (purebloods who don't buy the pureblood-superiority metanarrative), and they are *poor*. Draco is regularly goading Ron about his poverty. More than that, the Malfoys' financial status clearly buys them power and influence. Lucius occupies very influential roles in the Ministry, despite previous Death Eater status. He buys the Slytherin Quidditch team top of the line broomsticks in order to get his son on the team and give them an advantage over the other teams. Draco falsely associates this money with pureblood status, as if power, prosperity and privilege naturally follow from being pureblood; it's simply part of reality that purebloods have money and power. He and his family are later torn down in *Deathly Hallows*, under the subjugation of a half-blood (Voldemort)!

Disability is explored through the existence of Squibs, wizard-borns who do not demonstrate any magical power – the reverse of a muggle-born witch or wizard. Why is Argus Filch employed at Hogwarts? He's a bitter, mean old man; why would Dumbledore keep him around? Well, Dumbledore is an icon of tolerance and acceptance. But why is Filch bitter and mean? More likely than not, it's because he was bullied for being a Squib. When Mrs. Norris, his cat, is found petrified, he accuses Harry of doing it. Despite the fact that both Ron and Hermione are also on the scene, and that it's completely unrealistic that a second-year student could accomplish such Dark Magic, Filch protests.

> "She has been Petrified," said Dumbledore ("Ah! I thought so!" said Lockhart). "But how, I cannot say . . . ."
>
> "Ask him!" shrieked Filch, turning his blotched and tearstained face to Harry.
>
> "No second year could have done this," said Dumbledore firmly. "it would take Dark Magic of the most advanced -"
>
> "He did it, he did it!" Filch spat, his pouchy face purpling. "You saw what he wrote on the wall! He found – in my office – he knows I'm

a – I'm a -" Filch's face worked horribly. "He knows I'm a Squib!" he finished. (*Chamber* 142)

Filch seems downright irrational, but the reasoning makes sense if Filch was ridiculed and bullied for being a Squib. Harry *must* have done the deed; he found out Filch was a Squib. In Filch's mind, as soon as someone knows about his "disability," they begin bullying him. These two things are so linked in Filch's thinking that there can be no question in his mind – Harry petrified Mrs. Norris to pick on Filch for not being able to do magic.[2]

The Squib, Arabella Figg, plays a minor but important role. She seems content and happy in her life and status. As with Filch, the key player in her acceptance into the Wizarding World is Dumbledore. Mrs. Figg is a member of the Order of the Phoenix, and she is crucial to Harry's defense testimony in Book 5 following the incident with the Dementors in Little Whinging.

Race is the primary social justice issue of the books. Gender comes in a somewhat distant second. Class and disability are not as prominent, but they are there. Rowling has story-shaped answers to the inequalities constructed in the series, as well as in our own world.

The Social Justice Trio

Rowling carefully selected her heroic trio to set the social vision contained within the *Harry Potter* books. Concerning race: Ron is a pureblood, Harry is a half-blood, and Hermione is a Muggle-born. Concerning gender: Ron is in many ways a stereotypical guy (though he begins to break out of it a bit); Hermione is a strong female character (see chapter 14); Harry, though definitely male, is also the "Philosopher's Stone," the hermaphroditic perfect union of male and female, set within a cyclical female fairy tale (see chapter 14). Concerning class: Harry is independently wealthy; Hermione comes from what is likely a middle-upper or upper class family (her parents are dentists); Ron is poor. Concerning magical ability: Hermione is brilliant and talented; Harry is a fairly decent wizard with some obvious strengths and weaknesses; Ron appears to have no particular talent or outstanding magical ability at all. These three work, for the most part, in harmony together. While there is conflict between Ron and Harry over Harry's popularity and wealth, they eventually reconcile, underscoring their ability to work together regardless of differences.

The trio's supporting cast is a bunch of social outcasts as well. The other Weasleys belong to the same poor family as Ron. Ginny is a particularly powerful witch (of whom, unfortunately, we do not see enough). Luna is quirky and picked on, but pure of heart. Neville is afraid for the first decade and a half of his life that he's a Squib, and even refers to himself as "almost" a Squib in *Chamber of Secrets.*

In short, the rescuing of the Wizarding World is not going to be accomplished solely by wealthy superheroes or by the outcasts. It will be accomplished by all groups working together without prejudice, by the advantaged abandoning their own privilege for the pursuit of a better world, by the disadvantaged working hand-in-hand in harmony with others. It is a post-hierarchical cast of characters that comprise J.K. Rowling's heroines and heroes.

This social justice trio are placed by J.K. Rowling into a particular culture, not very unlike our own; but she also places them into a particular social vision. We turn now to the political philosophy embedded in the *Harry Potter* stories.

Chapter 11 Notes

1   This is not to say that this is the entire message of Jesus, nor to turn toward the classic "social gospel." This is not the place for that tired debate, nor to rehash the false dichotomy of "social vision" vs. "personal salvation." There are plenty of good books on that already, and I'd recommend the work of N.T. Wright as someone who gets it correctly.

2   Snape, while not a squib, has a similar reaction to being picked on, as evidenced by his "worst memory." When Harry invades his mind and sees the memory of his being bullied, all cool-headedness promptly leaves Snape, he rages against Harry, kicks him out of his office, and refuses to do what Dumbledore asked of him.

Chapter Twelve

Of Fountains, Fabians and Freedoms
Dumbledore's Deconstruction of the Wizarding World

"Sometimes God does his work with gentle drizzle, not storms. Drip. Drip. Drip." ~ John Newton to William Wilberforce in the film, *Amazing Grace* (2006)

Dumbledore, who we now know was once tempted and tried by power, became the deconstructor of the Wizarding World's "loathsome pecking order." Dumbledore is an advocate for Muggles, and his concern for house-elves and other magical brethren is so much a part of him that, staring at a boy who has just lost his godfather, Dumbledore finds it necessary to explain that Sirius's unkind behavior towards Kreacher drove the poor house-elf to treachery. In that moment, he explains that the fountain in the Ministry of Magic "told a lie." This is how the fountain was described earlier in the book, when Harry first saw it:

> Halfway down the hall was a fountain. A group of golden statues, larger than life-size, stood in the middle of a circular pool. Tallest of them all was a noble-looking wizard, with his wand pointing straight up in the air. Grouped around him was a beautiful witch, a centaur, a goblin, and a house-elf. The last three were all looking adoringly up at the witch and wizard. Glittering jets of water were flying from the ends of the two wands, the point of the centaur's arrow, the tip of the goblin's hat, and each of the house-elf's ears.... (*Order* 127)

The "lie" that this fountain told was that Wizards were naturally superior, and the other magical brethren were adoring subjects of the wise and benevolent rule of wizards. "We wizards have mistreated and abused our fellows for too long, and we are now reaping our reward," Dumbledore said (834). Dumbledore's destruction of the fountain which told the lie was a symbolic action, pointing to the truth that it was *that* lie that gave rise to Voldemort, that gave rise to enemies of the Wizarding World. As

Dumbledore and Voldemort dueled around the lying fountain, ideologies were at war: Voldemort, the Hitleresque racist and Slytherin, and Dumbledore, the Gryffindor Headmaster who believed that even Slytherin house had an important place at Hogwarts.   Dumbledore destroyed a fountain that upheld an oppressive social order of which Voldemort would approve.   Voldemort, through his puppet Pius Thicknesse, replaced that fountain with a statue far worse:

> The great Atrium seemed darker than Harry remembered it. Previously a golden fountain had filled the center of the hall, casting shimmering spots of light over the polished wooden floor and walls. Now a gigantic statue of black stone dominated the scene. It was rather frightening, this vast sculpture of a witch and a wizard sitting on ornately carved thrones, looking down at the Ministry workers toppling out of fireplaces below them. Engraved in foot-high letters at the base of the statue were the words MAGIC IS MIGHT....

> Harry looked more closely and realized that what he had thought were decoratively carved thrones were actually mounds of carved humans: hundreds and hundreds of naked bodies, men, women, and children, all with rather stupid, ugly faces, twisted and pressed together to support the weight of the handsomely robed wizards. (*Hallows* 241-42)

Apparently, things had to get worse before they started getting better.   At the time this statue was constructed, Dumbledore was no longer around to expose the lie; but he had left a legacy in place for Harry, one that Harry learned to take up, as evidenced by his leading the accused "Mudbloods" out of the Ministry to safety just an hour later.

We need to review where we've come thus far.   In the last chapter, it was argued that Rowling has written a fairy tale which, in L'Engle's words, "cries out for justice."   We also noted that Rowling agrees with the Christian commentator who said that *Harry Potter* was the biggest "missed opportunity" for the church in recent memory and argued that this "missed opportunity" was for Christians to join in this call for justice. We should note, in addition, that her belief that *Harry Potter* could be a "missed opportunity" for the church to regain is social justice bearings tells us something about the way Rowling views literature, including her own *Harry Potter* stories.   It tells us that Rowling believes story has the power to transform, and that what she wrote has transformational potential. Rowling has most certainly written stories with a moral purpose, even if she claims she did not intend to write morality tales.   In calling the stories "an extended argument for tolerance," she gives herself away. Stating the obvious, if the books are an "argument for tolerance," then, indeed, they *argue* for a specific moral vision. She may not have set her pen to paper with the purpose of writing a morality tale, but as morals were inevitably drawn, she ended up writing one anyway.

The use of *Harry Potter* as an agent for social change has already begun. The Harry Potter Alliance, founded by Andrew Slack and Paul DeGeorge, is an organization which rallies *Harry Potter* fans to fight for social justice and is rooted in the arguments for tolerance laid out by the words and example of Albus Dumbledore and Harry Potter (http://thehpalliance.org). It's not a specifically Christian organization,[1] but it does prove the point that a story has the potential to initiate change in the world. Not only this, but the Harry Potter Alliance advocates internal change leading to outward change; individuals much be transformed people before they can make a lasting difference in society. For example, in July 2008, their website sponsored an event called "11 Days of Breaking Through the Muggle Mindset," in which readers were encouraged to do certain exercises them would help them learn to think in a more magical, more hopeful way, and self-transformative way (http://www.thehpalliance. org/?p=139).

J.K. Rowling believes the same thing about inward change leading to outward change. At her 2008 Harvard commencement speech, she quoted Plutarch:

> One of the many things I learned at the end of that Classics corridor down which I ventured at the age of 18, in search of something I could not then define, was this, written by the Greek author Plutarch: What we achieve inwardly will change outer reality.

> That is an astonishing statement and yet proven a thousand times every day of our lives. It expresses, in part, our inescapable connection with the outside world, the fact that we touch other people's lives simply by existing. (http://harvardmagazine.com/go/jkrowling.html)

"What we achieve inwardly will change outer reality." That is a succinct summary of what is being argued for in the *Harry Potter* series, as well as what is being argued for in this book. That principle is at the root of a Christian social vision, because Christian theology calls for an inward change in the believer, producing a person who will work for justice and love mercy.

There is a political, though not specifically religious, group in England that espouses a similar doctrine – that inward change produces outward change in society – and Rowling has made some subtle links to this group in her stories. That group is the Fabian Society, an organization which began in the late 18th century and exists to this day. David Colbert found a few very interesting name connections between Rowling's Order of the Phoenix, and the Fabian Society (190). Consider the following:

- **Fabian Prewett** is one of the deceased members of the Order, and the connection to the Fabian Society is self-explanatory.

- **Sturgis Podmore** – One of the founding members of the Fabian Society was Frank Podmore. It was he who named the group after the Roman dictator and general Fabius Maximus, who became famous for his tactic of delaying battle against Hannibal, and in doing so, ended up winning the war against him.

- **Kingsley Shacklebolt** – Colbert suggests a name connection with, Kingsley Martin, a member of the Fabian Society who edited a "left-leaning political journal." Another possibility for Kingsley is Charles Kingsley. Charles was never a member of the Fabian Society, but he was a Christian socialist "who had preached Socialist ideas derived from the early Fathers, from St. Thomas Aquinas, from the Abbe Lammenais, and from the Rev. Rosmini-Serbati" (Fremantle 26). His ideas were part of the Christian socialist movement at the time which resulted in the formation of Thomas Davidson's "Fellowship of the New Life" (influenced by Rosmini's Christian socialism), out of which the Fabian Society grew. Frank Podmore was a regular attendee of these fellowship meetings, and it was he and Edward Pease who formed a break-off group which would come to be known as the Fabian Society.

- **Emmeline Vance** – Emmeline Pankhurst,[2] a women's rights activist, was one of the earliest members of the Fabian Society, and "vance" means "forward" (as in "advance"), which makes sense in light of their progressive political outlook (Colbert 190). The connection is made stronger by the fact that she is wearing a green shawl when Harry sees her, something commonly worn by suffragettes (Colbert 190).

Furthermore, many authors were among the early members – George Bernard Shaw, H.G. Wells, and Edith Nesbit, the latter being a favorite of Rowling's.

Many of the first Fabians began meeting when Thomas Davidson, the wandering scholar, visited London. Davidson was a Protestant who had abandoned his faith, but while searching for answers came across the teachings of Rosmini-Serbati, who we mentioned above was a key influence in Charles Kingley's Christian socialism. The Fabians, who formed out of this initial "Fellowship of the New Life," retained many of its principles, including the goal of "[t]he cultivation of a perfect character in each and all" (Pease 32). Christian socialism is part the DNA of the Fabian Society, though the Fabians did not maintain a specifically Christian outlook. Frank Podmore and Edward Pease were Spiritualists and discussed the idea of forming a society separate from Davidson's Fellowship while on an all-night ghost watch in Notting Hill (Pease 28). Later, Pease would abandon ghost-watching as "really foolish" (MacKenzie and MacKenzie 18). Still, Pease "believed that a change in personal values should precede reform of the social system," and in the period of time leading up to the formation of the Fabian Society, he sought like-minded people (21). Fabian historians Norman and Jeanne MacKenzie argue that this need for inward change to produce outward change "was a part of their Evangelical inheritance that persisted even when they rejected formal religion" (21).

Not all Fabians rejected religion. Many of the people active in the Fabian Society were also active in the Christian Socialist movement (McBriar 9). Some who attended early Fabian meetings were looking for an alternative to the socialism of the Social Democratic Federation, primarily because they were looking for something that recognized more than just materialism (MacKenzie and MacKenzie 42). William Clarke, for example, argued that socialism was getting it all wrong because it never "rose beyond the plane of the material;" he wrote to Davidson that the Marxists were "actively irreligious" and that they "desire revolution quite as much for the sake of overthrowing ethics and the spiritual side of things as for the sake of improving the material condition for the people" (42). Hubert Bland, one of the founding members and the husband of Edith Nesbit, "swung from Roman Catholicism to Atheism and then back again" (McBriar 4). Sidney Dark was "a lifelong Christian ... one of the High Church Fabians, and for many years was editor of the *Church Times*" (Fremantle 36). Sydney Olivier was "one of the managing group of the journal *The Christian Socialist* before joining the Fabians (McBriar 9). In the period of time leading up to World War I, the Fabians published six tracts on Christian socialism; they only published three others during this period of a philosophical nature (154). All six, one of which was a historical study on Charles Kingsley and Christian socialism, "were intended to prove to Christians that Christianity and Socialism or

Collectivism were compatible" (155). It seems fairly evident, at this point, that J.K. Rowling could have a political philosophy informed both by socialism and Christianity!

The Fabians, still active and influential today, were founded as a different kind of socialist than the Marxist revolutionary. The lingering Christian socialism of Davidson and the other Christian socialists of the time is likely one of the factors that influenced this socialism which required inward transformation leading to outward change.

What kind of socialists are the Fabians? Simply put, the Fabian Society believes in slow, gradual change, not revolution. This was one of their early defining characteristics. They are a socialist society, but different from Marxist socialism's belief that equity would come about by a lower-class revolution. Rather, the Fabians believe in gradual change over time. Sydney Webb, one of the original Fabians, wrote:

> [A]dvocates of social reconstruction have learned the lesson of Democracy, and know that it is through the slow and gradual turning of the popular mind to new principles that social reorganization bit by bit comes. ("The Basis of Socialism: Historic," in *Fabian Essays* I.1.8)

This gradual change must be "constitutional and peaceful" (I.1.8). Indeed, in needed to happen over time precisely because the inner character transformation of hte people needed to occur. No one could force socialism upon the people; they had to be ready for it. Sydney Olivier wrote that "not even ten percent of us are fit for a Socialist state yet" (MacKenzie and MacKenzie 62). At one point, Sydney Webb wrote that the moral transformation necessary to prepare the way for a just socialism would be so mjch of a challenge that it would be "easier to moralise the capitalist than to expropriate him" (61). What separated the Fabians from revolutionary socialists was that they sought no massive overthrow of the existing order, but slow, gradual change through transforming individual people.

> [T]here has been and is proceeding an economic evolution, practically independent of our individual desires or prejudices; an evolution which has changed for us the whole social problem by changing the conditions of material production, and which ipso facto effects a revolution in our modern life. To learn clearly what that revolution is, and to prepare ourselves for taking advantage of it in due course—this I take to be briefly what is meant by Socialism. The ignorant public, represented by, let us say, the average bishop or

member of Parliament, hears of the "Social Revolution" and instantly thinks of street riots, noyades, with a coup d'état: a 10th of August, followed perhaps by its nemesis in an 18th Brumaire. But these are not the Social Revolution. That great change is proceeding silently every day. (William Clarke, "The Basis of Socialism: Industrial" in *Fabian Essays* I.2.1)

Webb noted that "the inevitable outcome of Democracy is the control by the people themselves" and he bemoaned governments in which "[t]he nexus between man and man was essentially a relation of superiority and inferiority" (I.1.8-I.1.9). Webb also wrote, "Since 1832, English political history is the record of the reluctant enfranchisement of one class after another, by mere force of the tendencies of the age" (I.1.15). This is the postmodern claim about all of history that was discussed in the previous chapter. It may seem strange to the modern reader in a democratic society that a group of socialists could be championing freedom and attempting to overthrow oppression. Whether right or wrong, the Fabians did not believe capitalists were in error in their desire for a society characterized by freedom for all; they simply believed that capitalism could not accomplish that goal. Only their version of socialism could do that, they would argue.

What is the purpose of expounding these links to the Fabian Society? Is Rowling really a Fabian? Or might these links to early Fabians be mere coincidence of names? A few points weigh in favor Rowling being a Fabian gradualist.

Rowling has not made her political opinions unknown. After all, she did donate $1.83 million to the Labour Party – the political party which the Fabian Society helped found ("Reuters Entertainment Summary," September 22, 2008).

Her hero is Jessica Mitford, who was also a supporter of the Labour Party contra the British Fascists. Rowling calls Mitford "a self-taught socialist" (Fraser, "Harry and Me," November 2002). She named one of her daughters after Mitford, and interestingly, her love of Mitford is yet another nexus point for Rowling's thinking: the blend of her love of the classics with her political philosophy. In a review of Mitford's letters for *The Telegraph*, Rowling makes a point of noting in the opening paragraph that she learned about Mitford at the age of 14 from her great aunt, "who taught classics and approved of a thirst for knowledge" ("The First It Girl," November 26, 2006). It would be difficult indeed to argue that politically,

Rowling is anything other than a socialist, and that her understanding of both her Christian faith and her classics studies contribute to that political belief.

But she's not a Marxist, revolutionary socialist. She is most definitely a Fabian gradualist.

Rowling's set-up of the house-elf dilemma and the contrasting Hermione/Dumbledore responses to house-elf enslavement reveals a belief in gradualism. Consider her response to a question about Hermione's crusade to liberate the house-elves:

> Hermione, with the best of intentions, becomes quite self-righteous. My heart is entirely with her as she goes through this. She develops her political conscience. My heart is completely with her. But my brain tells me, which is a growing-up thing, that in fact she blunders towards the very people she's trying to help. She offends them. She's not very sensitive…. She thinks it's so easy. It's part of what I was saying before about the growing process, of realizing you don't have quite as much power as you think you might have and having to accept that. Then you learn that it's hard work to change things and that it doesn't happen overnight. Hermione thinks she's going to lead them to glorious rebellion in one afternoon and then finds out the reality is very different, but that was fun to write. ("J.K. Rowling Interview" CBCNewsWorld 2000)

This is Fabian thinking start to finish. The goal is noble and right; the methodology is entirely wrong, because it places the "cause" over the oppressed people themselves. More than that, Hermione attempts to solve the problem without any inward change in the either people who oppress the house-elves, or in the house-elves themselves.

The house-elves under Dumbledore's Headmastership at Hogwarts is an illustration of this. His treatment of the house-elves represents a slow-moving, transitional period for their kind, embracing a sensitive stance toward their psychological slavery, respecting their freedom of choice while allowing them to find their own desire and voice to work towards a time of greater freedom. Dumbledore doesn't lead a revolution like Hermione wants to do; he allows the change to happen slowly. He respects their free will choice to work while providing an atmosphere in which they are not required to submit to certain aspects of the house-elves' enslavement.

Dumbledore as Fabius Maximus

In the character of Albus Dumbledore we can find continuing evidence that the classics, Fabian gradualism, and a Christian social vision are the main ingredients in Rowling's political soup. Just because Dumbledore refused the position of Minister three times doesn't mean he was not a political figure. He held two very high-ranking positions: Supreme Mugwump of the International Confederation of Wizards and Chief Warlock of the Wizengamot. These two positions make sense, given Dumbledore's concerns: justice and international cooperation. But what exactly had Dumbledore done with those positions of influence? Fandom has been rife with complaints that Dumbledore did not use his political power to affect any lasting change. Indeed, some analyses of Dumbledore sound eerily similar to the Death Eater Amycus Carrow's charge against the headmaster on the Astronomy Tower: "Always the same, weren't yeh, Dumby, talking and doing nothing, nothing" (*Prince* 594). Popular Potter commentator Joyce Odell, known as "Red Hen" in Potter fandom, is representative of this position:

> Albus Dumbledore is one of the very biggest (non-chocolate!) frogs in the very small puddle which is the British wizarding world. And from what we saw in OotP it is clear that the British wizarding world is hopelessly *corrupt*. And it has *continued* to be so. On. His. Watch.
>
> Dumbledore is not a visionary outsider attempting to redress wrongs. He is the quintessential *insider* with his own clique of devoted followers, and he's had *decades* to work with them, from the inside of the system, and *this* is the result. ("Case in Point: Albus Dumbledore")

Dumbledore as Fabius Maximus of the Wizarding World is a better explanation than this. As noted previously, Frank Podmore named the Fabian Society after the Roman dictator and general who orchestrated the victory over Hannibal's invading armies. Fabius's strategy, which met with significant criticism, opposition, and even insubordination, ended up wearing down Hannibal and forcing him to retreat in the long run.

Rowling is likely familiar not only with the Fabians, but with Fabius himself, for she read Plutarch in her classics studies; as noted above, Rowling chose Plutarch's quote about inward achievements changing outward reality for her 2008 Harvard commencement speech. It is from Plutarch's *Lives* that we learn the most about Fabius. His "Life of Fabius" describes the methods of the man after whom the Fabian Society named itself, and we find much in common with Dumbledore. Consider, for example, Plutarch's description of Fabius's strategy against Hannibal:

> In this manner Fabius, having given the people better heart for the future, by making them believe that the gods took their side, *for his own part placed his whole confidence in himself,* believing that the gods bestowed victory and good fortune by the instrumentality of valour and of prudence; and thus prepared he set forth to oppose Hannibal, not with intention to fight him, *but with the purpose of wearing out and wasting the vigour of his arms* by lapse of time, of meeting his want of resources by superior means, by large numbers the smallness of his forces. (emphasis added)

Dumbledore is like Fabius in two respects here: his "confidence in himself" and his method in the war against Voldemort. Concerning the former, it should first be noted that Dumbledore does place trust in Harry, Ron, and Hermione to be able to decipher his plan and follow through; it should also be noted that Dumbledore *lacks* confidence in himself where he recognizes his own weakness, e.g., temptation to power. Nevertheless, no one knows the whole plan except Dumbledore – not even Snape or Harry, the two most vital elements. Dumbledore's plan is known only to him, and he trusts no one else with the entirety of the information. "For his own part he placed his whole confidence in himself."

Concerning methodology, the circumstances are vastly different, but as with Fabius, only Dumbledore knew that confronting Voldemort in open combat – which combat Dumbledore surely would have won – would not have ultimately defeated Voldemort. All Voldemort's resources – his horcruxes – had to be exhausted before the victory could be won. Instead, Dumbledore delayed and put the right pieces into place to rid Voldemort of his horcruxes and then deal with him for good.

Dumbledore was also much like Fabius in his patience with those who opposed him. Plutarch wrote of Fabius:

> The enemies of Fabius thought they had sufficiently humiliated and subdued him by raising Minucius to be his equal in authority; but they mistook the temper of the man, who looked upon their folly as not his loss, but like Diogenes, who, being told that some persons derided him, made answer, "But I am not derided," meaning that only those were really insulted on whom such insults made an impression.

Consider *Order of the Phoenix* in particular. Dumbledore is derided throughout the course of the book by the majority of the Wizarding World. He is considered either delusional or a power-seeking menace for his proclamation of Voldemort's return. But none of this was internalized by Dumbledore himself. The derision did not steer him off course in the least. Fudge greatly "mistook the temper of the man."

Ennius summed up Fabius's legacy in his *Annals:* "One man, by delaying, restored the state to us." Dumbledore's legacy is the same. While many criticized his methods, Book 7 demonstrated that he had put all the right plans in place. Frank Podmore made one of the most important early Fabian statements, underscoring his reason for choosing Fabius as the group's patron saint, so to speak: "For the right moment you must wait, as Fabius did most patiently, when warring against Hannibal, though many censured his delays; but when the time comes you must strike hard, as Fabius did, or your waiting will be in vain and fruitless" (quoted in Colbert 190-91). While many censured Dumbledore's delays, he patiently waited, and Harry Potter was Dumbledore's "right moment to strike."

Indeed, as Ennius said of Fabius Maximus, so it could be said of Albus Dumbledore: one man, by delaying, restored the Wizarding World to us. That's a gigantic claim, and likely to be rebuffed by criticism of Dumbledore's methods; he was "Machievellian," Rowling claims (Adler). The charge that "Harry was his puppet," made by Rowling herself, is somewhat surprising. What choice, exactly, did Dumbledore – or Harry – have? Dumbledore did not create the Harry-Horcrux. Harry had to face his own death in order to bring Voldemort down. This was a non-negotiable, as defeating Voldemort was of the utmost priority. While arguments could be made on either side of the question of whether or not Dumbledore should have told Harry *sooner*, that is hardly the point. Dumbledore delayed in striking Voldemort down previously, because he suspected that Voldemort had been dabbling in Horcruxes. He delayed in communicating everything to Harry in order to set the perfect plan in place for Voldemort's downfall, so that all Voldemort's resources would be exhausted, and he would be able to be finished. But whether or not Harry would be put in the place of having to choose his own death was inevitable, not a Machiavellian move on his part. And keeping Snape out of the loop makes perfect sense; if Voldemort ever began to suspect Snape's allegiance to Dumbledore, Snape could not have the knowledge of the Harry-Horcrux inside him. Nor was Dumbledore necessarily lying to Snape, using him, as Snape accused; for even Lily would have known and accepted what Harry had to do. "You've been so brave," were Lily's words when she was summoned by the Stone as Harry walked to his death (*Hallows* 699).

Libertarian Elements

There are Rowling's actual political views, and then there are the *Harry Potter* stories themselves. Here the reader gets two interesting nuggets in one package – two opposing views of the political outlook of *Harry Potter*, and they're based on two different kinds of reading. The first view, which has just been expounded, takes very seriously the author's intentions and personal viewpoints when writing a text. If Rowling is a socialist, then the political foundation of her series is socialist. It would be difficult indeed to argue that Rowling is really a libertarian in disguise, and that because of her own bad experiences with government as a struggling, single mother, she therefore believes all big government to be bad.

The second view, which follows, considers the text itself the authority. While there is plenty of Fabian gradualism throughout the series, as we've already seen, there is hardly a hint of the idea that government is very much good for anything in the first place. In other words, as Benjamin H. Barton has said, "Rowling may do more for libertarianism[3] than anyone since John Stuart Mill" ("Half-Crazed" 1526).

What is libertarianism? Barton summarizes its two foundational principles:

> The libertarian movement relies upon two interrelated concepts to recruit: (a) "[t]hat government is best which governs least;" and (b) self-reliance and respect of individual rights should be paramount. (1537)

How can we possibly have gone from Fabian socialism to free market capitalism and still be talking about the same series of books? The Fabians did not embrace these libertarian principles, but rather repudiated the "Administrative Nihilism" of what they called anarchic individualism, the result of the Industrial Revolution's "massive deregulation of the economy and of manufacturers" (Webb, I.1.15 – I.1.21). In short, the radical individualism and commitment to free market capitalism of the libertarians does not jive with Fabian socialism; they believed that while tyranny was the oppression of the rulers over the people, capitalism was the oppression of the wealthy over the poor. Now, since John Stuart Mill eventually became an economic socialist, the Fabian founders might not be too upset with Barton's comparison. Sydney Webb would probably argue that a libertarian Harry would eventually end up a socialist anyway ("Historical" I.1.49 – I.1.52). Indeed, there is very little upon which Fabians and libertarians could agree.

Nevertheless, despite the obvious contradiction here, the *Harry Potter* stories themselves have plenty of material to make a libertarian happy. Barton summarizes the message about government coming from the *Harry Potter* stories:

> In a nutshell, Rowling has very little use for central government, and through satire and later, darker commentaries, draws a portrait of government as a non-democratic, inefficient, and frequently, a flatly dishonest bureaucracy. ("Miserable Ministry" 441)

Andrew P. Morris concludes similarly:

> The Ministry of Magic regulates cauldron bottoms, organizes wizard tournaments, and is run by the bumbling and officious Cornelius Fudge. It does not catch, or even seem to slow down, Lord Voldemort's many attempts to return to power. Indeed, it does not seem to perform any functions critical to everyday life.
>
> More importantly, the state is not even an essential ally in the battle against evil. (479)

Indeed, the Ministry seems entirely incapable of doing anything right, even in the rare instance that they're trying to do the right thing. Barton catalogues the things done by the Ministry:

- tortured children for lying
- designed its prison specifically to suck all life and hope out of the inmates
- placed citizens in that prison without a hearing
- ordered the death penalty without a trial
- allowed the powerful, rich or famous to control policy
- selectively prosecuted crimes (the powerful go unpunished and the unpopular face trumped-up charges)
- conducted criminal trials without defense counsel

- used truth serum to force confessions
- maintained constant surveillance over all citizens
- offered no elections and no democratic lawmaking process
- controlled the press ("Half-Crazed" 1523-24)

That's a rough list, and Barton wrote it before *Deathly Hallows!* With that book, we could add more of the same, along blatantly racist policies and the almost complete silencing of all opposition. Even prior to *Deathly Hallows,* when at least in name the Ministry is not under the direct influence of Voldemort, they bungle everything up. From their pathetic attempts to make the Wizarding community feel safe through instructional leaflets to their terribly unjust policies of holding innocent people to make it look like they're doing something, the more power the Ministry takes, the more foolish they look.

There's even economic material in play for the libertarian reader of *Harry Potter.* The Weasley twins' entrepreneurial venture with their private small business, Weasley's Wizard Wheezes, is meant not only to be seen as a glowing success, but as a vindication of their brilliance, despite not getting good grades in school. Percy's report on cauldron bottom thickness is ridiculed by the twins, and it's easily interpreted as a jab at absurd over-regulation by a government that has assumed too much power and has too much time on its hands.

Dumbledore seems to be something of both a Fabian and a libertarian. Certainly, he is the "Fabius Maximus" of the war against Voldemort. In patiently waiting and putting the pieces into place, he brought about not just a temporary victory over Voldemort, but a decisive and final victory. "Dumbledore the Delayer" would be a fine nickname for him; for though Voldemort was afraid of him, and Dumbledore would more than likely have won a duel as he did against Grindelwald, that would have done little more than delay yet another rebirth, and future accompanying terror. He is likewise a "Fabius Maximus" when it comes to social change; he believes that hearts and minds must be changed over time, and that in the end a greater victory will be won in this way.

But on several other counts, he's much more libertarian-minded – a man who, despite having tremendous power, influence, and authority, thinks it's best to leave people to make their own choices, *whatever they are* (whereas the Fabians want to *influence* people to *want* and *choose* socialism in particular). Dumbledore's willingness to let people under his charge live and be free – despite potentially negative consequences – is evident in several points of the story.   Right from the beginning, he makes a choice about Harry's life that is questioned: he leaves him at the Dursleys.

> "I've come to bring Harry to his aunt and uncle. They're the only family he has left now."
>
> "You don't mean -- you can't mean the people who live here?" cried Professor McGonagall, jumping to her feet and pointing at number four. "Dumbledore -- you can't. I've been watching them all day. You couldn't find two people who are less like us. And they've got this son -- I saw him kicking his mother all the way up the street, screaming for sweets. Harry Potter come and live here!" (*Stone* 13)

Dumbledore knew the kind of life into which he was sending Harry. He knew that Harry would be neglected and abused; but somehow he also knew that Harry would have the resilience to make it.   In other words, Dumbledore knew that he could not micromanage Harry's life to keep him from pain, and that to do so would deprive him of many important life-shaping experiences.   Dumbledore's penchant for doing this shows up again in the same book.   Reflecting on his showdown with Voldemort over the Philosopher's Stone, the trio have the following conversation about Dumbledore's plan in the whole thing:

> "D'you think he meant you to do it?" said Ron. "Sending you your father's cloak and everything?"
>
> "Well, " Hermione exploded, "if he did -- I mean to say that's terrible -- you could have been killed."
>
> "No, it isn't," said Harry thoughtfully. "He's a funny man, Dumbledore. I think he sort of wanted to give me a chance. I think he knows more or less everything that goes on here, you know. I reckon he had a pretty good idea we were going to try, and instead of stopping us, he just taught us enough to help. I don't think it was an accident he let me find out how the mirror worked. It's almost like he thought I had the right to face Voldemort if I could...." (*Stone* 302)

The Dumbledore vs. Hermione contrast is set up way back here at the conclusion to Book 1.   Hermione, social crusader and moral legislator, is appalled at the idea that Dumbledore would allow Harry the freedom to fight Voldemort.   His safety should have been micromanaged by the Headmaster; Harry was not ready for that sort of responsibility, in Hermione's view. Dumbledore, on the other hand, had faith in an eleven-year-old boy. It's not difficult to see a small-government libertarian vs. big-government socialist in the Dumbledore/Hermione contrast.

J.K. Rowling, reflecting on Dumbledore's loneliness after the release of *Half-Blood Prince* said:

> I see him as isolated, and a few people have said to me rightly I think, that he is detached. My sister said to me in a moment of frustration, it was when Hagrid was shut up in his house after Rita Skeeter had published that he was a half-breed, and my sister said to me, "Why didn't Dumbledore go down earlier, why didn't Dumbledore go down earlier?" I said he really had to let Hagrid stew for a while and see if he was going to come out of this on his own because if he had come out on his own he really would have been better. "Well he's too detached, he's too cold, it's like you," she said!" [Laughter] By which she meant that where she would immediately rush in and I would maybe stand back a little bit and say, "Let's wait and see if he can work this out." I wouldn't leave him a week. I'd leave him maybe an afternoon. But she would chase him into the hut. (Anelli and Spartz, 2005)

It might seem strange to disagree with Rowling about her own character, but it seems just as likely that Dumbledore has faith in Hagrid. After all, he had no problem making his way down to the hut later in the year when Buckbeak was going to be killed. "Let's wait and see if he can work this out" is part of being libertarian, at least philosophically; one does not micromanage, but rather, lets a person grow and learn to work through struggles. It's the "self-reliance" that we noted above was one of the two main points of libertarian philosophy.

When it comes to how he runs his school, Albus Dumbledore is once again libertarian-minded. Where, precisely, is Dumbledore throughout most of the series? He's hardly ever prominently on the scene at Hogwarts. Dumbledore allows much to go on under his watch that a micromanager would never allow, the pedagogy of Severus Snape being the most obvious example. Rowling was asked about Dumbledore's permitting Snape to teach in a *Barnes & Noble* chat:

> lhhicks99 asks: Why does Professor Dumbledore allow Professor Snape to be so nasty to the students (especially to Harry, Hermione, and Neville)?
>
> jkrowling_bn: Dumbledore believes there are all sorts of lessons in life...

jkrowling_bn: horrible teachers like Snape are one of them! ("Barnes and Noble & Yahoo! chat")

This is a striking claim, because Snape's bullying is quite emotionally abusive at times. Hermione's teeth. Neville (his toad, and in *Prisoner*). And you will notice the question is not, "Why does Dumbledore allow Snape to *teach* at Hogwarts?" but "Why does he allow him to be nasty to students?" In other words, why doesn't Dumbledore protect the students from Snape's bullying behavior? Dumbledore's basic strategy as Headmaster is to have faith in the development of the students themselves. He does not intervene in the classrooms, set teaching standards, or micromanage curriculum. There are no lesson plan submissions, scheduled observations, or annual performance evaluations. Dumbledore believes that students' learning to cope with bad teachers is part of life. Watching his teaching style with Harry in *Half-Blood Prince,* it's obvious that not a single teacher at Hogwarts who has been there for any length of time teaches according to Dumbledore's style. But Dumbledore does not mandate one style of teaching. While Rowling offers scathing critique of government-mandated, standardized, exam-based education through her portrayal of the Ministry and some of the Hogwarts teachers, Dumbledore would not use such methods. None of this proves Dumbledore would vote libertarian; we are, after all, talking about the way he runs a school. But the libertarian-minded tendencies are there.

Concerning progress toward social justice also, while being in many ways a Fabian gradualist, Dumbledore shows libertarian tendencies. He clearly believes house-elf enslavement is wrong, but almost the entirety of the Wizarding World – even the "good guys," including members of the Order – thinks differently. Dumbledore wants to see change happen because people – wizards and house-elves – *freely choose* change, not because it's forced by the government. Wizarding dominance over house-elves is entirely immoral, Dumbledore believes, but then there's the dilemma: house-elves also have a will, and most house-elves want their enslavement. It's a horrifying picture, and if Rowling had done it with humans, we'd be appalled. By writing the comical but sad house-elves,[4] she gives us an extreme caricature to make the point about how an oppressed group begins to take on the identity forced upon them by their oppressors.

Dumbledore knows that all of this is very complex, and he's not going to pretend it's easy. Change will take a long time; hearts and minds of both the Wizarding community and the house-elf community will have to change. So what does Dumbledore do? He creates an atmosphere in which house-elves are permitted to do what they *want* to do (work as servants at Hogwarts), but are not bound by the typical rules (they may speak ill of Dumbledore; they may have pay and vacation if they want it). He refuses to insult their own choices, just as he refuses to let Sirius' treatment of Kreacher off the hook, just an hour after his death, and in the face of his grieving godson, no less.

Dumbledore is always set in stark contrast to the methods and beliefs of the Ministry of Magic. There are significant aspects Rowling's portrayal of government which lends the series toward a libertarian reading of government. The incompetence of the Ministry was chronicled earlier. The only exception to the ridicule of government seems to be Arthur Weasley; his Muggle Protection Act is looked on favorably by Dumbledore. It's likely true that Rowling sees bigger government as a good thing as long as good people inhabit its positions; but this is not to be found in the *Harry Potter* series itself apart from Arthur. And even so, it might be argued that the Muggle Protection Act is hardly outside the realm of libertarian political philosophy, for it does little more than protect Muggles from attack by Wizards. In essence, it places a firm limit on magical power to dominate others, which is an important Libertarian idea. Furthermore, it does not infringe on civil liberties as far as we know, and it falls under the category of national protection – by way of non-interventionism![5]

If this is an accurate reading of the series itself, then there is some contradiction of messages – Fabian vs. libertarian. None of this is to assume that Rowling would identify herself politically as a libertarian, and there are no deliberate links to libertarian political philosophers or activists as there are with the Fabians. Nevertheless, both Fabian and libertarian elements are evident in the series.

Dumbledore is something of a Fabian and something of a libertarian – which makes him something of a contradiction. But perhaps not as much as one might think (there is, in fact, a strain of libertarianism which embraced Fabian methodology called "Fabian Libertarianism[6]" – the belief that libertarianism can gain a foothold over time, gradually). Dumbledore wants to see authentic, lasting change come to society, but he knows enough about the temptations of power to avoid it himself. Though he may believe that a better person, like Harry Potter, could do well with power, he ultimately sees the micro-management of people to be a very harmful thing. Dumbledore shares J.R.R. Tolkien's political philosophy. Compare Dumbledore's statement on power with Tolkien's:

Dumbledore: "It is a curious thing, Harry, but perhaps those who are best suited to power are those who have never sought it. Those who, like you, have leadership thrust upon them, and take up the mantle because they must, and find to their own surprise that they wear it well." (*Hallows* 718).

Tolkien: The most improper job of any man, even saints, is bossing other men. Not one in a million is fit for it, and least of all those who seek the opportunity." (in a letter to his son Christopher in 1943)

Tolkien is far less optimistic than Dumbledore, but the essence of their statements are the same: power is a terrible temptation, and the ones who are drawn to seek it are likely to abuse their powers oppress others. Dumbledore, even skeptical of a belief that seeks to legislate good intentions, knows that people need to experience grief, pain, frustration, and even bullying. He'd prefer, of course, a world in which none of that happens. But you can't legislate pain out of existence. Dumbledore is libertarian-minded because he knows, first hand, the corrupting potential of power.

Andrew P. Morris summarizes why the libertarian element is so crucial to the plot and morality of *Harry Potter:*

A world which allows moral calibration is a world in which individuals are free. They are not able to rely on the state or grownups to solve their moral dilemmas for them nor can they put problems off on others. One crucial thing readers can thus learn from the Harry Potter books is that moral choices require liberty. (480)

The greatest vindication for libertarianism is in the character of Harry Potter himself, for in the end, the young hero who stands up to the abusive Ministry makes his own choices as a private citizen to fight evil. No government helps him along the way, and indeed, he has to rescue innocents from the government at one point in the story. It is the courageous actions of individuals that wins the day against Voldemort.

No matter the political persuasion of the reader with regard to libertarianism, one lesson can be drawn from this that all can agree upon, even where political philosophy differs: heroes and heroines need to have liberty in order to make truly courageous and moral choices. That's a lesson from *Harry Potter* worth taking into our political discussions. Indeed, the freedom to transform one's character and make moral choices is a common element among Fabianism, libertarianism, and a Christian social vision.

Fabianism, Libertarianism, and Christian Social Vision

Character transformation – or transfiguration – is one of the fundamental themes of the *Harry Potter* stories, so it should be no surprise that it's fundamental to Rowling's social vision.   As noted previously, Rowling quoted Plutarch at the 2008 Harvard commencement speech, and that quote is telling: "What we achieve inwardly will change outer reality." This is the fundamental insight of Rowling's social vision, and it brings together the three key threads: Fabianism, libertarianism, and Christian social vision.

The London School of Economics and Political Science, which was started by four early Fabians, notes the following:

> The Fabian Society grew out of the Fellowship of the New Life in 1883, the object of which had been 'The cultivation of a perfect character in each and all.' Members of the Fabian Society also argued that '*the end of the State…is, in fact, the development of character.*' Not only was character – national, individual, moral – a Victorian preoccupation, but its development in the individual was perceived by social reformers as a form of liberation from oppression. Cultivating character involved education and achieving bias-free judgement, and social reform aimed to build a society where altered political and social circumstances improved the conditions of those whom society could and should help. ("The Fabian Society" http://www.lse.ac.uk/resources/LSEHistory/fabian.htm)

Character transformation should be the business of the State, according to the Fabians, and this puts them at severe methodological odds with libertarians. But there is some common ground in the contradiction. Libertarians are not going to legislate morality, unless it has to do with physical protection of a nation's citizens, primarily because freedom to choose good or bad for oneself is a fundamental moral and human right in the first place.   Nevertheless, for any positive social change to occur in a libertarian framework, individual character transformation *must* take place, for the government will not be stepping in to legislate morality – apart from those things that keep people safe. Individuals need character transformation in order to choose the good for themselves.

Taking the common ground on the matter of character development – that in both cases, any change that comes about must occur in the hearts and minds of individuals first – the political key to the social vision of the *Harry Potter* series can be discovered. Change happens by the slow influence, the changing of hearts and minds and development of character (Fabian); the freedom of individuals to make their own choices must be protected in order for societal change to be authentic and not forced by people in power (libertarian). And transformation comes through the transfiguration of the soul from selfishness to self-sacrificial love (Christian). This is a succinct summary of the political philosophy underlying the *Harry Potter* series.

Fabian methodology and libertarian philosophy work together nicely in the Christian social vision presented in the *Harry Potter* series. The transformation of character is a central part of Christian spirituality, as is the need for the free will of a human to act in accordance with the self-sacrificial, compassionate will of God. St. Paul's beliefs and methodology about slavery and gender issues in the first century are primary examples. St. Paul clearly believed that in the eyes of God, there is no inequality: "There is neither Jew nor Greek, slave nor free, male nor female, for you are all one in Christ Jesus" (Galatians 3:28). At the same time, he did not lead early Christians in a radical, revolutionary overthrow of social mores. Instead, within the existing sociological framework, St. Paul initiated a subtle subversion of oppressive norms. Notice his carefully chosen words to slaves and masters:

> Slaves, obey your earthly masters with respect and fear, and with sincerity of heart, just as you would obey Christ. Obey them not only to win their favor when their eye is on you, but like slaves of Christ, doing the will of God from your heart. Serve wholeheartedly, as if you were serving the Lord, not men, because you know that the Lord will reward everyone for whatever good he does, whether he is slave or free. And *masters, treat your slaves in the same way.* Do not threaten them, since you know that he who is both their Master and yours is in heaven, and there is no favoritism with him. (Ephesians 6:5-9, NIV)

Rather than overthrow the existing, sinful social order, St. Paul calls on individual slaves and masters to live in a Christlike, self-sacrificial way toward each other, effectively undermining the oppressive nature of the relationship. Over time, hearts and minds could and would be changed; in the meantime, the gospel would do its transformative work in individuals and communities.

St. Paul created the same kind of situation with husbands and wives a few verses earlier. Wives, in standard first century house codes, were ordered to "submit" to their husbands, and Paul retained this language

(Eph. 5:22). But he coupled it with a call for mutual submission amongst all believers (5:21) and a command for husbands to lay down their entire lives in self-sacrificial love for their wives, just as Christ did for the church (5:25) – again, effectively subverting any societal subjugation along gender lines (subsequent church abuse and misapplication of these verses notwithstanding). Why did St. Paul choose this course of action? Because he knew that revolutionary political overthrow and legislated morality held no power for lasting change; only the self-sacrificial gospel held that power. Instead of large-scale political revolution, St. Paul looked for gradual change rooted in gospel-centered character transformation.

So, with the knowledge in hand that social evils are battled by the self-sacrificial, willing work of individuals and communities, and that for real and lasting change to occur, hearts and minds must change, we press forward and begin to explore two important and parallel trains of thought: the social injustices of the Wizarding World, and their counterparts in our own "Muggle" world.

Chapter 12 Notes

1   And, indeed, it takes positions on sexuality that are contrary to traditional Christian morality.

2   Emmeline Pankhurst only remained with the Fabian Society for 10 years. After joining in 1890 with her husband Richard, she left the party in protest in 1900, because of the Society did not officially oppose the Boer War.

3   The reader will note that I'm deliberately using the lower-case "l" for "libertarianism." There is, indeed, a Libertarian Party in the U.S., but I'm referring to the general principles of libertarianism on the whole, held both by small-government conservatives who call themselves libertarians (without belonging to the LP), as well as official members of the Libertarian Party.

4   I take issue with one particular house-elf moment from Rowling – that of their strange, kitchen-knife-wielding behavior in the Battle of Hogwarts. I write about this in detail in the next chapter.

5   Non-interventionism is the belief that it is not the moral obligation of a sovereign nation to meddle in the affairs of another country, and that doing so results in unintended consequences which turn out to be bad for the nations involved. While Dumbledore calls for international cooperation, this is not outside the realm of libertarianism, non-interventionist foreign policy believes in the importance of friendship with all nations, but "entangling alliances" with none.

6   The belief does not abandon Libertarian principles in favor of Fabian ones, but embraces Fabian methodology for implementing Libertarian ideas. To an extent, this is what is being launched in the current "Ron Paul Revolution," a movement inspired by the Libertarian-Republican candidate after which it is named. The goal is to slowly but steadily "Take back the GOP," and in doing so, win a wide variety of voters through Libertarian principles and eventually downsize American government and move back toward an originalist interpretation of the Constitution. Paleo-libertarians such as the late Murray Rothbard reject the notion, believing that Fabian methodology works for socialists because rulers want more power anyway, so they'll naturally follow a socialist agenda, whereas Libertarianism requires less and less governmental power and authority, and it's therefore harder to convince the politicians, however slowly, that this is the way to go.

Chapter Thirteen

How Half-Bloods Became Purebloods
(and what that says about race in the wizarding world)

Nobody who ever fought to separate people into superiors and
inferiors ever came up with the novel idea of categorizing their own
into the ranks of the inferiors.

~ Adam-Troy Castro, "From Azkaban to Abu Ghraib," pg. 121

The new statue at the Ministry of Magic, set up by Pius Thicknesse
and the cohorts of Voldemort, is an appalling example of racism.
Wizarding dominance, literally built on the backs of Muggles, captioned
with "Magic is Might," points to a directly racist agenda: Voldemort
intends to ascend to power by subjugating Muggles, Muggle-born witches
and wizards, and anyone who will stand in his way. It also stands as
something of a materialistic agenda: magic is no longer something that
incarnates love, but something that oppresses; in short, it's the attempted
victory of Voldemort's kind of magic over Dumbledore's. But perhaps the
most shocking aspect of the new statue is that it was erected in the context
of the *existing* Ministry (after the death of Rufus Scrimgeour); Voldemort
was not Minister of Magic. While a puppet minister was in control, the
same staff that had inhabited their positions for years either sat idly by or
encouraged the building of the statue, as well as the building of the racist
agenda. Those who were supposedly opposed to Voldemort were quite
ready to carry his agenda.

The new statue was so easily accepted, because it was simply one more
natural ideological step in the direction of the previous statue, destroyed
in *Order of the Phoenix,* which depicted the magical brethren adoring the
wizard – which Dumbledore called "a lie." These two statues tell lies of
Wizarding superiority – over Muggles and over all other magical brethren.
These lies have parallels in our own world as well, and they open the doors
for important conversations on the problem of racism.

Wizards vs. Muggles

Wizards vs. Muggles is obviously the first area of prejudice we see in the Wizarding World. This is a complex matter. Prior to *Deathly Hallows*, it could have been argued that Wizards vs. Muggles was peripheral to the story, but Book 7 changes the way we look at the entire series.

Some, particularly anti-Potter fundamentalists (but not limited to them), have criticized Rowling for painting all Muggles with a broad, prejudiced brush, thereby being guilty of the very prejudice she seeks to dismantle.[1] This is an unfortunate reading. Dumbledore, the most prejudice-free character in the series, the "epitome of goodness," and Harry's moral model, is described as a "muggle-lover," and he clearly is concerned, at the end of *Chamber of Secrets*, about anything that might hinder Arthur Weasley's "Muggle Protection Act." We're also intended to think well of Hermione's parents, who appear to be models of progressive thinking, based on the kind of social conscience developing in Hermione.

What makes the Wizards vs. Muggles issue complex is that it's an opportunity to look at things from the point of view of the oppressed, which is a difficult thing for the privileged to do. In other words, Rowling has accomplished a profound feat, at least with her readers who belong to any sort of privileged, dominant culture: she's put us on the side of the oppressed group! This leads to interesting analyses that carry over into our own Muggle discussions. Memory modification, for example, is a difficult issue: does it constitute oppression of Muggles? How can it, when it is absolutely necessary for the survival of the Wizarding World? After all, the Wizarding World is in hiding because of the oppression of Muggles! Without hiding, and without memory modification, the Wizarding World would be found out. Despite their magical powers, the miniscule Wizarding World would stand no chance against vast Muggle armies. Secrecy is absolutely necessary for the survival of the Wizarding World.

Yet it's the Wizarding World's combination of secrecy and power t makes them so potentially dangerous to the Muggle world, should Muggle-haters take control. In a most extreme example, recall Bob 's visit to the House of Gaunt. Morphin was to be brought up on of using magic on a Muggle. We see that even the great Albus lore was at one point lured by the idea that Wizarding power sed to rule over Muggles. It is complex, and no fixed solution ma will be offered here; we do well to let its difficulty sink into our thinking before rushing to solutions. Yet, what Rowling has accomplished in making us relate to the dilemmas of an oppressed group opens up many avenues for conversation. Some of her most important commentary, however, is to be found in the divisions within the magical world itself.

Purebloods, Half-Bloods, and Muggle-borns

The Pureblood, Half-Blood, and Muggle-born conflict is clearly the central power story of the series. It is the fundamental rift in the Wizarding World, and the backstory to the entire conflict at Hogwarts and beyond. What is told in the 7 years of the series is a story founded upon the division, along the lines of views of "blood-status," between two former best friends: Godric Gryffindor and Salazar Slytherin.

What we find in the Harry Potter books is a fairly nuanced view of racism that even finds some similarities with current progressive thinking on the issue. There have been complaints about how Rowling addresses race in the series. But we can take a look at the series through this lens and find some profound insight into the problem of racism.

There is, of course, the standard criticisms of bigotry. Once Voldemort has taken over the Ministry, there's a very bigoted statue put in the place of the old one: Wizards sitting on thrones made up of Muggles. It doesn't get more blatantly prejudiced than that! There is a significant amount of blatant prejudice in the series – quite obvious when it comes from the mouth of Voldemort, less obvious, but still rather clear, when coming from the mouths of folks like Ron and Hagrid, who both hold wizarding prejudices (as it relates to house-elves, for example), while being part of "othered" groups (poor and half-giant, respectively) . Yet, for the most part, as it relates to the question of Wizards vs. Muggles, or even Purebloods vs. Muggle-borns, there is a general perception in the Wizarding World that this kind of prejudice is a bad thing. Why, then, does the racism persist?

Clearly, there is still prejudice, despite it being, in general, a social taboo to be prejudiced. Horace Slughorn is the perfect example of this. He has evidently accepted some deeply ingrained prejudices against Muggle-borns, based on his conversation with Harry in which he seems a little too surprised at a Muggle-born's magical mastery. "You mustn't think I'm prejudiced," Slughorn protests (*Prince* 71). We'd all say that, wouldn't we? Because it's quite virtuous not to be prejudiced, and our social conscience tells us that prejudice is wrong. And the argument could be made successfully that he's not really all that prejudiced. After all, as long as a Muggle-born works hard and achieves high marks and does well in the Wizarding World, Slughorn is quite impressed with the individual. He isn't so prejudiced against Muggle-borns that he deliberately fails to recognize excellence in someone like Hermione. In that case, he's far beyond the Malfoys, many Slytherins, and the Ministry under Voldemort's control. And after all, he does fight against Voldemort in the end.

But Slughorn is prejudiced, because he clearly expects wizards with magical blood to be naturally more skilled, and he is surprised to find Muggleborns with tremendous talent. Slughorn, of course, loves his creature comforts. So he's very much willing to accept Muggleborns into the Slug Club, providing that they will get him solid connections in the future. But he doesn't drop his prejudice on principle.

But the presence of wizards like Slughorn does not explain an entire Wizarding World's willingness to move back in the wrong direction concerning race, when bigotry is, on the whole, socially unacceptable (otherwise, Slughorn would have not protested at the idea of being considered prejudiced). How do we explain the perpetuation of racial divisions within a society that has dropped open and outright bigotry? Joyce E. King's notion of "dysconscious racism" is helpful here:

> Dysconsciousness is an uncritical habit of mind (including perceptions, attitudes, assumptions, and beliefs) that justifies inequity and exploitation by accepting the existing order of things as given…. Dysconscious racism is a form of racism that tacitly accepts dominant White norms and privileges. (King 133)

In U.S. culture, there is an incredibly important factor in the social construction and perpetuation of racism that is usually missed by Whites: the fact that racism put Whites at a socio-cultural advantage over members of other races. Whites like myself are used to their advantages; we are so used to them we don't even realize they are White advantages. We legitimize ourselves with the metanarrative of the American Dream, the "myth of meritocracy," i.e., that if we just work hard enough, we'll achieve our dreams, and if you fail, it's because you didn't work hard enough.

Instead of being something that is inherent to human nature, "race" is a social construct. To illustrate the point, note what Kenneth Roberts wrote in 1922:

The American nation was founded and developed by the Nordic race, but if a few more million members of the Alpine, Mediterranean and Semitic races are poured among us, the result must inevitably be a hybrid race of people as worthless and futile as the good-for-nothing mongrels of Central America and Southeastern Europe. (Roberts, in Brodkin 25). [2]

So, race wasn't always black and white, was it? Roberts is referring to ethnic groups now included in the "White" category, who less than a hundred years ago were not "white" enough. The mentality found in this statement is the same kind of thing Slytherin would have said about Wizards marrying Muggles. Indeed, it's the same type of sentiment that opens up *Deathly Hallows*, and it's the motivation for Voldemort's murder of the Muggle Studies teacher, Charity Burbage.

The Kenneth Roberts quote above is taken from Karen Brodkin's work, *How Jews Became White Folks and what that Says about Race in America*, in which she argues based on the fact that not all "whites," in the current use of the term, were always consider "white." There was a time when only folks who looked like the Malfoys (blond haired, blue-eyed, Aryan whites) were considered white. What changed? Brodkin argues that a decisive factor in the assimilation of many European ethnic groups into dominant white culture was the post-WWII GI Bill. The benefits provided to all men – except black men – pushed many European-Americans into the middle class – underscoring the intersectionality of the oppressive "isms" (racism, classism, sexism) and the fact that race constructs shift based on power and privilege, which are, of course, linked to money.

It is interesting to note that by *Deathly Hallows*, there is no more talk of the problem of half-bloods. Any witch or wizard who can prove any magical blood in their family history is acceptable in the Nazi-like, Voldemort-controlled Ministry. Why? If Muggle blood is a problem, why are half-bloods accepted? The answer is really quite simple: the number of purebloods who remain are so few that they would not have the power to maintain their advantage; Ron affirmed as much in *Chamber of Secrets*: "Most wizards these days are half-blood anyway. If we hadn't married Muggles we'd've died out" (116). Hence, "races" were shifted in the public consciousness to maintain pureblood power and advantage.

The lesson here is this: Race is socially constructed. By whom? By the people who are advantaged by the oppression of others. Some of the most important insight into this in our own Muggle world came with

Peggy McIntosh's now well-known essay, "White Privilege: Unpacking the Invisible Knapsack." Ms. McIntosh is a white female who unpacked all of the privileges she had received, without even realizing it, simply because she's white. Without even thinking about it, the norm in America is, quite frankly, that middle class white is considered "normal," and everything else is "different."

Beverly Daniel Tatum gives the following definition to racism:

> Many people use the terms prejudice and racism interchangeably. I do not, and I think it is important to make a distinction. In his book Portraits of White Racism, David Wellman argues convincingly that limiting our understanding of racism to prejudice does not offer a sufficient explanation for the persistence of racism. He defines racism as "a system of advantage based on race." In illustrating this definition, he provides example after example of how Whites defend their racial advantage – access to better schools, housing, jobs – even when they do not embrace overtly prejudicial thinking. Racism cannot be fully explained as an expression of prejudice alone. (Tatum 7)

Tatum is right on the mark here. People do not subjugate other people for the fun of it; they do so for the purpose of creating some kind of economic advantage for themselves. Once the subjugation is called "evil" in a society, it begins the process of breaking down; but it does not magically go away. Those who have advantage continue to dig their heels in, whether they realize it or not, to maintain that advantage; this happens at personal and institutional levels, and the invisible walls of racism remain long after legislation has been enacted to tear down the walls at a civic level.

A subtle example of institutionalized racism in the Wizarding World – one that maintains pureblood advantage – is the enforcement of the restriction against underage wizardry:

> "So if you're underage and you do magic inside an adult witch or wizard's house, the Ministry won't know?"
>
> "They will certainly be unable to tell who performed the magic," said Dumbledore, smiling slightly at the look of great indignation on Harrys face. "They rely on witch and wizard parents to enforce their offspring's obedience while within their walls." (*Prince* 368)

What makes the enforcement of this law racist is this: by its very nature, it can only be enforced upon Muggle-borns, because it is only in a Muggle-born's home that the Ministry can be sure that it was the underage wizard performing the magic. As such, the Ministry is able to turn a blind eye to underage witches and wizards of magical families practicing over the summer.

While bigoted thinking about blood-status has become something of a cultural taboo, its effects are still potent, even at the institutional level; it is, sadly, all too often the same in our own world.

Wizards vs. Non-human Magical Brethren

We can further consider the problem of wizarding advantage when thinking of the way the various magical brethren have been oppressed. They are forbidden wands, which prevents them from rising to a great power, therefore keeping them in check. The enslavement of the house-elves is an obvious example of oppression in which wizarding advantage that is maintained – even by the "Good Guys" of the series, like Ron and Hagrid – by very racist thinking. In fact, it might be argued, based on the way the majority of the Wizarding World thinks about house-elves, that the social conscience of the Wizarding World is a few hundred years behind our own.

As noted in Chapter Four, many traditionally scary or evil characters are not such in Rowling's world. Giants and werewolves are only on Voldemort's side because, as Dumbledore argues, he is the only one who will treat them with respect and give them the freedom they deserve as beings with souls. In an ironic twist, Cornelius Fudge is entirely unwilling to break ranks with the Dementors, who are Voldemort's "natural ally," while simultaneously not sending "envoys to the giants," whom Dumbledore believes would join with the Wizarding World against Voldemort if they were offered their freedom.

Goblins offer a particularly interesting window into oppressive structures in the Wizarding World. Remaining in the background until *Deathly Hallows*, the reader follows the Wizarding World's basic suspicion of goblins that he was exposed to in Hagrid's initial warnings about them way back in *Philosopher's Stone*. Getting to know Griphook, however, makes the reader have to rethink. After Harry buries Dobby and calls Griphook in to discuss breaking into a Gringott's vault, Griphook will not allow Harry to get the discussion started until making a point: "You are an unusual wizard, Harry Potter" (*Hallows* 486). What makes him so unusual is his willingness to care for, to rescue, and to fully respect other non-human magical brethren.

With Griphook, we get a close look at wizarding oppression from the goblin perspective. Griphook refers to wizards as "wand-carriers" (*Hallows* 488). "The right to carry a wand," Griphoook notes, "has long been contested between wizards and goblins" (488). Ron, ever the voice of passive racism, cites the regular justification that goblins can do magic without wands. This is not the point, however, and Griphook presses forward: "Wizards refuse to share the secrets of wandlore with other magical beings, they deny us the possibility of extending our powers" (488). Ron continues to protest, noting that goblins don't share their knowledge either.

The conversation is highly informative from a standpoint of race conversation. Clearly, the animosity is shared between wizards and goblins, and each have complaints about the other; there are obvious cultural clashes, particularly concerning beliefs about ownership (goblins believe the true owner of an object is its maker, while wizards believe the true owner is the one who paid for the item). But the ones who set the rules, create the laws, and govern relationships is the wizarding community. Non-human magical brethren have no say in such matters, by law, and the wizarding metanarrative, told by the Fountain of Magical Brethren, is that goblins, house-elves, and centaurs *prefer* it that way. It's Dumbledore's "for the greater good" justification all over again. Wizards have been given power and the right to rule, and any oppression along the way is justified, because wizards know what's best for the entire magical community.

Harry tries to interject at this point in the conversation that this issue isn't about "race relations," so to speak. How often this is the default position of the privileged; those for whom power and privilege are the norm rarely see how much race plays a role in every aspect of society. Harry betrays dysconscious racism in his attempt to quell the race discussion, and Griphook rebukes him firmly, noting that the conversation *must* be about these power relationships: "As the Dark Lord becomes ever more powerful, your race is set still more firmly above mine! Gringotts falls under Wizarding rule, house-elves are slaughtered, and who amongst the wand-carriers protests" (488-89)?

This is illustrative of a subtle form of racism, called by Bonilla-Silva "color-blind racism."³ In summary form: the argument is that not talking about race problems, taking a "color-blind" approach to race, will simply ensure that dominant white culture will remain dominant. Norms will be tacitly accepted, stereotypes advanced and embraced, and dysconscious racism encouraged, because people will be *discouraged* from thinking about race for the stated reason that *it is racist* to talk about race at all. If we are unable to talk about lingering race problems for fear of being accused as a racist, or accused of "playing the race card," problems of racism will remain. It's important to note here that it is easy for whites (and for wizards) to simply "turn off" the race discussion. Chris Rice writes about "White blinders," and the commentary is insightful for the discussion at hand:

> Probably the most glaring example of White blinders is the fact that as the majority culture, we don't have to deal with race. We say "I don't see color," but the reality is we don't have to see color. I can walk away from…Black people and the whole mess of race any time I like. I can cross town tomorrow and enter the White world and know I will be treated well and not be denied opportunities because of my color. But my Black friends don't have that option. (116-17)

Harry is able, in his conversation with Griphook, to default to "Wizard blinders," so to speak. For a wizard, it is easy to say, "Let's not talk about race; that's not the point." This is not easy for those who are oppressed. A mere five years after civil rights legislation was passed, Patrick Moynihan wrote in a memo to President Nixon, "The issue of race could benefit from a period of benign neglect."⁴ This is easy for a white man to say; it is most definitely not easy for a black person.

Embracing "Mudblood"

At this point, there is only one member of the human Wizarding community present who has a leg to stand on: Hermione Granger, the "Mudblood." Hermione does a fascinating thing in this moment: She calls *herself* a "Mudblood;" and when Ron protests, she retorts:

> "Mudblood, and proud of it! I've got no higher position under this new order than you have, Griphook! It was me they chose to torture, back at the Malfoys'" (489)!

In White-Black relations in the United States, there is a word that parallels "Mudblood" in Rowling's world: "Nigger." That word has become as vile as any swear word in the U.S., and for a white person to say it of a black person is considered a terrible offense. At the same time, many black folks use it in conversation with each other, referring to each other. To the white on-looker, this is hypocritical. If the word is such an insult, why use it with each other? Whites are fairly critical of this practice; but just as Harry was comfortable trying to skirt the race conversation because of his privileged status as a wizard, so whites are able to entirely miss the point: blacks have taken a word that was hurtful, damaging, and representative of a whole history of oppression, embrace that word and transform it. It's the concept of "naming" that was discussed in Chapter Three. The pain has been named and transformed. This is precisely what Hermione does with the term "Mudblood."

It was Hermione's deliberate embrace of the painful term "Mudblood," and her association with the oppressed that finally convinced Griphook to discuss the matter of breaking into Gringotts. While Harry is, in many ways, becoming as free of prejudice as Dumbledore was, only Hermione can see the difference between prejudice and racism; that difference is about who holds the power and privilege.

The Death of Dobby

The question can be and has been asked: Did J.K. Rowling succeed? Did she leave us a hopeful picture concerning racial justice? There were many complaints about Rowling's handling of racial issues in the mid-series analysis. What did she leave us with after a full series? There are some legitimate complaints. Rowling may have missed a golden opportunity just prior to the Battle of Hogwarts, when Slytherins were told to choose their side and *none* of them, save Slughorn, stayed to fight Voldemort. She gave in to house-elves-as-comic-relief when they joined the Battle of Hogwarts; instead of using their powerful magic, which readers already know they possess, they come slashing at Death Eaters with kitchen utensils. This was a particularly sad missed opportunity for Rowling. Here is the house-elf revolt:

> The house-elves of Hogwarts swarmed into the entrance hall, screaming and waving carving knives and cleavers, and at their head, the locket of Regulus Black bouncing on his chest, was Kreacher, his bullfrog's voice audible even above this din: "Fight! Fight! Fight for my Master, defender of house-elves! Fight the Dark Lord, in the name of brave Regulus! Fight!"

They were hacking and stabbing at the ankles and shins of Death
Eaters their tiny faces alive with malice…. (*Hallows* 734-35)

On first read, it might be a rather humorous scene – until you begin
to think about the power of house-elf magic. They are not subject to
the blocked apparition rules at Hogwarts or anywhere else. Dobby was
powerful enough to stop Lucius Malfoy from harming Harry. Even if it
could be argued that their power was weakened because of their servitude
– kitchen utensils? At the very least, Rowling could have spent a few more
sentences on the house-elves here; imagine, for example, a description of
their apparating and disapparating all over the Great Hall, so quickly that
the Death Eaters couldn't possibly match their agility and attack strategy!
Alas, we get kitchen utensils instead; comic relief won out in a moment of
great opportunity to vindicate the house-elves' unique power. There might
actually be a powerful message even in this: the house-elves are using the
tools of oppression against their subjugators, much in the same way that
Hermione embraced and transformed the term "Mudblood." Still, the
description of the house-elves, including the repeated emphasis on their
"tiny" stature, leans toward the comical and even patronizing. One would
hope to see some real power from the house-elves in this moment.

Yet even with this missed opportunity, Rowling has laid the
groundwork for a future of social justice for house-elves and other magical
brethren. Not all agree with this statement (which I shall support below).
One essayist summarized his complaints this way:

> And then there is the hope for the "And Justice for All" ending (or
> at least a path to a brighter future). It died! It died when Grawp
> was given no leadership role within the population of Giants. It
> died when Remus was killed and left Fenrir as the werewolf leader.
> And it died when Bellatix's knife killed Dobby. And this was the
> cruelest blow of all. Dobby had been, for us, the symbol of potential
> freedom for the house elves and others. Dobby died and with him
> the hope for a bright and shining future for all died with him.
> (eroej_kab)

Alas, this is a sadly mistaken criticism, and it misses the entire point
of the series – to get to the end of the Harry Potter series and think that
death ends hope is to have missed Rowling's greatest lesson. Indeed, the
most significant moment for house-elves, and symbolically for racial justice
issues in the Wizarding World, is not in Kreacher's sudden transformation
or in the house-elf attack on the Death Eaters in the Battle of Hogwarts,

but Dobby's death. This is by far the moment with the most transformative power for the house-elves' future. Dobby's epitaph, created by Harry, is the key to this transformative power: "Here lies Dobby, a Free Elf." One can be sure that Harry will be certain to spread Dobby's story far and wide. It is one of the two most important moments of decision for Harry in the entire series (the other being the King's Cross waiting room decision to return and face Voldemort again). Harry has been wrestling for months with whether or not he can trust Dumbledore and the plan he laid out. It is watching Dobby's willing sacrifice on his behalf that motivates Harry to trust the flawed, wise man.

How did Dobby's death accomplish this? Harry's internal struggle was between the pursuit of Horcruxes and the pursuit of the Deathly Hallows. He was not far from possessing all three, with which he, not Voldemort, would be the immortal one. Possessing all three Hallows would make him seemingly invincible against Voldemort. This was not Dumbledore's plan. Dobby's death accomplished the rescue of Harry and the others from certain death at the hands of Voldemort – and, of course, the failure of the only three people with the knowledge to bring about his downfall. When Harry saw what could be accomplished through death, a lesson he had already learned from his mother, he knew that seeking immortality was not the right path. Dumbledore knew that even better than Harry did, and Harry would trust in Dumbledore.

Why is this significant for house-elves? Dobby accomplished this crucial task as "a free elf." Harry was already a significant hero in the world of house-elves. In *Chamber of Secrets*, Dobby clearly venerates him, and he explains to Harry that Harry had no idea what it was like, how badly house-elves were treated when Voldemort was in power. Harry's victory over Voldemort years ago had been "a new dawn" for house-elves (*Chamber* 178). Most definitely, Harry's victory over Voldemort would become legendary; but it seems a very fair speculation to think that Dobby's death will also become legendary, especially among the house-elves. Their great hero, Harry Potter, was saved by the sacrifice of a *free* house-elf. Harry set Dobby free; Dobby died to save Harry's life. One might balk at this idea: Dobby died in the service of a wizard. But surely he died out of free choice and not out of forced servitude. Dobby died because he knew that things would be worse for his kind if Voldemort were in power, and that future freedom was possible with Voldemort out of the way. Surely that will be a rallying point and an inspiration for future house-elf liberation movements – indeed, inspiration enough to cause more house-elves to *want* to be free.

Little Victories

Rowling, then, does not give us an overarching transformation of the Wizarding World. It is much better that she did not. Much injustice, prejudice, and institutionalized racism still exists. House-elves are still enslaved at the end of seven novels, and even our hero is wondering whether the house-elf he owns would want to make him a sandwich (though it should be noted that Harry wondered if Kreacher would *want* to, and didn't end up asking him at all). One might be tempted to be frustrated with Rowling here, complaining that she left us a world in which much injustice still exists, and yet she can finish her story with the phrase, "All was well."

But Rowling chose wisely; this is her Fabian gradualism at work, and the libertarian element is present as well. To wrap up the story of house-elves, eliminate all prejudice and slavery, and create peace and harmony in the world in that one final year would be an utter insult to the depth of the problem of racism. To say, "See? Racism can be solved by the brave acts of three teenagers in the span of one year! It's that easy!" would be an insult to all those who still suffer the effects of institutionalized racism. And Rowling trusts her readers to be able to discern what evil still exists in the Wizarding World and what could be done about it.

She has left us hopeful symbols: wizards like Ron, whose perspective began to shift by the end of the year; the sacrifice of Dobby; the feast at the end of the book, in which members of all houses sat intermingled, not separated; Hermione, who embraced and transformed the hurtful word "Mudblood." It's all transformation in the hearts and minds of people which will lead to a better society in the future. The transformations are not complete. Ron's stance toward the house-elves, for example, fails to recognize them as powerful creatures who could contribute to the battle against Voldemort; he sees them instead as helpless creatures in need of rescue. The whole scene is a step in the right direction for both Ron and Hermione. Ron has at least begun to care for house-elves. Hermione is able to recognize someone's care for them, even if that concern is not part of an S.P.E.W. legislative revolution. In both cases, more work is needed; but it has begun. These symbols of transformation, placed alongside a world that is still made up of injustice, provides hope and opens up conversation for our own world, which, alas, is so much like the Wizarding one.

Chapter 13 Notes

1   Richard Abanes is one of the worst offenders here here: "Muggles are consistently portrayed by Rowling as a narrow-minded and callous group of persons unable to grasp the glory of magic" (*Harry Potter and the Bible: The Menace Behind the Magick*. Camp Hill, PA: Christian Publications, Inc., 2001. p. 16). The statement is so profoundly mistaken, it doesn't deserve a response.

2   Kenneth Robert's book, *Why Europe Leaves Home*, educates readers about the refugee problems in Europe circa 1920, in Russia during/after the Bolshevik Revolution, in Poland, in Greece and in Scotland. The book was carefully researched during his European travels. Roberts is acutely aware of bigotry as a cause of conflict. On page 227 he writes: "These people were Greeks, and the people responsible for their pitiful state were Greeks." Referring to the Russian refugees he writes "Meanwhile, the refugees live on from day to day. Poor people! God help them - if nobody else will! (p. 220) and on page 153: "The Russians have no consuls to whom they can go, no country to which they can return. They've got to find work; and if they can't find work, they've got to beg or die." Throughout the book, Roberts credits the work of the American Red Cross and other humanitarian relief efforts. With the exception of the paragraph quoted by Boder, there is no further evidence that Roberts is a racist. Robert does argue that America cannot absorb all the unfortunate refugees of the world without creating serious problems for itself - a topic of concern in American politics even 90 years later.

Roberts was a trained newspaper journalist and an Army lieutenant in the Russian Civil War (1919). He won the Pulitzer Prize in 1957 for his work as a novelist of American history. His most famous novel, *Northwest Passage*, was made into a movie starring Spenser Tracy in 1940. However admirable the work of this first-rate historical scholar and novelist, it is clear that he lapsed in making a bigoted statement in at least this one instance.

3   See his book, *Racism Without Racists: Color-blind Racism and the Persistence of Racial Inequality in the United States.* Rowman and Littlefield, 2006.

4   Quoted in Traub, James. "Daniel Patrick Moynihan, Liberal? Conservative? Or Just Pat?" *The New York Times*. September 22, 1990.

Chapter Fourteen

The Witching World?
Gender in Harry Potter

> All of the great mythologies and much of the mythic storytelling of the world are from the male point of view. When I was writing *The Hero with a Thousand Faces* and wanted to bring the female heroes in, I had to go to the fairy tales.
>
> ~ Joseph Campbell, *Pathways to Bliss*, pg. 145

In a male-dominated world full of male heroes and male adventure stories, why did a single mother of one daughter begin writing yet another one? Why is Harry not Harriet? Why is it called the "Wizarding World" rather than the "Witching World?" After all, if you're going to use the controversial term "witchcraft" with historical references to past witch hunts and everything, why not stick with a matriarchal motif? Why is the Headmaster of Hogwarts, the Minister of Magic, and every other key authority figure in the series male? Are the *Harry Potter* books sexist?

As J.K. Rowling is a woman writing in a context of the deconstruction of metanarratives, certainly there must be some deliberate commentary on gender in the series. Indeed, there is, but it's a bit more subtle than race. The fundamental argument of this chapter is that, while certain stereotypes are reinforced and certain traditional hierarchies observed, there is an underlying feminism to the series that is set in the context of a male-dominated society, making it an effective commentary on our own. "Though the magical world, like the Muggle world, suffers from gender stereotyping and sexism, it is a world in the process of change" (Gallardo-C. and Smith 203). While Rowling does not present us with an ideal world (she never does), she lays the groundwork for change. To answer the pressing question above: No, the *Harry Potter* series is not sexist, even if the Wizarding World is.

It is important to spend time hearing female – and feminist – voices in response to the *Harry Potter* series. Feminists are divided on the issue of gender in the *Harry Potter* series, and this makes perfect sense, since the term "feminism" does not itself refer to one unified theory (Dresang 216).

There are feminists who dislike the gender representations in the series, and there are feminists who love it. As far as the story itself goes, there seems to be unity among feminists that *Harry Potter* is not strictly feminist literature (see below). The division begins when considering how the books should be responded to from a feminist point of view, given what they are. There is plenty of discontent with how J.K. Rowling handles issues of gender in the series. Let's begin with some of the complaints.

Tison Pugh and David L. Wallace argue that though many female characters are presented throughout the series in a sort of "post-feminist way" (meaning, equal opportunity is a given in the Wizarding World), that all the female characters remain in subjugation to men (268-71). Molly and Petunia are both stay-at-home moms. There is only one historical Hogwarts Headmistress mentioned. Even Hermione's considerable talent and strength are only worth anything insofar as they help Harry's quest. Christine Schoefer argued in "Harry Potter's Girl Trouble" that Hermione, while strong and smart, is portrayed as annoying; indeed, that all of the stronger women are simultaneously rule-loving nags, trying to keep the boys from adventure; that the girls at Hogwarts do too many girly thinks like "screaming" and "giggling" and standing on the sidelines while boys have all the fun; that McGonagall "defers to [Dumbledore] in every respect;" that Ginny is portrayed as stupid and foolish; and that in general, the books are filled with incessant gender stereotypes. Natasha Whitton, upon reading the first four books, called the series "seemingly devoid of non-stereotypical females." More than that, she argues that "Rowlings (sic) presents us with a world of doting fools, overweight loud-mouths, simpering girls, crazy witches and old women." Elizabeth E. Heilman argues that not only is femininity portrayed stereotypically and negatively, but that only brute, dominant masculinity is validated (232-33). She states that in the series, "Males are represented as wiser, braver, more powerful, and more fun than females" (223).

These are fairly strong claims and very serious charges in many respects. If they are entirely true, the claim that *Harry Potter* is potentially detrimental to gender equality should be entertained. Not all feminists are agreed, however. Some feminists are adamant that the *Harry Potter* books present a picture of equality that exceeds our own world. Mimi R. Gladstein's thesis is that in the magical world, "women...are anything but second class citizens" and that "equal opportunity among the sexes is a given" (49). She notes that every aspect of the Wizarding World permits equal status for women, from the co-education of Hogwarts to the international Quidditch pitch, from the Order of the Phoenix to the Death Eaters (55-59). Sarah Zettel, a "*bona fide* feminist," argues that while the series is not feminist, neither is it sexist (83). "To be a feminist work, a story has to be specifically about issues unique to girls and women and usually has a female protagonist as the main point of view" (84). The fact of the third-person, limited omniscient view through Harry's eyes (or what's been called, "the Harry filter") disqualifies the series as strictly feminist literature. Nevertheless, the clear message of the series is that "no matter who you are, you can be yourself and still be a worthy person," and Zettel "cannot think of a better message for the girls and young women of the world" (99).

In some critiques, feminist frustration with the Harry Potter series is simply trying too hard. Whitton, for example, neglects the fact that Quidditch is a clear example of "equal opportunity," even at the professional level (Moran, excellent player for the Irish in the World Cup, is a female), and makes this statement: "Angelina Johnson is a chaser for the Gryffindor House team, but Wood the Captain addresses the team as men and has to be corrected." The clear buffoon in this instance, however, is Wood; Rowling seems rather to be presenting a world in which equal opporunity is evident, and chauvinistic men have to realize that "the times, they are a-changing." Whitton even goes so far as to say that the animals are treated in a sexist way: Hedwig's sole purpose in life is to carry messages for Harry, and Mrs. Norris is evil. Whitton conveniently ignores that Fang is a coward, and that Errol and all other owls in the entire Wizarding World have the same job, regardless of gender; it would be better to argue that even the animals are "equal opporutunity" in the Wizarding World! Zettel, who freely admits that if she found the books to be sexist, it would ruin her enjoyment of them (83) is on the mark on this point: Rowling balances her stereotypical and derisive references to women with the same sorts of thing with men (98).

The *Harry Potter* series presents neither an entirely sexist world nor an ideal situation for women. There are legitimate complaints that do not need interpretive gymnastics to find. It is absolutely the case that "the Harry Potter books feature females in secondary positions of power" (Heilman 223). There is altogether too much "shrieking" and "squealing" and "giggling" going on; these are stereotypical and "weak" descriptors used for women, and Rowling most often uses these terms for women (226-27). These are fair enough complaints, as there do seem to be moments in which Rowling defaults very quickly to gender stereotypes that reinforce certain dominant views of gender. Some, of course, simply make sense as descriptions of reality: 11 to 17 year-old girls *do* gather and giggle, just as 11 to 17 year-old boys get together and act in stereotypically male ways. It should be noted that older men are also described as "squeaking" at times (as when Dedalus Diggle came to get the Dursleys in the beginning of *Deathly Hallows)*. The list of complaints in the opening paragraph of this chapter need answering, in one way or another.

It's quite possible – indeed, likely – that J.K. Rowling remains an ardent feminist and has some very good reasons for utilizing gender stereotypes that ultimately serve to highlight and exonerate the exceptions while maintaining a realistic commentary on society in its current state. There are at least six promising approaches to the Harry Potter series, with significant overlap, that serve as helpful ways to understand gender in the books: (1) Harry as the hermaphroditic Philosopher's Stone; (3) Ginny as "Susan Pevensie, vindicated;" (3) Hermione as maturing feminist; (4) Harry as "Cinderfella" (Galllardo-C. and Smith); (5) Kathryn McDaniel's "The Elfin Mystique" argument; (6) Harry's mother-archetypes, and how they create a subtle subversion of patriarchy.

Harry as Philosopher's Stone

John Granger's work on alchemy in *Harry Potter*, as already argued, is fundamental to understanding the series. It also contains symbolically what carries some of the better potential for a feminist reading of the series. Gallardo-C. and Smith recognized this:

> Somewhere in that 'other' land, between the advice of his best friends Ron and Hermione, between the masculine and the feminine, Harry stands as a true symbol of the possibility of the Philosopher's Stone (201).

So just what is all this "hermaphrodite" talk about? John Granger explains:

> The activity of alchemy is the chemical marriage of the imbalance ("arguing couple") of masculine sulfur and feminine quicksilver. These antipodal qualities have to be reconciled and resolved, 'die' and be 'reborn' after conjunction before recongealing in a perfect golden unity....

> The end of alchemy is the Philospher's Stone which is the transcendence of this imbalance, impurity, and polarity. It is also

about the creation of the transcendent alchemist, the saintly God/ Man often represented by a Hermaphrodite or "S/He," a person who is both male and female. Here polarity is not resolved as much as it is transcended and embodied in harmonious unity, and incarnation of love and peace. (*Unlocking* 73)

If there's any doubt that Rowling had this in mind when she made Dumbledore an alchemist, read carefully this statement by Rowling in answer to why Slytherin is allowed in the school:

But they're not all bad [the Slytherins]. They literally are not all bad. Well, the deeper answer, the non-flippant answer, would be that you have to embrace all of a person, you have to take them with their flaws, and everyone's got them. It's the same way with the student body. If only they could achieve perfect unity, you would have an absolute unstoppable force, and I suppose it's that craving for unity and wholeness that means that they keep that quarter of the school that maybe does not encapsulate the most generous and noble qualities, in the hope, in *the very Dumbledore-esque hope that they will achieve union, and they will achieve harmony. Harmony is the word.* (Anelli/Spartz, 2005, emphasis added)

Indeed, it might be noted here that, surpassing all the culture war debates surrounding Rowling's statement about Dumblerdore's being "gay," there may be no better explanation for why she thought of him as gay than his role as the master alchemist of the series. This is not meant to say that alchemy produces a gay orientation as the human ideal, but that the idea of a gay male alchemist might work symbolically in Rowling's mind.

The Philosopher's Stone is the perfect harmony of opposites, including male and female. Indeed, the alchemical process not only reconciles male and female, but the four elements (to which the four houses correspond) also. This builds an organic link between Rowling's comment above about the harmony of the houses and the harmony of male/female:

The contrary qualities of the four elements are likened to quarreling foes who must be reconciled or united in order for harmony to reign.... The circulation of elements is identical with the process the alchemists describe as the conversion of body into spirit, and spirit into body, until each is able to mingle together, or *unite in the chemical wedding* to form a new perfect being, the Philosopher's Stone.... (Lyndy Abraham, quoted in Granger, *Unlocking* 138, emphasis added).

This is precisely why Harry is not allowed to take Ginny with him. He must complete his transformation into the hermaphroditic Philosopher's Stone between the conflict of the "quarreling couple," Ron and Hermione, as the alchemical process necessitates. This is how Harry, though male, serves not as a typical male-hero, but as a hero who transcends the male/female opposites and serves as a perfect harmony between the two. This is an interpretive key for a feminist reading of *Harry Potter;* it signifies that J.K. Rowling did not intend, with this series of stories, to enter into and take sides on a debate about gender roles, but rather to transcend that debate with her hero. Once again, the "social justice trio" motif should be mentioned: Ron is stereotypically male in some ways, Hermione stereotypically female in some ways; Harry symbolically transcends gender and becomes a perfect harmony of male and female. In postmodern parlance, one could say it's a post-feminist way of approaching gender issues.

Ginny: Susan Pevensie, Vindicated

This Harry-as-Philosopher's-Stone motif works its way out in the rest of the story. As mentioned, Ginny did not accompany the trio in Book 7. Wasn't this a missed opportunity for Rowling? Adding Ginny would have put the focus on another strong woman in the series and balanced out the male/female disparity in the series' heroes. But if Harry is to be the symbolic, hermaphroditic Philosopher's Stone, his "other half" can't be with him. So Ginny's not being added makes sense.

Her inclusion in the story, however, as Harry's girlfriend, and later, wife, also makes sense from a feminist point of view. We've already looked at her role as Harry's anima in Chapter 7. But as an individual, Ginny represents a powerful woman, and her character is something of a vindication of female sexuality.

In an interview shortly after the release of *Half-Blood Prince,* she repeats an old line of complaint against C.S. Lewis' *Narnia* series:

> "There comes a point where Susan, who was the older girl, is lost to Narnia because she becomes interested in lipstick. She's become irreligious basically because she found sex," Rowling says. "I have a big problem with that." (Grossman, "Hogwarts and All," 2005)

This is an unfortunate reading of Lewis on this point (it wasn't sexuality, but her abandonment of belief in Narnia that got her excluded).

Nevertheless, if Rowling believes this, it might make a lot of sense for her to create Ginny the way she has. Ginny has certainly "found sex," and she's teaching it to Harry, our inhibited hero (not that they've slept together at all. Rowling has gratefully stayed clear of that).

Ginny is a young woman who knows how to "use her sexuality" – or, better, be sexual; in other words, what is specifically female about her is powerful. She is, of course, very attractive; even the Slytherin boys think this, though she is a "blood traitor" (*Prince* 150). She is also portrayed as passionate and fiery, and able to be sexual while not being promiscuous. Ginny is simply attempting to be herself, and Rowling is trying to communicate that being sexual is a good thing:

> "I never really gave up on you," she said. "Not really. I always hoped ... Hermione told me to get on with life, maybe go out with some other people, relax a bit around you, because I never used to be able to talk if you were in the room, remember? And she thought you might take a bit more notice if I was a bit more – myself."
>
> "Smart girl, that Hermione," said Harry, trying to smile. (*Prince* 647)

Some, undoubtedly, will recoil at the idea of Ginny's fiery sexuality being a good thing, but the cultural context for this is important. A male-dominated society tends to reward men for promiscuity, excusing sexual obsession as simply part of being male. Females, on the other hand, become outcasts for the same thing. There are no male-equivalent terms of disparagement like "slut," or "whore" which carry the same power to tarnish a reputation. Indeed, while it is to be desired that both male and female sexuality be less on display and considered more sacred in society (according to Christian theology, a sacred thing shared between husband and wife), Rowling has not attempted to advocate for sexual promiscuity with Ginny. She's simply saying that female sexuality is not a bad thing.

While the Pevensies are four (Lucy, Edmund, Susan, and Peter), the Hogwarts heros are three (Harry, Ron, Hermione) except for a short spell in Book 6. Making Ginny the fourth (though not included in the quest, for reasons mentioned above) might be her subtle, or even subconscious way of saying, "Susan should have been included."

Hermione, Feminist

Something the careful reader will notice about much of the critique of gender in *Harry Potter* is that it was done, like so much of the published analysis, after the release of Book 4. There was a three year wait in between books 4 and 5, and given the unprecedented popularity of the series at the time, that interlibrum was flooded with books and articles. What is significant about this as it pertains to gender is that earlier studies were unable to consider Hermione's development as a character past the first four years. Some, indeed, ignored it even during those four years. Schoefer's article, for example, was written after she had read the first four books, but she chose to focus only on Book 1; that an 11-year old girl does a lot of girly things should not surprise us too much. But where does Hermione go from here? Schoefer's ignoring of the three subsequent books skews her thinking on the matter, because there is a markedly different Hermione even in Book 4 from the Hermione of Book 1 – not a forced, unnatural difference, but the evidence of a maturing feminist.

There has been no shortage of criticism for Rowling's portrayal of Hermione, mixed in with some praise. Dresang is a balanced example, considering Hermione a strong character but lamenting the out-of-character moments:

> For Hermione the bossy, assertive champion of rights and problem solver, these words ["shriek," "squeak," "wail," "squeal," and "wimper"], at least in some contexts, seem unbelievable and completely out of character.... Her hysteria and crying happen far too often to be considered a believable part of the development of Hermione's character and are quite out of line with her core role in the book. (223).

Here again the notion of Harry as Philosopher's Stone is helpful. The "Chemical Wedding" of alchemy is the "central symbol of alchemy" (*Unlocking* 103). Bill and Fleur's wedding was clearly an alchemical wedding to at the start of *Deathly Hallows*, the final stage of Harry's alchemical transformative process (the Red Stage). But Harry's actual character transformation has been taking place in the middle of the Ron/Hermione (sulfur/mercury) contrast. Hermione is, undoubtedly, a strong character, and the reasons will be enumerated below. But the stereotypical, "weaker" aspects of Hermione can be explained by Rowling's need to have the female part of the "quarreling couple" be *stereotypically*, or "cartoonish or caricatured" female (*Unlocking* 105). But the fact that Hermione was a strong female character at all, and not "pretty" in the pop culture sense indicates that Rowling's feminist agenda may have even overruled an alchemical necessity. Hermione is nothing at all like Fleur. But Ron? He's a fairly stereotypical male, at least in attitude, all the way through the series; he is, after all, Bill's brother.

One of the most crucial aspects of the quest for equality is the need for equal access for all groups of people. If minority groups are to remain in their subjugated state, then access to social capital, as well as the things that produce social capital (wealth, education, etc.) will be made impossible or more difficult by the members of dominant culture. The things that are valued in a white-male-dominated society are easily accessed by white men, whereas women and minority groups cannot access these things as easily. It's already been demonstrated that Hogwarts provides greater access for minority groups – "equal opportunity." But McGonagall and Hermione can be seen as behind-the-scenes, colluding to give themselves even greater access, and therefore greater power for women, in *Prisoner of Azkaban*. McGonagall is another character over whom feminist analysis has been conflicted. As noted above, some think she is simply a woman with strength, but who is ultimately in deference to Dumbledore, thereby undermining the message of equality. Hermione's and McGonagall's teamwork to gain better access for women tells a story not of quiet submissiveness, but of subtle subversion of a male-dominated society.

"Hermione's secret" to making it to all her classes turns out to be a Time-Turner, a small, charmed necklace that gives her the power to go back in time. How did McGonagall attain her status as a tremendously powerful witch and Deputy Headmistress? The readers are led to believe through Hermione's reverence for McGonagall that they are kindred spirits – women who see learning as fundamentally important. But access to learning is a step towards power for women; undoubtedly, Hermione and Minerva McGonagall are two of the most powerful magical people of their age, and a good deal brighter than a majority of wizards. That Hermione's access to knowledge is potent is demonstrated illustratively in the fact that Hermione's possession of the Time-Turner – and Dumbledore's trust in her to use it well – is the key element to subverting injustice and releasing two falsely condemned prisoners, Buckbeak and Sirius Black. In *Prisoner of Azkaban*, Hermione's access to knowledge literally is female power to overturn the injustice perpetrated by cranky, old, white men in power. Once again, this is Fabian gradualism at work.

Hermione further develops in *Goblet of Fire* as a powerful woman. Dresang notes the following about Hermione of Book 4:

> Rowling, consciously or unconsciously, is letting go of the stereotypical language and giving her the freedom to subvert the stereotypical behavior assigned to her in the early books. Hermione cries less readily and is described less frequently using the weak verbs and adjectives in book four than in any of the previous three books. She "shrieks" and "squeaks" only once, does not wail or squeal at all, and is not described as "timid" in *Goblet of Fire*, compared to the more than fifteen such descriptions in *Prisoner of Azkaban*. (224)

Indeed, it is in Book 4 that Hermione takes on the role of political liberator with S.P.E.W., even though it is clear that she has a lot to learn about herself and about social justice. While she continues to struggle with stereotypical versus subversive behavior in the following books, by *Deathly Hallows*, she has become so strong and independent that she all but takes on the leader role in the first half of the novel. Harry and Ron are utterly clueless about the way in which to begin the Horcrux hunt; Hermione has things well-planned. Without Hermione, the plot falls apart, and Voldemort remains in power, plain and simple. Sarah Zettel nicely sums up Hermione-as-feminist; this is lengthy, and it's only part of Zettel's extensive argument, but it gets the point across:

> Hermione publicly and unashamedly pursues the course she knows to be right, even when it costs her her friends or the regard of male authority figures. She is not deterred by the prevailing opinion of society. If she is not initially effective, she tries other methods to achieve her right ends. She is, in the main, highly confident in her own understanding, and that confidence frequently pays off. She forcefully argues her points and does not back down when ignored. She brings every weapon she's got to bear into her particular fight, and she succeeds, even if it takes a while. She is also conscious that the boys have some blinders when it comes to the abilities of girls, and she does not take this lightly. In *Half-Blood Prince*, it's Hermione, true to form, who works out that "Prince" might be a woman's surname rather than a man's title. The boys sneer at the notion. Also as usual, Hermione ignores their derision and goes forward on her own path, because she's certain she might be right, and this is important, so she will pursue it.... Hermione makes the first real, open challenge to Delores Umbridge. Hermione is the one who refuses to cower and be silent when threatened by Rita Skeeter's pen. (95-96)

It's no wonder that Rowling has frequently referred to Hermione as a "strong female character," particularly when referring specifically to feminism (Interview with Oprah, 2001).

What's King Arthur Doing Living with a Wicked Stepmother?

Ximeno Gallardo-C. and C. Jason Smith have introduced one of the more interesting feminist readings of the series, namely, "Cinderfella" – the argument that Rowling placed Harry not in the traditional male-hero story, but in the cyclical female-hero story:

> [C]yclical moves from passive subject at home (Cinderella as servant) to active subject at Hogwarts (Cinderella at the ball) drive the series and inevitably lead to the hero's "blooming." This tie to a traditionally "girl tale" feminizes Harry in ways that allow female readers to identify strongly with a male protagonist. (pg. 191)

This fits nicely with the Philosopher's Stone reading, because it highlights the feminine elements of Harry's nature and story. Not only does it fit nicely, it's a very accurate reading of the series. If you're thinking of the Disney rendition of Cinderella, you're wondering how the tale is "cyclical" – after all, she only heads off to the ball and returns once, to be later found and whisked away to live "happily ever after." But the older versions of the Cinderella story are not like the Disney version; Gallardo-C. and Smith refer specifically to the Grimm Brothers' "Aschenputtel," in which a magical tree planted on her mother's grave (lingering magic from a deceased mother!) grants her the ability to "repeatedly attend the royal ball" (195). Petunia is a classic wicked stepmother with a favored child and a mistreated child (192). Harry is given all the chores and is hidden when important guests come over, while Dudley is praised simply for existing and allowed to become absurdly fat and have anything he wants.

Interestingly, after each cyclical pattern, Harry becomes more in control at the Dursleys. After the first year, he finally gets his own bedroom. After the second, he's become confident and self-sufficient enough to simply leave after blowing up Aunt Marge. After the third, he makes arrangements to leave for the remainder of the summer, even convincing the Dursleys to let a Wizarding family in their house. After the fourth year, Harry deals with the invasion of Dementors and frequent owl post right in Little Whinging. After the fifth, Dumbledore shows up on the Dursleys' doorstep, and an entire conversion – including a momentary visit from Kreacher – happens right in the Dursleys' living room. Finally, after the sixth year, Harry is entirely the one in control, deciding for the Dursleys that they must leave and accept protection from the Wizarding World.

While the Arthurian backdrop for much of the series was explained in part in Chapter 5, the story's structure does not follow Arthur: Harry does not move from orphanhood and anonymity to king and hero. He moves in cycles, and each cycle makes him stronger. He achieves Arthurian virtue, but he does so as Aschenputtel.

Kathryn McDaniel's "The Elfin Mystique"

Kathryn McDaniel's essay about house-elves in *Past Watchful Dragons* is creative and fascinating. Her thesis is basically this: the house-elves are written by Rowling to symbolize "'unliberated' women, shackled by the chains of tradition to a circumscribed role in the domestic sphere" (185). McDaniel enumerates the parallels between house-elves and house-wives: house-elfs, though gendered, are somewhat androgynous, sometimes being called "it;" they are "feminized as a group;" they are "caretakers of the home" and "constrained within this domestic role;" and, like 20th century women during second wave feminism, liberation is "not unequivocally desired" (185-86). Dobby, of course, serves as the ultimate example of a free elf experiencing the "Elfin mystique" – he has achieved liberation, but in many ways he is still shackled psychologically that says his place and security are to be found in his role as subordinate caretaker of the home (192-93).

Instead of giving away the entirety of McDaniel's argument – indeed, it's a brilliant and nuanced essay with excellent further reflections on Dobby, Winky, Kreacher, and oppressive structures within the Wizarding World, and I commend the work to your careful attention – we should pause and note both an objection to this reading, and in answering that objection, we will find the greatest value in McDaniel's reading.

First, the objection: J.K. Rowling says that the house-elves stand symbolically "for slavery" (Edinburgh "cub reporter" press conference, *ITV*, 16 July 2005). That should settle the matter, right? It might be argued that scholars like McDaniel are simply trying to salvage the series from the obvious criticism that Rowling has created an utter abomination with "happy slaves," entirely subverting her tolerance message and creating an ugly message for her readers.

We have to take the long way around in answering that objection. Some fairly simple observations could help take the objection straight on: it's a magical world, and house-elves are not African-Americans in the U.S.; they are quirky magical creatures, therefore serving as a loose thematic parallel, not an allegory for slavery. But to dismiss the complaints with those arguments is to miss out on the most important parts of McDaniel's thesis, namely, the vast complexity and difficulty of these sorts of social justice issues, and the intersectionality of oppression.

As argued in the previous chapter, racism is not first and foremost about a prejudice against a physical characteristic – it is a system of advantage, privilege, power. As with racism, so with sexism; the key element in all forms of oppression is not simple bigotry, but the advantage that is gained by the oppressor. This is the insidious secret that keeps certain "types" of people in subordinate positions. As such, there is an organic link between racism and sexism, for they both serve to keep a white-male-dominated culture intact. Even though house-elves, in Rowling's mind, allude to slavery, they contain thematic elements that have everything in common with racism and slavery – and indeed, with the house-elves in particular, the intersectionality between oppression of a race and oppression of a gender is profound, for all the reasons Dr. McDaniel has noted. McDaniel is not alone in noticing this parallel between the house-elf slaves and the subordination of women. Gallardo-C. and Smith write, "The house-elves are the 'women' of Hogwarts, regardless of their sex" (202). As such, the house-elves become a sort of nexus of oppression, a symbolic stand-in for the ways that dominant groups oppress all others; Rowling has managed to write the entire complex theme of oppression into the seemingly simple-minded house-elves, and that is an important contribution to the discussion of oppression in our own society.

The other important observation of McDaniel's is that Rowling is perfectly within her right to write a world that reflects not an ideal situation, but a description of the gross and complex injustices of our own world. She writes:

> Many of Rowling's critics seem to wish she were more "fantastic" in depicting the world as they believe in should be and not in the full light of its real paradoxes and contradictions (204).

It is better that Rowling has written her story honestly and not idealistically. Indeed, Rowling has given us a gift in doing so: "the reader's ability to see the flaws in the fantasy world (as perhaps they cannot in their own) may serve to highlight those aspects of the "real world" that need to be attending to and changed" (184). This is precisely what we've been arguing for all along in Part III, but it's particularly poignant when considering the house-elves, because they are such troubling examples of the effects – both physical and psychological – of longstanding oppressive structures. Those who have complained that Rowling hasn't provided us an ideal world – indeed, that she's written an unjust one with seemingly tacit acceptance of oppressive norms – miss the point that this might have been Rowling's plan all along: lay those things out in her world, so that we can recognize them both there and in our own.

Subverting and changing longstanding oppressive and often invisible social structures is not something that occurs overnight. Granger rightly observes that "the harmony of elves, goblins, centaurs, and magical folk... seems a noble ambition that might take generations to realize" (*Unlocking* 89). There's nothing simple about liberating oppressed groups; it's very messy business, and "often encounters reluctance from both those who enslave and those who are enslaved" (McDaniel 185). Rowling is under no delusion that *Harry Potter* will topple all the world's oppressive structures; but if it can open up conversations that lead in that direction, then she has accomplished her "extended argument for tolerance."

Harry's Moms

One of Rowling's more clever ways of subverting patriarchy is in her portrayal of fathers and mothers in the series. Undoubtedly, she sticks, by and large, to "traditional" patriarchal "gender-roles;" this will be addressed at the end of the chapter. But returning to our archetypal thinking from Part II, when we examine the mother archetype, we find an interesting pattern in the concept of motherhood in Rowling's work.

Jung wrote of the mother archetype:

> This is the mother-love which is one of the most moving and unforgettable memories of our lives, the mysterious root of all growth and change; the love that means homecoming, shelter, and the long silence from which everything begins and in which everything ends. Intimately known and yet strange like Nature, lovingly tender and yet cruel like fate, joyous and untiring giver of life--*mater dolorosa* and mute implacable portal that closes upon the dead. Mother is mother-love, *my* experience and *my* secret. Why risk saying too much, too much that is false and inadequate and

beside the point, about that human being who was our mother, the accidental carrier of that great experience which includes herself and myself and all mankind, and indeed the whole of created nature, the experience of life whose children we are? The attempt to say these things has always been made, and probably always will be; but a sensitive person cannot in all fairness load that enormous burden of meaning, responsibility, duty, heaven and hell, on to the shoulders of one frail and fallible human being--so deserving of love, indulgence, understanding, and forgiveness--who was our mother. He knows that the mother carries for us that inborn image of the *mater natura* and *mater spiritualis*, of the totality of life of which we are a small and helpless part. (*Four Archetypes* 26)

The mother figure is a crucial aspect of Harry's hero development. The point of Jung's words is that the place of the mother in the life of the hero is both fundamental and indescribable. The best that an author can do is demonstrate through the plot the importance of the mother; it can hardly be accurately described theoretically. Undoubtedly, the love of a mother is central to the *Harry Potter* books, and this stems directly from the experience of J.K. Rowling, who has confessed the extent to which the loss of her mother affected the stories (Greig).

There is only one clear-cut example of an altogether nasty mother figure in the entire series: Kreacher's mistress, Sirius's mom, that awful screeching woman in the portrait. She's a terrible old woman. Petunia is a bad mother in that she spoils Dudley and so ruins him as a person; but Rowling even induces sympathy for Petunia by the end. Furthermore, she's not part of the magical world, wherein the archetypes are found. Narcissa is a pompous and vain woman, but her love for her son causes her to help Harry in the end, and at a crucial moment. Merope is not a good mother in the least, but most certainly much of this is her having been abused. The only other treacherous women in the text – Alecto Carrow and Bellatrix LeStrange – are not portrayed as mothers at all. Carrow we simply don't know enough about, but Bellatrix doesn't seem to have children at all, which makes sense. She never really loved Rodolfo. She has a disgusting obsession with Voldemort instead. This is why Rowling's attempted parallel between the twisted love of Bellatrix and the motherly love of Molly doesn't quite hit home the way she had hoped. Sure, it's pure love versus demented love. But Bellatrix is not a bad mother, because she's not portrayed as a mother at all.

Most importantly, there is never even a hint at a deconstruction of Lily. She's as perfect in Harry's and our minds at the end of the seven books as she was at the beginning. This is a significant observation, for the same cannot be said of fathers in the series. For Harry, as a young boy, his parents are idealized in his mind, because he never knew them and instead grew up with the abusive Dursleys. Harry's idealization of his father is torn to shreds in his fifth year; not so with his mother. And Harry's mother-figures in the series, though flawed, do not ever deconstruct for him the very basic belief that mothers are loving, brave, nurturing, and heroic. Fathers come into question: his own, Marvolo Gaunt, Tobias Snape, Lucius Malfoy. But "his own" is the most important. Whether you think this breakdown of good mothers vs. bad fathers is correct or a stretch, it is not a stretch to say that Rowling smashed Harry's hagiographic view of his dad, but she never did so with his mom. Lily is far, far more prominent as a heroine, a mother, and a powerful witch than James, who appears to be little more than an arrogant bully who wised up and became a fairly noble guy before he died – and that because of Lily.

Mrs. Weasley is easily the most important Mother-influence on Harry, despite the fact that he's around Professor McGonagall more often. Undoubtedly, Molly sees Harry, in some sense, as one of her own, and to an extent she pays more attention to Harry than to Ron. This doesn't help Ron's insecurity, of course, but it *does* help Harry's. While there is an extent to which Molly's care over Harry is a bit too much, and she treats him like a child (which she does with her own children as well), she plays a vital role: Harry knows and feels that he is loved.

Professor McGonagall represents for Harry a mother's loving discipline. While she is stern – sometimes a bit too stern – she is a powerful disciplinarian who simultaneously demonstrates genuine care and compassion, not least when Harry and Ron tell her the lie that they were going to visit the petrified Hermione in *Chamber of Secrets*. McGonagall is wise, explaining to Harry the complexity of the situation in *Order of the Phoenix* under Umbridge's control, and compassionate, understanding how difficult that situation is for Harry, who is being smeared by the majority of the Wizarding World as a liar and a fraud for his claim that Voldemort has returned.

Hagrid is a Great Mother figure. That's a strong claim, but there it is. From start to finish, Hagrid has strong mothering tendencies. His care for dangerous magical creatures, not least Norbert(a) the Norwegian Ridgeback, is illustrative of this. This is not meant to be sexist (consider the claim being made here before making that charge!), but Hagrid fulfills some traditional "mothering" roles – compassion, nurture, and comfort. He is quick to make tea and offer food when the trio have come to him with questions and concerns – exactly what we see Mrs. Weasley doing in similar situations. Others have seen female characteristics in Hagrid. John Granger, for example, speculating on the alchemical "Rebis" or "hermaphrodite" in the final installment during the interlibrum, wrote, "He's a mommy," and then quoted correspondence with Dr. Danelia Teodorescu who noted Hagrid "knitting," his mothering nature toward Norbert and other creatures, and his "cooking with a flowery apron" (*Unlocking* 114-15).

So it could be said that Harry's most fundamental, life-shaping influences, apart from Dumbledore (whose hagiographic status in Harry's mind is also is torn down by the end), are all mothers. In other words, Harry is primarily the product of a community of matriarchal influence.

What About Mrs. Weasley?

A final objection should be taken up before concluding: if Rowling is a feminist, and we've just argued that house-elves demonstrate some interesting parallels with traditional female subordination, why are the Weasleys such a "traditional" family? Why is Mrs. Weasley the cooking, cleaning, stay-at-home mom while Mr. Weasley is the "breadwinner"? Feminist Sarah Zettel takes up this issue:

> How do you portray a traditionally structured family? You can't pretend they don't exist. No one will believe you.... I've thought a lot about this, as a feminist, and as an author.... The best way to do it is what Rowling does – to show the traditional role as one possibility among many, and to show it as both negative and positive according to the choices of the person playing the role. (91-92)

Or, as Madeleine L'Engle writes:

> Several women have written to me to complain about *A Swiftly Tilting Planet*. They feel that I should not have allowed Meg Murry to give up a career by marrying Calvin, having children, and quietly helping her husband with his work behind the scenes. But if women are free to choose to pursue a career as well as marriage, they must also be free to choose the making of a home and the nurture of a family as their vocation; that was Meg's choice, and a free one, and

it was as creative a choice as if she had gone on to get a Ph.D. in quantum mechanics." (*Walking* 98-99).

Conclusion

Rowling made a very subtle move in describing the Fountain of Magical Brethren that most commentators miss:

> Halfway down the hall was a fountain. A group of golden statues, larger than life-size, stood in the middle of a circular pool. *Tallest of them all was a noble-looking wizard*, with his wand pointing straight up in the air. *Grouped around him was a beautiful witch*, a centaur, a goblin, and a house-elf. The last three were all looking adoringly up at the witch and wizard. Glittering jets of water were flying from the ends of the two wands, the point of the centaur's arrow, the tip of the goblin's hat, and each of the house-elf's ears.... (*Order* 127)

We move so quickly to thinking about the "last three" who are "looking adoringly up at the witch and wizard" that we miss the subtle but important fact that the witch is "grouped around" the wizard along with the other magical brethren. We don't hear Harry considering the implication of this positioning, though he does realize, upon reflection, that the witch is "wearing a vapid smile like a beauty contestant," pointing to the common patriarchal valuing of a woman if she happens to be "pretty" by some imposed cultural standard (156). If this fountain really told a lie, it told a lie about gender relationships as well, for it communicated the natural superiority of a wizard over a witch, a male over a female.

To repeat the thesis, *Harry Potter* is not sexist, even if the Wizarding World is; and this is precisely the point that makes it most effective. Gellardo-C. and Smith write, "Although Rowling draws long and deep from a fairy-tale and fantasy tradition steeped in misogyny and gender stereotyping, she is seldom at its mercy" (203). By placing the subtle subversion of subordination in the context of a sexist world, she creates an atmosphere not at all unlike our own. As with the subject of racism, Rowling has written a series that opens up significant conversation about sexism and gender equality. Racism is treated in more detail than sexism, to be sure: "Books are necessarily of a finite length and complexity, and an author, even of fantasy, must choose which ethical questions to present in detail. Rowling chose to make racism the major ethical theme of the Harry Potter books" (Zettel 84). But embedded within the series is, as we've demonstrated, an underlying, effective commentary on gender.

Chapter Fifteen

Wizards at War
Harry Potter as a Commentary on the War on Terror

After the release of *Half-Blood Prince*, a writer calling herself "Bookworm" published an article in *The American Thinker*, "Harry Potter and the War on Terror," arguing that the *Harry Potter* stories, along with *Narnia* and *Lord of the Rings*, contains a message that supports the U.S./British policy toward international terrorism:

> [E]vil exists...and the only thing to be done against evil is to attack it, root and branch. A war against evil is a total war, from which one cannot walk away.

> It is therefore a great comfort to me that the most popular and compelling products our children devour affirm values that will aid America in the fight against the Islamist forces arrayed.

"Bookworm" calls *Order of the Phoenix* "a perfect analogy to the situation the West faces today, in the real world, in its War against Islamofascism." She argues that the Ministry of Magic parallels the anti-war movement in the U.S. which is "bound and determined to explain away or ignore the evil in its midst," and Dumbledore and Harry parallel those like George W. Bush and Tony Blair who recognize evil and are prepared to do whatever it takes to fight it.

It's likely that Rowling, and therefore both Dumbledore and Harry, would be a little disturbed by the comparison.

The tragedy of September 11, 2001, occurred in between Books 4 and 5, and it affected the entire world, including the Wizarding World. J.K. Rowling can hardly be described as a fan of the Bush-Blair response to international terrorism, despite the radical evil of that terrorism. While

Voldemort certainly has Hitleresque, Nazi tendencies, there are just as many parallels between Voldemort and Osama bin Laden. As *Half-Blood Prince* opens up, acts of terrorism are plunging both Muggle and Wizarding worlds into chaos, and Voldemort is nowhere to be found. Rowling has created the same sort of atmosphere, once Voldemort's return is publicly acknowledged by the Ministry, as we are experiencing in the world today. Where is Osama bin Laden? Where was Voldemort? In hiding, ordering acts of terrorism in their names.

Furthermore, like terrorists, the Death Eaters are not an army with a "homeland." It's not as though the country of Death-Eaterdom is plotting a world takeover. They are an army with an ideology, but they are in hiding, striking whenever they can at their perceived enemies. So Rowling has effectively created in the Wizarding World the same type of atmosphere we experience in our own.

Bookworm's move from there to advocacy for the current methodologies in the War on Terror, however, is a bit of a leap. In the first place, she seems to miss a fundamental point in all three stories she cites. If, for example, the message of *The Lord of the Rings* is supposed to be that evil is attacked "root and branch," without mercy, one wonders what she makes of Gollum. For, indeed, it was an act of mercy toward an evil character that ultimately brought down Sauron; had Frodo not shown mercy to Gollum, he would have failed, and Sauron succeeded. *Narnia*, too, does not tell a story of all-out-attack on evil, but one in which the determining factor in the battle against evil is Aslan's willing self-sacrifice – a deliberate submission to the enemy. These stories are far more nuanced than the "Good" people attacking and defeating the "Evil" people, "root and branch."

Several themes we've already discussed converge in Rowling's critique of the Bush/Blair response to terrorism. Fearing fear itself is key: Harry's fear is not of Voldemort. Rowling's hero, the model for our behavior, is not acting out of fear of a perceived (and very real!) threat. Why is this significant? The concept of fearing fear itself is rooted in the fact that fear causes one to do things that one would not normally do. This is precisely the case in times of war, when fear is used in order to justify actions which, outside of wartime, would never be permitted. The "ticking time bomb" scenario of the television series *24* is a perfect example of this. The dilemma is this: a time bomb is about to go off in a major city. You have custody of someone with alleged terrorist associations, and he may, or even probably does, have information about that bomb that can save human lives. In the regular workings of justice, torture is considered wrong and immoral; but if it can convince the accused terrorist of giving out important information about the bomb, is it still wrong?

We dare not make light of the dilemma; it's a difficult one. How often this *actually happens*, however, is a different story, as opposed to how often the perceived *fear* of the ticking time bomb is used to justify torture. This is precisely Fudge's argument about the use of dementors:

> "Voldemort has returned," Dumbledore repeated. "If you accept that fact straightaway, Fudge, and take the necessary measures, we may still be able to save the situation. The first and most essential step is to remove Azkaban from the control of the dementors -"
>
> "Preposterous!" shouted Fudge again. "Remove the dementors? I'd be kicked out of office for suggesting it! Half of us only feel safe in our beds at night because we know the dementors are standing guard at Azkaban!" (*Goblet* 707)

Here, Fudge's argument is simple: the dementors make the Wizarding World feel safe, because, far away from everyone sleeping in their beds, they are torturing the "bad guys," day and night. Dumbledore, on the other hand, has always thought the Wizarding World's alliance with the dementors was a very bad thing; they are Voldemort's "natural allies," and one does not make friends with pure evil. This is a powerful parallel between Dumbledore and Gandalf:

> You can't fight the Enemy with his own Ring without turning into an Enemy, but unfortunately Gandalf's wisdom seems long ago to have passed with him into the True West. (Tolkien, quoted in Purtill 72).

One could hardly imagine either Gandalf or Dumbledore engaging in torture in order to defeat the enemy, for torture is the activity of the enemy. Torture is dehumanizing. This is precisely Harry's reasoning for not killing Stan Shunpike; while the good guys argue that it's war, and the normal rules of morality don't apply, Harry disagrees, refusing to become like Voldemort in any way:

> "I saw Stan Shunpike . . . . You know, the bloke who was the conductor on the Knight Bus? And I tried to Disarm him instead of – well, he doesn't know what he's doing, does he? He must be Imperiused!"
>
> Lupin looked aghast.

"Harry, the time for Disarming is past! These people are trying to capture and kill you! At least Stun if you aren't prepared to kill!"

...

"So you think I should have killed Stan Shunpike?" said Harry angrily.

"Of course not," said Lupin, "but the Death Eaters – frankly, most people! – would have expected you to attack back!" ...

"I won't blast people out of my way just because they're there," said Harry, "That's Voldemort's job." (*Hallows* 70-71)

Harry, like Gandalf and Dumbledore, refuses to fight the enemy with their "ring," their methodology; his use of *expelliarmus*, even when battling Voldemort, is evidence of this. The atmosphere of fear that is created during times of external threat and war is frequently used as justification for encroachments on civil liberties and the setting aside of social justice work in order to deal with the seemingly more important, more pressing need to eradicate the Voldemorts of the world. Harry doesn't agree.

What is particularly dangerous about beginning to let fear encroach upon liberty is that this process, historically, has led to fascism. This is not to say that either the U.S. or England have become fascist countries; that's not the argument. But security against external or internal threats often becomes the justification for moves in that direction. Some, indeed, are bristling at the association of antiterrorist torture policies with the justification for fascism, but it should be remembered that fascism rarely takes over a country in a day. As Adam-Troy Castro argues, "[I]t's perfectly possible for freedom to fail overnight, but it usually takes an invading army. More dangerous fascist movements proceed with caution, instituting their abuses incrementally" (125). No, nations currently fighting this "War on Terror" are not fascist, and the justification for eradicating terrorism is, indeed, the preservation of freedom. Nevertheless, Rowling is arguing through Harry and Dumbledore, whether you agree with them or not, that it is dangerous to fight the enemy with his own ring.

Eliminating Freedom

Despite the Ministry's denial of Voldemort's return throughout *Order of the Phoenix*, they are beginning to act in a fascist way based on a perceived threat: Fudge believes Dumbledore is raising up an army of students to launch an attack on the Ministry and grab Fudge's power.

It's absurd, but it becomes the justification for all of the heavy-handed work of the Ministry through Umbridge. Here is where the concept of the metanarrative comes in: all of the Ministry's activities are justified by lofty language. If Umbridge showed up at the school and said, "Here are the new rules, and anyone who disobeys them will be forced to write lines with a pen that will cut your hand over and over, using your own blood for ink," she wouldn't have lasted a day. She had to use the language of lofty, admirable goals. Castro notes that Umbridge's earliest rule changes "carefully couched in obfuscatory language" (125). Her initial speech was about "a new era of openness, effectiveness, and accountability," and only Hermione saw through the trap. This is the same kind of trap into which Dumbledore fell as a youth and upon which Grindelwald rose to power: oppression "for the greater good" is justifiable.

If the Ministry desires to keep its people in check, of course there is no better place to start than with education. If one can get full control of what is taught there, one can eventually turn an entire culture in whatever direction one wants. Castro notes the importance tyrants place on gaining control of education, or squashing it altogether, by pointing to "the revolt at China's Tiananmen Square" and "the Khmer Rouge, who upon taking power in Cambodia began a bloody purge against anyone foolish enough to admit to having an education" (123). It can happen violently like that, or in much more subtle fashion – as in taking complete control of the educational process, often under the stated intention of making it better. As evil slowly takes over the Wizarding World, Rowling parallels that track with increased Ministry involvement in education at Hogwarts. As already stated, Umbridge's initial speech at Hogwarts set the tone: "We're doing this for your own good." With this as justification, accompanied by fear of an uprising from Dumbledore, Umbridge is named "High Inquisitor," given power to set new rules and to hire and fire Hogwarts staff. Fudge's real goal in all of this is to keep his own power. In order to do that, dissent must be squelched, and the goal of education, instead of producing thoughtful and active members of a democratic society, becomes "raising a class of obedient little functionaries" (Castro 127). Defense Against the Dark Arts, under Umbridge's tutelage (if one could call it that) becomes theory-centered, so as to make sure the students never have the practical ability to revolt against the Ministry. It is no surprise then, that as Voldemort takes over the Ministry, freedom is taken away from parents and students, and attendance at Hogwarts becomes mandatory (*Hallows* 210).

Outside the school setting, the Ministry is involved in many other activities that reinforce its own power at the expense of others. *The Daily Prophet* has come under the heavy influence of Fudge, and it runs incessant smear pieces on Harry and Dumbledore in order to discredit their claims of Voldemort's return. Scapegoating plays a huge role in this: When Griselda Marchbanks resigned from the Ministry in protest, *The Daily Prophet* ran the story, but not without a list of her "links to subversive goblin groups" (*Order* 308). The power of scapegoating should not be underestimated. A study was conducted by Paul Rozin at the University of Pennsylvania in which the effect of perceived contamination was measured. Students were offered a series of choices: for example, two glasses of juice, one in which a sterilized cockroach had been dipped; a glass of water labeled "sucrose" and one labeled "cyanide;" a sweater briefly worn by someone with AIDS, and a sweater briefly worn by someone without the virus. In every situation, students most often took the one without the "negative" label, despite the fact that there was no actual difference between the two choices. (Rozin et al, cited in Nacify 214).

Scapegoating and suppression of non-wizard magical brethren is part and parcel of the problems of the Wizarding World, a glaring Muggle-world parallel being the Nazi scapegoating of the Jews in the last century. Fudge, right after Voldemort's return – and ironically, right after defending his alliance with the evil dementors – recoils in horror when Dumbledore urges him to "send envoys to the giants," offering them freedom:

> "The second step you must take - and at once," Dumbledore pressed on, "is to send envoys to the giants."
>
> "Envoys to the giants?" Fudge shrieked, finding his tongue again. "What madness is this?"
>
> "Extend them the hand of friendship, now, before it is too late," said Dumbledore, "or Voldemort will persuade them, as he did before, that he alone among wizards will give them their rights and their freedom!"
>
> "You - you cannot be serious!" Fudge gasped, shaking his head and retreating further from Dumbledore. "If the magical community got wind that I had approached the giants - people hate them, Dumbledore - end of my career -" (*Goblet* 708)

With scapegoats firmly in place – Dumbledore, Harry, goblins, werewolves, centaurs, and giants – Fudge is able to point the finger at every imaginable perceived threat as justification for the Ministry's freedom-quelling activity at Hogwarts and in the Wizarding World. Fudge wants, more than anything else, to keep his own power and to make sure it is not threatened. He has always felt intimidated by Dumbledore, and he knows full well that the Wizarding World asked Dumbledore to be Minister three times before Fudge got the job.

When Voldemort's return finally becomes evident to everyone, Dumbledore's deconstruction of the Wizarding World is something that politicians would jump all over. While not in the least negating the true evil that is Voldemort, Dumbledore explains that the Wizarding World's mistreatment of the magical brethren is one of the primary causes for the evil about to be visited upon them. In U.S. politics, if a candidate were to make a statement on par with this – say, for example, that American foreign policy played a motivational for terrorists to launch the attack of 9/11 – that candidate would immediately be branded "anti-American" or would be labeled a "blame America first" candidate. But that's hardly the point. Dumbledore is not saying, "The Wizarding World is primarily culpable for Voldemort, and we just need to try to understand him better and be nice to him." Rather, he is saying, "The prejudiced Wizarding World created an atmosphere in which the Dark Arts could flourish and find motivation for their terror."

Rufus Scrimgeour hardly does better than Cornelius Fudge. His first line of action seems to be a pamphlet teaching members of the Wizarding World how to be safe. This is Rowling's satirizing of a similar pamphlet sent out by the British government called "Preparing for Emergencies – what you need to know" (Rauhofer 101). The Ministry's pamphlet contains a chilling line: "Should you feel that a family member, colleague, friend, or neighbor is acting in a strange manner, contact the Magical Law Enforcement Squad at once. They may have been put under the Imperius Curse (see page 4)" (*Prince* 42). While the concern about the Imperius Curse is realistic enough, the implication is somewhat frightening: due to fear of Death Eater activity, people can start turning other people in on suspicion.

The consequence of that is false imprisonment, of course, and that is precisely what we see. The injustice of Azkaban as a means of dealing with crime and terror is evident enough early in the series. The first two Azkaban residents we meet are Hagrid and Sirius, and both were falsely imprisoned: Hagrid, without a trial and so that it would look like Fudge was "doing something," and Sirius also without a trial. Stan Shunpike's imprisonment is utterly absurd, and everyone knows it; Harry is still challenging Scrimgeour on it by the end of *Half-Blood Prince*. While the Ministry goes about trying to look like it's doing something, it is sacrificing justice in the process. Certain people can be spared or sacrificed, as long as the people's fear is alleviated and they have some confidence that the Ministry is working for them.

This is precisely why it's so easy to get anti-Muggleborn legislation passed in *Deathly Hallows*. Muggleborns are scapegoated as thieves of magic, and therefore turned into a perceived threat. During a time of war and terror, attempts will be made to eliminate all perceived threats; social justice and civil liberty begins to fall away, as long as people feel safe. In order to track and round up perceived threats, the "Undesirables" list is created, and Harry finds himself at the top, along with files on other undesirables including Arthur Weasley, in Umbridge's Ministry office (*Hallows* 25-52). This "Undesirables" list is very much like the "Terror Watch Lists" that are used today.

"But," one might object, "That was Umbridge! Under Voldemort's control because Pius Thicknesse was Minister!" Indeed, but that's precisely Rowling's – and Tolkien's – point. You cannot fight the Enemy with his own Ring without becoming like him.

Here is the reason that it's so easy for the Wizarding World, as well as many in our own world, to accept the loss of civil liberties during a time of war: the members of the dominant culture are almost always unaffected. When people are ready and willing to accept encroachments on civil rights for the sake of security, they do so because they simply do not believe that such measures will actually encroach upon *their* liberties – only the liberties of the scapegoat. And if they get a few wrong, so be it – it's better than having lots of people from dominant culture die.

There is nothing easy about these matters; they are complicated. But it simply cannot be argued that *Harry Potter* supports the current U.S. policy toward terrorism. Rather, as Benjamin Barton argues:

> Rowling taps into the current general distrust of government in the United States and the United Kingdom and creates a Ministry of Magic that simultaneously echoes and critiques our own governments. On the one hand, she creates a government that is repulsive in its structure, personnel, and actions. On the other, she crafts this government to appear closely related to our own government. This juxtaposition creates a powerful and subtle critique of government. ("Half-Crazed" 1537)

What, then, is Rowling's answer to the current evils in the world? It can hardly be argued that Rowling is 100% anti-war. Dumbledore and Harry both firmly believe that Voldemort must be taken out, finished, killed. Even so, there is a definite hope toward a peaceful future (which hope, of course, we all have), most powerfully symbolized by Harry's "signature move," *Expelliarmus*. It's a disarming charm, which is a clear reference toward disarmament being a wise direction in which to head. While governments continue to stockpile weapons that could literally destroy the entire world, Rowling is saying, through Harry, that you do not fight the enemy with the Killing Curse. She built the tension very well. First, Harry used the Imperius Curse at Gringotts; then, just a few hours previous, he had used the Cruciatus Curse on Alecto Carrow. Would he use the third? Would he fire the Killing Curse at Voldemort? He did not; instead, he disarmed, and the symbolic meaning of that moment was this: Voldemort died from his own Killing Curse. Yes, practically speaking, it comes to the same thing: Harry knew Voldemort would die. But Harry offered him the opportunity for redemption – "Try for some remorse, Riddle" (*Hallows* 741) – and then aimed to disarm, while Voldemort effectively was destroyed by his own method of murder.

So, the overarching lesson of *Harry Potter* is this: evil must be confronted and fought. But it must be done so self-sacrificially, and it should never be done with the enemy's own weapon. Otherwise, we become like the evil we are trying to defeat. And while the obvious evil (Voldemort) is being challenged, Rowling might also encourage us to be a good Weasley twin and disrupt any Umbridge-like policies that we meet along the way.

Chapter 16

The Last Enemy
Learning to Imagine Better on the Way Between Two Worlds

We do not need magic to change the world, we carry all the power we need inside ourselves already: we have the power to imagine better. ~ J.K. Rowling, 2008 Harvard Commencement Speech

John Granger wrote in *Unlocking Harry Potter*,[1] prior to Book 7's release:

> Harry will forgive Severus Snape and embrace the Slytherin aspect of Hogwarts to transcend his Gryffindor prejudices, either during the story in order to become the Androgyn Vaquisher or after the story to vanquish forever the partisan metanarrative that we readers have adopted along with wizard kind. (172)

Alas, while the former part of Mr. Granger's prediction became true, the latter did not follow, at least on the pages of the story itself. Harry did, indeed, forgive Severus Snape: "Albus Severus," he named his second son after the "Slytherin" who was "probably the bravest man I ever knew" (*Hallows* 758). Harry also embraced Slytherin, transcending his Gryffindor prejudices; to Albus Severus, who worriedly proposed a hypothetical situation in which he was sorted into Slytherin, " – then Slytherin House will have gained an excellent student" (758). And though Harry goes on to inform Albus Severus that he can actually *choose* Gryffindor, the point is forcefully made: being sorted into Slytherin is not a bad thing.

But there's no indication whatsoever that the world has been made right, that oppressive metanarratives have ceased, that house-elves have been liberated, and that there are no more unjust power structures. Indeed, the fact that the students act as if being sorted into Slytherin were a *bad* thing proves just the opposite. Why? If Rowling is writing a story of hope, and "an extended argument for tolerance," why leave so much undone? Why, in heaven's name, conclude the book with the words, "All was well," when so much was *not* well?

Because Rowling knows better.   She knows that problems like slavery, racism, sexism, and all other forms of discrimination, when deeply embedded into the DNA of a society, do not going away in a year – or even in nineteen years. She's a Fabian at heart, and Harry Potter, though a decisive blow against evil, is just one of many transformative moments needed for widespread, lasting societal change.

It is telling that Rowling chose 1 Corinthians 15:26 for the Potter's epitaph: "The *last* enemy that shall be defeated is death." "Last" implies that there are other enemies that will be defeated along the way, until that final enemy is dealt the decisive blow. In so many ways, this is precisely where Rowling is most closely tracking with Christian theology.

Human beings have a certain good purpose and place in the midst of a beautiful, wild, wonderful world (creation). There is also, alas, evil in the world, and it entered the world because of human choices (the Fall). These evil choices result in dehumanization, in the move away from created intent into selfishness and grabs at power at the expense of others (corrupt governments, world orders, etc. – the "nations raging" of Psalm 2). There is hope for redemption, and it is accomplished through self-sacrificial love (Christ on the cross). While death is tragic, to the "well-organized mind" it need not be feared; indeed, one day, it will be defeated. Harry became the first person ever to "defeat" death – once because of the self-sacrificial love of his mother, and once because he willingly sacrificed himself. In our lives, we may contribute to the evil of the world, in all its various shades and nuances (whether as heinously as Voldemort or as subtly as Ministry officials; whether throughout outright acts of evil or through cowardice), or we may love self-sacrificially, and work toward changing hearts and minds before our time here is done. Rowling's story path in *Harry Potter* is, essentially, the path I've been describing in this book. Each of my chapters illustrates one aspect of our journey."

I wrote in the introduction that Harry Potter is for real life. We belong to a world that is full of wonder and of magic; with imaginations re-awakened, and perspective transformed to see the more permanent things, we must move beyond mundane, mechanical existence and see the world as a wild place (Chapter One). We live between two worlds: this imperfect one which is mixed with evil and good, and the day when all evil will be defeated and good will triumph; on the battleground of grace and evil, we become conduits of the grace of the future world making its way into the struggles of the current fallen world (Chapter Two). The evil in this world is frightening, and there are forces at work that could potentially destroy us, throw us into depression and despair, and drive us toward cowardice and evil (Chapter Three). We make evil choices when we are afraid to be vulnerable, to be hurt, and when we are prone to self-preservation, rather than self-sacrifice; we hurt others in order to keep from being hurt (Chapter Four). A life of courage is to be preferred to a life of fear; a courageous life is one that seeks virtue and goodness in the face of temptation to evil (Chapter Five). A courageous person is willing to go to the very end in the fight against evil, willing to give himself or herself up for the greater good (Chapter Six).

There is no other way to reach virtue, courage, and self-sacrifice than by embracing grief, letting it refine us, and emerging, like a phoenix, as a stronger person; with imagination alive, we become creative heroes in the fight against evil (Chapter Seven). In choosing to be refined by grief instead of being plunged into despair and self-preservation, we expose and take control of our shadow side, the evil that exists in each one of us that fights for domination, as Harry did with his inner Voldemort (Chapter Eight). As Harry with Dumbledore, we cannot do this alone, but must listen to those who have gone before us, who are older and wiser, and who have set an example for us; but we also need to learn from their faults, and become better people (Chapter Nine). Like Harry needed to do with Severus Snape, we must have our own perceptions and prejudices challenged, and be prepared to believe in and hope for redemption of those around us – including those who have harmed us personally (Chapter Ten).

As this character develops within us, we become enabled to recognize injustice and oppression in the world and to fight against it with our own stories; we become the kind of creative people who cry out for justice (Chapter Eleven). In doing so, we must be careful not to tread on the moral freedom of others, but to work for genuine character transformation in ourselves and in those around us that will lead to outward change (Chapter Twelve). In seeking to change hearts and minds concerning injustice, we recognize the oppressive metanarratives about class, disability (Chapter Twelve), race (Chapter Thirteen), and gender (Chapter Fourteen), and we seek for lasting change. Finally, when the world is threatened by an evil of Voldemortian proportions, we do not embrace evil in order to defeat evil; we never fight the enemy with his own weapons, for greater evil must be fought with greater love (Chapter Fifteen).

This is the great place of imaginative literature in the world – to re-awaken our imaginations, to produce inward change in ourselves leading to the transformation of outward reality. We learn to imagine better.

Until the time comes when the last enemy is defeated, we can join Frodo, Sam, and Gandalf, Aslan and the Pevensie children, Charles Wallace, Meg, and Calvin, Harry, Ron, and Hermione, and all the heroes and heroines found in fairy tales – for, through their examples, we will find courage to fight evil with self-sacrificial love

Chapter 16 Notes

1   The reader should note that Mr. Granger is revising *Unlocking Harry Potter*, which means two things: the page numbers cited in this book will not match up, and the predictions he wrote during the Book 6-7 interlibrum will be replaced with more of his must-read analysis.

Afterword:

Conversations at the Hog's Head

"You get a lot of funny folk at the Hog's Head." ~ Hagrid

If you've found the subject matter of this book – fairy tales and culture – to be as fascinating a topic as I do, I cordially invite you to join the conversation at The Hog's Head (http://thehogshead.org), the blog I run along with the Blogengamot – a council of Harry Potter bloggers. Together, we continue analysis of the series, setting it in the various spaces in which it belongs: fairy tales, English lit, children's lit, pop culture, education, theology, postmodern discourse, and a wide variety of other subjects. I also run, from that same site, The Hog's Head PubCast, a podcast that is available through free subscription in iTunes, Odeo.com, or free download through The Hog's Head. I think you'll enjoy the commentary, and I invite you to bring your comments, questions, and disagreements to the discussion in the comments sections at The Hog's Head.

There are people without whom I'd have never written this book, and they deserve special mention. First and foremost among these is Tricia, my wife and my love. Her support and her influence is all over this book. Second, my daughter Sophia, who is two years old at this volume's completion. Even when she interrupts Daddy's writing, she's thoroughly magical. Neither my wife nor my daughter blog, so I've nowhere to point you to except my own writing, for they are an integral part of it.

Among those who write about *Harry Potter* (from an informed and intelligent perspective) is John Granger. His work on the series inspired me to seriously examine the books for myself. Granger is to *Harry Potter* what Michael Ward is to *The Chronicles of Narnia*: he is the one who discovered the series' *kappa* element, the concealed but foundational secret imaginative key to the entire series. His work on literary alchemy in *Harry Potter* is the most important element of the series' analysis. Be sure to pick up, read, and re-read his books on the series (*Unlocking Harry Potter, How Harry Cast His Spell, The Deathly Hallows Lectures*), and you can keep up with his regular commentary at his blog, Hogwarts Professor (http://hogwartsprofessor.com). The conversation there is always worth your time.

The Blogengamot, my council of bloggers at The Hog's Head, deserve special mention. Matthew Boyd, the moderator, has keep the site running beautifully. Dave Jones's insight is all over this book, having read the first manuscript and offered his invaluable suggestions and editorial help; and it is a better book because of Dave. You can read his writings at The Hog's Head and also at his blog Nowhere On the Ohio River (http://ohioriverutopia.wordpress.com). Johnny Chavez has written some of the better commentary I've read on Christian themes in *Harry Potter.* He blogs at Behold a Phoenix (http://beholdaphoenix.blogspot.com) as well as at The Hog's Head. Behind the scenes at The Hog's Head are (voluntary, free) tech-elves Jonathan Lane and Ben Spearman, without whose tech support the site would have fallen apart long ago. And the artist responsible for that great and beautiful banner at the top is Michael Politakis. I must also give special thanks to all the Hog's Head patrons. They make Potter discussion challenging and fun, and they make the Hog's Head some of the best literature discussion on the web. Without the supportive and brilliant Hog's Head community, this book would not be what it is.

Dr. Amy H. Sturgis, professor at Belmont and scholar of Native American studies as well as literature, runs the LiveJournal "Redecorating Middle-Earth in Early Lovecraft" (http://eldrichhobbit.livejournal.com). From there, you can keep up with her regular blogging as well as link to her official site with her published works referenced and, in the case of some articles, linked. Her review and comments of chapters 1-3 of this book were invaluable to their formation.

Greg and Penny Gershman also deserve a mention and a recommendation. They are friends and colleagues of mine in Harry Potter fandom. They run the popular Harry Potter Prognostications podcast (http://hpprogs.com), and you'll have a great time listening to their excellent episodes, insightful and often humorous commentary.

Special thanks for the support and encouragement from my family and friends. Thanks to Bob Trexler of Zossima Press for his help in making this book a reality, and for his very helpful insights and editorial work.

And to you, dear reader – thank you for taking the time to read this book. I would greatly appreciate your feedback. Come to thehogshead. org, join the discussion, and send an "E-Owl" with your comments and questions about *Harry Potter and Imagination: The Way Between Two Worlds.*

See you at The Hog's Head.

~ Travis Prinzi

Bibliography

"Harry Potter Author Works Her Magic," Family Education website, 1999.

Adler, Shawn. "'Harry Potter' Author J.K. Rowling Opens Up About Books' Christian Imagery." MTV News. http://www.mtv/news/articles/1572107/20071017/index.jhtml. October 17, 2007.

Adler, Shawn. "'Harry Potter' Author J.K. Rowling Meets With L.A. Students, Plots Her Next Move." MTV.com, 15 October, 2007

Anelli, Melissa and Emerson Spartz. "The Leaky Cauldron and MuggleNet interview Joanne Kathleen Rowling: Part Two," The Leaky Cauldron, 16 July 2005.

Babinski, Edward T. "Lovecraft's Theology of Fear and Williams's Theology of Romance." The Crypt of Cthulhu, Volume 2, Number 5, 1983. pp. 16-22.

Barnes and Noble interview, March 19, 1999. http://www.accio-quote.org/articles/1999/0399-barnsandnoble.html

Barnes and Noble & Yahoo! chat with J.K. Rowling, barnesandnoble.com, 20 October, 2000

Barton, Benjamin H. "Harry Potter and the Half-Crazed Bureaucracy." Michigan Law Review 104, May 2006:1523-1538.

Barton, Benjamin H. "Harry Potter and the Miserable Ministry of Magic." Texas Wesleyan Law Review Volume 12, Number 1. 2005. pp. 441-443.

Beam, George. *Fact, Fiction, and Folklore in Harry Potter's World*. Hampton Roads Publishing Company, 2005.

Blackmore, Leigh D. "Middle-Earth, Narnia, and Lovecraft's Dream World: Comparative World-views in Fantasy." *The Crypt of Cthulhu* Volume 2, Number 5. 1983. pp. 6-15.

Brodkin, Karen. *How Jews Became White Folks and What That says about Race in America*. Rutgers University Press, 1998.

Card, Orson Scott. "Scott. "Who is Snape?" http://hatrack.com/misc/who-is-snape.shtml

Carey, Brycchan. "Hermione and the House-Elves: The Literary and Historical Contexts of J.K. Rowling's Anti-Slavery Campaign" in in *Reading Harry Potter: Critical Essays*. Ed. by Giselle Liza Anatol. Westport, CT: Praeger Publishers, 2003. pp. 103-116.

Castro, Adam-Troy. "From Azkaban to Abu Ghraib" in *Mapping the World of Harry Potter*. Ed. by Mercedes Lackey. Dallas: Benbella Books, Inc. 2006. pp. 119-132.

Chang, Maria Hsia. "A Study in Evil: Voldemort, Malignant Narcisist." Mugglenet. http://www.mugglenet.com/editorials/editorials/edit-changm01.shtml

Cheeser. "Transcripts of JK Rowling's charity reading Q&A." Aug 10, 2006. http://hpna.com/news.1954.html

Chesterton, G.K. "The Ethics of Elfland" in *Orthodoxy*. http://ccel.orgccel/chesterton/orthodoxy.vii.html

Clement. "The Letter of the Church of Rome to the Church of Corinth, Commonly Called Clement's First Letter" in *Early Christian Fathers* ed. by Cyril C. Richardson. New York: Touchstone, 1996. pp. 43-73.

Clute, John and John Grant. *The Encyclopedia of Fantasy.* New York: St. Martin's Griffin, 1997.

Cockrell, Amanda. "Harry Potter and the Secret Password: Finding Our Way in the Magical Genre" in *The Ivory Tower and Harry Potter*. Ed. Lana A. Whited. Columbia: University of Missouri Press, 2002. pp. 15-26.

Colbert, David. *The Magical Worlds of Harry Potter*. Tandem Library Books, 2002.

Cruz, Juan. "Ser invisible...eso seria lo mas." http://www.elpais.com/articulo/cultura/Ser/invisible/seria/elpepicul/20080208elpepicul_1/Tes. February 8, 2008. Translation: http://www.snitchseeker.com/harry-potter-news/entire-spanish-j-k-rowling-interview-54113/. 2/10/2008.

de Bertodano, Helena. "Harry Potter Charms a Nation." Electronic Telegraph, 25 July 1998. http://www.accio-quote.org/articles/1998/0798-telegraph-bertodano.html

Diagnostic and Statistical Manual of Mental Disorders: DSM-IV. American Psychiatric Association: 1994.

Dresang, Eliza T. "Hermione Granger and the Heritage of Gender" in *The Ivory Tower and Harry Potter*. Ed. Lana A. Whited. Columbia: University of Missouri Press, 2002. pp. 211-242.

Duriez, Colin. *A Field Guide to Harry Potter*. Downers Grove: InterVarsity Press, 2007. Edinburgh "cub reporter" press conference, ITV, 16 July 2005.

eroej_kab, "Deathly Hallows, Disappointments, Plot Holes, and More." http://community.livejournal.com/hp_essays/236424.html. August 12, 2007.

eToys interview transcript, etoys.com, Fall 2000. http://www.accio-quote.org/articles/2000/fall00-etoys.html

Ford, Paul. *Companion to Narnia*. San Francisco: HarperSanFrancisco, 2005.

"The Fabian Society." The London School of Economics and Political Science. http://www/lse/ac.uk/resources/LSEHistory/fabian.htm

Franklin, Nancy. "The Social Dynamics of Power and Cooperation in the Wizarding World" in *The Psychology of Harry Potter*. Ed. by Neil Mulholland. Dallas: Benbella Books, Inc. 2006. pp. 169-173.

Fraser, Lindsay. Conversations with J.K. Rowling. New York: Scholastic, 2001.

Fraser, Lindsay. "Harry Potter - Harry and Me." The Scotsman. Nov. 2002. http://www.accio-quote.org/articles/2002/1102-fraser-scotsman.html

Freemantle, Anne. *This Little Band of Prophets.* New York: Mentor Books, 1959.

Fry, Stephen. "J.K. Rowling at the Royal Albert Hall," 26 June 2003. http://www.accio-quote.org/articles/2003/0626-alberthall-fry.htm

Fry, Stephen. "Living with Harry Potter," BBC Radio4, December 10, 2005. http://www.accio-quote.org/articles/2005/1205-bbc-fry.html

Gallardo-C., Ximena and C. Jason Smith, "Cinderfella: J.K. Rowling's Wily Web of Gender" in *Reading Harry Potter: Critical Essays.* Ed. by Giselle Liza Anatol. Westport, CT: Praeger Publishers, 2003. pp. 191-206.

Granger, John. *The Deathly Hallows Lectures: The Hogwarts Professor Explains the Final Adventure of Harry Potter.* Allentown, PA: Zossima Press, 2008.

Granger, John. *How Harry Cast His Spell.* Carol Stream, IL: Tyndale, 2008. (revised/updated edition of *Looking For God in Harry Potter*)

Granger, John. *Looking for God in Harry Potter.* Carol Stream, IL: Tyndale, 2004.

Granger, John. *Unlocking Harry Potter: Five Keys for the Serious Reader.* Wayne, PA, Zossima Press, 2007.

Gray, E.A., trans. Cath Maige Tuired: The second battle of Mag Tuired. Naas: Irish Texts Society v. 52, 1982.

Greig, Geordie. "There would be so much to tell her..." http://www.accio-quote.org/articles/2006/0110-tatler-grieg.html

Grimes, M. Katherine. "Harry Potter: Fairy Tale Prince, Real Boy, and Archetypal Hero" in *The Ivory Tower and Harry Potter.* Ed. Lana A. Whited. Columbia: University of Missouri Press, 2002. pp. 89-124.

Grossman, Lev. "J.K. Rowling Hogwarts And All," *Time Magazine*, 17 July, 2005.

Heilman, Elizabeth E. "Blue Wizards and Pink Witches: Representations of Gender Identity and Power" in *Harry Potter's World: Multidisciplinary Critical Perspectives.* Ed. by Elizabeth E. Heilman. Taylor and Francis Books, Inc. 2003. pp. 221-240.

Hook, Misty. "What Harry and Fawkes Have in Common" in *The Psychology of Harry Potter.* Ed. by Neil Mulholland. Dallas: Benbella Books, Inc., 2006. pp. 91-104.

"Harry Potter: Everyone's Wild About Harry," CNN News, 18 November, 2001. http://www.accio-quote.org/articles/2001/1101-cnnnews.htm

Holcomb, Justin. "Responding to Carl Trueman - Christianity is NOT a Metanarrative." Common Grounds Online. http:/commongroundsonline.typepad.com/common_grounds_online/2007/05/editors_note_ju.html. 9 May 2007.

Jensen, Jeff. "Rowling Thunder (parts 1 & 2)," Entertainment Weekly, August 4, 2000.

J.K. Rowling at the Edinburgh Book Festival, Sunday, August 15, 2004. http://www.accio-quote.org/articles/2004/0804-ebf.htm

"JK Rowling Chat," AOL Live, May 4, 2000. http://maxpages.com/hpnetwork/JK_Rowling.

"J.K. Rowling Interview," CBCNewsWorld: Hot Type, July 13, 2000.

J.K. Rowling on The Diane Rehm Show, WAMU Radio Washington, D.C., October 20, 1999 (re-broadcast December 24, 1999). URL: http://www.accio-quote.org/articles/1999/1299-wamu-rehm.htm.

"J.K. Rowling reçoit le Prix James Joyce : la Retranscription," La Gazette du Sorcier. http://www.gazette-du-sorcier.com/J-K-Rowling-recoit-le-Prix-James,1037 April 2, 2008.

"J.K. Rowling's Books That Made a Difference." *O, The Oprah Magazine* January 2001. http://www.accio-quote.org/articles/2001/0101-oprah.html

Jones, Malcolm. "The Return of Harry Potter," *Newsweek*, 10 July, 2000. http://www.accio-quote.org/articles/2000/0700-newsweek-jones.html

Jordan, James. "Concerning Halloween." *Biblical Horizons*. August, 1996. http://www.biblicalhorizons.com/open-book/no-28-concerning-halloween/

Jung, C. G. (1969). *Four archetypes: Mother/rebirth/spirit/trickster* Princeton, NJ: Princeton University Press.

Jung, Carl. "New Paths in Psychology" (1912). In CW 7: Two Essays on Analytical Psychology.

Jung, Carl. "On the Psychology of the Unconscious" (1912). In CW 7: Two Essays on Analytical Psychology.

Jung, Carl. "Psychology and Religion" (1938). In CW 11: Psychology and Religion: West and East.

King, Joyce E. " Dysconscious Racism: Ideology, Identity, and the Miseducation of Teachers." *The Journal of Negro Education*, Vol. 60, No. 2 (Spring, 1991), pp. 133-146.

King, Larry. "J.K. Rowling Discusses the Surprising Success of 'Harry Potter'," Larry King Live (CNN), 20 October 2000

Kovacs, Maureen Gallery, transl. with intro. (1985,1989). *The Epic of Gilgamesh*. Stanford University Press: Stanford, California.

Le Guin, Ursula K. *A Wizard of Earthsea*. New York: Bantam Books, 1968.

LeLievre, K. A. (2003). Wizards and wainscots: Generic structures and genre themes in the Harry Potter series. *Mythlore*, 24, 25-38.

L'Engle, Madeleine. *Many Waters*. New York: Square Fish, 1986.

L'Engle, Madeleine. *A Swiftly Tilting Planet*. New York: Square Fish, 1978.

L'Engle, Madeleine. A Wind in the Door. New York: Square Fish, 1973.

L'Engle, Madeleine. *A Wrinkle in Time*. New York: Square Fish, 2007.

L'Engle, Madeleine. *Walking on Water*. Colorado Springs: Shaw Books, 2001.

Lewis, C.S. *Letters to Malcolm, Chiefly on Prayer*. New York: A Harvest Book, 1964.

Lewis, C.S. *Mere Christianity*. New York: Touchstone, 1980.

Lewis, C.S. "On Stories" in *Of Other Worlds: Essays and Stories*. New York: A Harvest Book, 1966. p. 3-21.

Lewis, C.S. "On Three Ways of Writing for Children" *Of Other Worlds: Essays and Stories*. New York: A Harvest Book, 1966. p. 22-34.

Lewis, C.S. *Prince Caspian*. New York: HarperTrophy, 1979.

Lewis, C.S. "Sometimes Fairy Stories May Say Best What's to be Said." *Of Other Worlds: Essays and Stories*. New York: A Harvest Book, 1966. p. 35-38.

Lewis, C.S. *The Abolition of Man*. New York: Collier Books, 1947.

Lewis, C.S. *The Lion, the Witch, and the Wardrobe*. New York: HarperTrophy, 1978.

Lewis, C.S. *The Last Battle*. New York: HarperTrophy, 1984.

Lewis, C.S. *The Magician's Nephew*. New York: HarperTrophy, 1983.

Lewis, C.S. *The Problem of Pain*. New York: Touchstone, 1996.

Lindermans, Micha F. "Benu." Encyclopedia Mythica. 22 June 1997. 3 August 2007.

Lindermans, Micha F. "Feng-Huang." *Encyclopedia Mythica*. 16 January 2004. 3 August 2007.

Lindermans, Micha F. "Phoenix." *Encyclopedia Mythica*. 09 June 2004. 12 May 2006.

Lydon, Christopher. J.K. Rowling interview transcript, The Connection (WBUR Radio), 12 October, 1999. http://www.accio-quote.org/articles/1999/1099-connectiontransc2.htm

Loomis, R.S. *Celtic Myth and Arthurian Romance*. New York: Columbia University Press, 1926.

Lovecraft, H.P. "Supernatural Horror in Literature." http://gaslight.mtroyal.
ab.ca/superhor.htm

Lyotard, Jean-Francois. *The Postmodern Condition*. Manchester University
Press, 1984.

MacDonald, George. "The Fantastic Imagination." [S.I]: Gaslight, 2005.
,http://www.mtroyal.ab.ca/gaslight/ortsx14.htm.

MacKenzie, Norman and Jeanne. *The First Fabians*. London: Quartet Books,
1977.

McBriar, A.M. *Fabian Socialism & English Politics: 1884 - 1918*. Cambridge
University Press, 1966.

McDaniel, Kathryn. "The Elfin Mystique" in *Past Watchful Dragons*.
Mythopoeic Press, 2007.

McGrath, Alister E. *The Christian Theology Reader*. Blackwell Publishers,
2006.

Miller, John J. "Xmas in Narnia." National Review Online. December 22,
2005. http://www.nationalreview.com/miller/miller200512220847.
asp

Millman, Joyce. "To Sir, With Love" in *Mapping the World of Harry Potter*.
Ed. by Mercedes Lackey. Dallas: Benbella Books, Inc. 2006.
pp. 39-52.

Mills, Alice. "Archetypes and the Unconscious in Harry Potter and Diana
Wynne Jones's Fire and Hemlock and Dogsbody" in *Reading Harry
Potter: Critical Essays*. Ed. by Giselle Liza Anatol. Westport, CT:
Praeger Publishers, 2003. pp. 3-13.

Morris, Andrew P. "Making Legal Space for Moral Choice." *Texas Wesleyan
Law Review* Volume 12, Number 1. 2005. pp. 473-480.

Morris, Tom. "The Courageous Harry Potter" in *Harry Potter and Philosophy:
If Aristotle Ran Hogwarts*. Ed. by David Bagget and Shawn E.
Klein. Chicago: Open Court, 2004. pp.9-21.

"Mother of all Muggles," *The Irish Times*, July 13, 2000. http://www.accio-
quote.org/articles/2000/0700-irishtimes.html.

Myers, Doris T. "The Compleat Anglican: Spiritual Style in The
Chronicles of Narnia" in Paul Ford, *Companion to Narnia*. San
Francisco: HarperSanFrancisco, 2005. pp. 473-488.

Nacify, Siamak Tundry. "The Werewolf in the Wardrobe" in *The Psychology
of Harry Potter*. Ed. by Neil Mulholland. Dallas: Benbella Books,
Inc., 2006. pp. 207-219.

Natov, Roni. "Harry Potter and the Extraordinariness of the Ordinary." *The
Lion and the Unicorn* 25.2 (2001) 310-327.

Naughtie, James. "James Naughtie talks to JK Rowling about one of her
novels, *Harry Potter and the Philosopher's Stone*," Radio 4's Book
Club programme, August 1, 1999. URL: http://www.accio-quote.
org/articles/1999/0899-bbc-naughtie.htm.

Nel, Philip. "Is There a Text in This Advertising Campaign?: Literature, Marketing, and Harry Potter." *The Lion and the Unicorn* - Volume 29, Number 2, April 2005, pp. 236-267.

Nesbit, Edith. *The Enchanted Castle and Five Children and It.* New York: Barnes and Noble Classics, 2005.

Nicol, Patricia. "Boy wizard frees trapped mother," *Sunday Times* (London), December 6, 1998. http://www.accio-quote.org/articles/1998/1298-sundaytimes-nicol.html.

Odell, Joyce. "Case in Point: Albus Dumbledore." Red Hen Publications. October 31, 2007. http://www.redhen-publications.com/Dumbledore.html

Ostry, Elaine. "Accepting Mudbloods: The Ambivalent Social Vision of J.K. Rowling's Fairy Tales" in *Reading Harry Potter: Critical Essays.* Ed. by Giselle Liza Anatol. Westport, CT: Praeger Publishers, 2003. pp. 89-102.

Pearce, Joseph. *Tolkien: Man and Myth.* San Francisco: Ingatius Press, 1998.

Pearce, Joseph. "Why Tolkien Says The Lord of the Rings Is Catholic." *National Catholic Register* (January 12-19, 2003). http://catholiceducation.org/articles/arts/al0161.html.

Pease, Edward R. *History of the Fabian Society.* London: Fabian Society, 1925.

Peck, M. Scott. *People of the Lie.* Simon and Schuster, 1983.

Pennington, John. "From Elfland to Hogwarts, or the Aesthetic Trouble with Harry Potter." *The Lion and the Unicorn* 26.1 (2002) 78-97.

Pharr, Mary. "In Media Res: Harry Potter as Hero-in-Progress" in The Ivory Tower and Harry Potter. Ed. Lana A. Whited. Columbia: University of Missouri Press, 2002. pp. 53-66. "Potter debate still brewing." Times-Mail News. 3 August 2007. 23 August 2007.

Pugh, Tison and David L. Wallace. "Heteronormative Heroism and Queering the School Story in J. K. Rowling's Harry Potter Series." Children's Literature Association Quarterly 31.3 (2006) 260-281.

Purtill, Richard. *J.R.R. Tolkien: Myth, Morality, and Religion.* San Francisco: Ignatius Press, 2003.

Pyle, Howard. *The Story of King Arthur and His Knights.* New York: Dover Publications, 1965.

Ramos, Andreas. "The Trouble with Harry Potter – Teaching our Children Sexism." Advancing Women 30 October 2000 http://www.advancingwomen.com/womsoc/review_potter.htm

Rauhofer, Judith. Defence against the dark arts: how the British response to the terrorist threat is parodied in J K Rowling's "Harry Potter and the Half Blood Prince." *Int. J. Liability and Scientific Enquiry*, Vol. 1, Nos. 1/2, 2007

Red Nose Day Chat, BBC Online, March 12, 2001. http://www.accio-quote. org/articles/2001/0301-bbc-rednose.htm.

Renton, Jennie. "The story behind the Potter legend: JK Rowling talks about how she created the Harry Potter books and the magic of Harry Potter's world," *Sydney Morning Herald*, October 28, 2001. http:// www.accio-quote.org/articles/2001/1001-sydney-renton.htm

Rowling, J.K. *Harry Potter and the Chamber of Secrets*. New York: Scholastic, Inc., 1999.

Rowling, J.K. *Harry Potter and the Deathly Hallows.* New York: Scholastic, 2007.

Rowling, J.K. *Harry Potter and the Goblet of Fire*. New York: Scholastic, Inc., 2000.

Rowling, J.K. *Harry Potter and the Half-Blood Prince*. New York, Scholastic Inc., 2005.

Rowling, J.K. *Harry Potter and the Order of the Phoenix*. New York: Scholastic, Inc. 2003.

Rowling, J.K. *Harry Potter and the Sorcerer's Stone*. New York: Scholastic, Inc., 1997.

Rowling, Joanne Kathleen. "Fighting In A Battle That Will Never Be Won" (Príncipe de Asturias Prize acceptance speech), 25 October 2003. URL: http://www.accio-quote.org/articles/2003/1025-princeasturias-speech.htm

Rowling, J.K. "The First It Girl." *The Telegraph.* November 26, 2006. URL: http://www.telegraph.co.uk/arts/main.jhtml?xml=/ arts/2006/11/26/bomit05.xml

Rice, Chris and Spencer Perkins. "Reconciliation: Loving God and Loving People" in *Restoring At-Risk Communities.* Ed. by John R. Perkins. Grand Rapids: Baker Books, 1995. pp. 107-138.

Runcie, James. "J.K. Rowling: A Year in the Life." http://www.tvcatchup. com/watch/15050/. January 1, 2008.

Sanyal, Sumanta. "Garuda." *Encylopedia Mythica*. 29 March 2005. 1 August 2007.

Scamander, Newt. *Fantastic Beasts and Where to Find Them*. New York: Arthur A. Levine Books, 2001.

Schoefer, Christine. "Harry Potter's Girl Trouble: The World of Everyone's favorite Kid Wizard is a Place where Boys come First." *Salon* 30 October 2000 http://www.salonmag.com/books/ feature/2000/01/13/potter/

Scott, Jr., Daniel L. and Cagle, Austin. "A Cat Sat on a Mat: Education in a World Without Wonder - Looking at Modern Western Education Through the Eyes of C.S. Lewis" in *Past Watchful Dragons*, ed. by Amy H. Sturgis. Altedena: The Mythopoeic Press, 2007. pp. 125-135.

Shippey, Tom. *J.R.R. Tolkien: Author of the Century*. New York: Houghton Mifflin Company, 2000.

Simpson, Anne. "Face to Face with J K Rowling: Casting a spell over young minds," *The Herald*, 7 December 1998. URL: http://www.accio-

Smith, Mark Eddy. *Tolkien's Ordinary Virtues*. Downers' Grove: InterVarsity Press. 2002. p. 112.

Squire, C. *Celtic Myths and Legends*. New York: Gramercy Books, 1994.

Sturgis, Amy. "'Art in its Most Essential Sense:' H.P. Lovecraft on the Imaginative Tale" in *Cthulhu's Grandfather*, ed. by Geoffrey Girard, Apex Books, 2008.

Sturgis, Amy. "Harry Potter Is A Hobbit: Rowling, Tolkien, and The Question of Readership," *CSL: The Bulletin of the New York C.S. Lewis Society* (May/June 2004).

Sturgis, Amy. "The New Shoggoth Chic: Why H.P. Lovecraft Now?"Apex Science Fiction and Horror Digest, Vol. 1 Issue 4 (Winter 2005).

Tatum, Beverly Daniel. Why Are All the Black Kids Sitting Together in the Cafeteria? (New York: Basic Books, 2002).

"The Fabian Society." The London Society of Economics and Political Science. 2000. http://www.lse.ac.uk/resources/LSEHistory/fabian.htm)

Ward, Michael. "C.S. Lewis and the Star of Bethlehem." *Books and Culture*. January/February 2008. http://www.christianitytoday.com/bc/2008/001/15.30.html.

Ward, Michael. *Planet Narnia*. New York: Oxford University Press, 2008.

Whitton, Natasha. "Me! Books! And Cleverness!:" Stereotypical Portrayals in the Harry Potter Series." *Women Writers*. May 15, 2004. http://www.womenwriters.net/summer04/reviews/HarryPotter.htm

Williams, Donald T. "Sons of Adam and Daughters of Eve" in *Past Watchful Dragons*, ed. by Amy H. Sturgis. Altedena: The Mythopoeic Press, 2007. pp. 23-40.

"World Exclusive Interview with J K Rowling," South West News Service, 8 July 2000. URL: http://www.accio-quote.org/articles/2000/0700-swns-alfie.htm

Wright, N.T. *Surprised by Hope*. Harper One, 2008.

Vieira, Meredith. "Harry Potter: The Final Chapter" Dateline (NBC) , 29 July 2007.

Vieira, Meredith. "JK Rowling One-On-One: Part One." *Today Show* (NBC) , 26 July 2007

Zettel, Sarah. "Hermione Granger and the Charge of Sexism" in *Mapping the World of Harry Potter*. Ed. by Mercedes Lackey. Dallas: Benbella Books, Inc. 2006. pp. 83-100.

Scripture quotations taken from the following translations:

Quotations marked "NIV" taken from The Holy Bible, New International Version. International Bible Society, 1984.

Quotations marked "ESV" taken from The Holy Bible, English Standard Version. Crossway Bibles, 2001.

Quotations marked "NLT" taken from The Holy Bible, New Living Translation. Tyndale House Publishers, 2004.

Index

Zossima Press Titles

A professor of literature for over thirty years, Dr. James W. Thomas (Pepperdine University) takes us on a tour back through the Potter books in order to enjoy them in different ways upon subsequent readings. Re-readers will be pleasantly surprised at what they may have missed in the books and at what secrets Rowling has encoded for us to decode as we revisit these rich texts. The professor's informal discussions focus on puns, humor, foreshadowing, literary allusions, narrative techniques, and various other aspects of the *Potter* books hard-to-see on the hurried first or fifth reading. Throughout, Dr. Thomas also draws parallels between passages in Harry's story and various literary classics. Dr. Thomas shows us  too that a "serious" reading of literature can be as much fun as it is edifying and rewarding.

 In THE DEATHLY HALLOWS LECTURES, John Granger reveals the Potter finale's brilliant details, themes and meanings. Even the most ardent of Harry Potter fans will be surprised by and delighted with the Hogwarts Professor's explanations of the three dimensions of meaning in DEATHLY HALLOWS to include why Ms. Rowling chose to make Lily's eyes green, why Harry buried Moody's eye where and when he did, and why Ollivander prefers the three wand cores he does. Ms. Rowling has said that alchemy sets the "parameters of magic" in the series; after reading the chapter-length explanation of DEATHLY HALLOWS as the final stage of the alchemical Great Work, the serious reader will understand how important literary alchemy is in understanding Rowling's artistry and accomplishment.

Here is a modern-day parable of a modern-day cat with modern-day attitudes. Riverboat Dan is a "cool" cat on a perpetual vacation from responsibility. He's The Cat on the Catamaran – sailing down the river of life. Dan keeps his guilty conscience from interfering with his fun until he runs into trouble. But will he have the courage to believe that it's never too late to change course? (28 pages, 18 illustrations)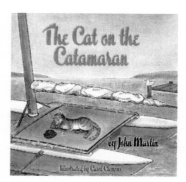

"This book is a joy, and as companionable as a good-natured cat."
Walter Hooper, author of *C.S. Lewis: Companion and Guide*.

Daily reflections by two poets from different times and places, but with a common love.

Betty Aberlin's close readings of George MacDonald's verses and her thoughtful responses to them speak clearly of her poetic gifts and spiritual intelligence.

Luci Shaw, poet

To Love Another Person:
A Spiritual Journey Through Les Miserables
by John Morrison

"I've just put down your manuscript. I had not got far into it before I knew that I was sitting at the feet of an excellent teacher, theologian, and literary and drama critic. Quite seriously – I feel that I have no possible comment on your work except, "Publish it! Whenever you can!"

Thomas Howard, author

Fourteen essays that truely place MacDonald in context. Important, challenging, and exciting.

This comprehensive collection represents the best of contemporary scholarship on George MacDonald.

Rolland Hein, author

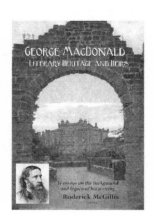

Sixteen of the best presentations from the international C. S. Lewis convention in Wake Forest, NC.

Walter Hooper shares his important essay "Editing C. S. Lewis," a chronicle of publishing decisions after Lewis' death in 1963.

"A magisterial work, chock full of fresh historical tidbits and penetrating analysis."

> David Baggett
> editor of *C.S. Lewis as Philosopher*

"Indispensible"
James Como

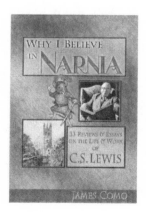

Why I Believe in Narnia:
*33 Essays and Reviews
on the Life and Work of C.S. Lewis
by* James Como

"A valuable, wide-ranging collection of essays by one of the best informed and most astute commentators on Lewis' work and ideas."

Peter Schakel, author
Imagination & the Arts in C.S. Lewis

About the Author

Travis Prinzi is a Harry Potter pundit whose weblog, TheHogsHead.org, enjoys an international readership because of his insights, humor, and challenging responses to Potter news and theories. Prinzi holds an M.A degree in Theological Studies and an M.S degree in Teaching and Curriculum, English - adding to his insights about Harry's adventures at Hogwarts and the intersection of theology, literature, and education. A popular speaker at libraries, churches, schools, and universities, he has given presentations and Keynote talks at four different Potter conferences in the U.S. and Canada. In addition to *Harry Potter and Imagination*, Mr. Prinzi is the editor of a collection of cutting-edge essays in Potter scholarship, *Hog's Head Conversations* (Zossima Press, March 2009). He lives in Rochester, NY, with his wife and daughter.

If you would like to schedule Mr. Prinzi to speak at your library, church, school, or university, contact him at thehogshead.org. Click on "E-Owl."

CPSIA information can be obtained at www.ICGtesting.com
Printed in the USA
LVOW07s1743231215

467601LV00002B/75/P

9 780982 238516